The European Union and the Supra-Religion:

Setting the Stage for the Final Act?

A Biblical Perspective

—⟋⟍—

Robert R. Congdon

Copyright © 2007 by Robert R. Congdon

The European Union and the Supra-Religion:
Setting the Stage for the Final Act? A Biblical Perspective
by Robert R. Congdon

Printed in the United States of America

ISBN 978-1-60266-679-5

Unless otherwise indicated, Scripture quotations are from the *King James Authorized Version* of the Bible. Copyright ©1987-2005 Online Bible Edition version 2.00, Jan. 19, 2005. Winterbourne, ON. Canada.

Cover Pictures: Pictured are the European Union's Parliament Building in Strasburg, France; and *Europa*, an EU sculpture outside the entrance of the European Council of Ministers EU building in Brussels Belgium. Photo Credit: R. Congdon.

www.xulonpress.com

DEDICATION

—∿∿—

This book is dedicated to my wife Pam, my best friend.

My helpmeet who meets me where I need help.

Without her encouragement and help,
this book could never have been completed
and our ministry could not exist.

TABLE OF CONTENTS

—⁓⁓—

ABBREVIATIONS

—ᘻᘻ—

BDB—Francis Brown, S. R. Driver, & C. A. Briggs, *Hebrew and English Lexicon of the Old Testament.* Oxford: Clarendon Press, 1907.

JFB—*Jamieson, Fausset, Brown Commentary.* CD-ROM. Online Bible Edition version 2.00, 19 Jan. 2005. Winterbourne, ON. Canada: Online Bible, 1992-2005.

K&D—C. F. Keil & F. Delitzsch. *Commentary on the Old Testament, 10 vol.* Peabody, MA: Hendrickson Publishers, 2001.

Strong's—James Strong. *Strong's Exhaustive Concordance of the Bible.* CD-ROM. Online Bible Edition version 2.00, 19 Jan. 2005. Winterbourne, ON. Canada: Online Bible, 1992-2005.

TWOT—R. Laird Harris, ed., Gleason L. Archer, Jr., assoc. ed., Bruce K. Waltke, assoc. ed., *Theological Wordbook of the Old Testament, 2 vol.* Chicago: Moody Press, 1980.

ACKNOWLEDGEMENTS

—〰—

I thank the Lord Jesus Christ for allowing me the time to study and grasp God's great plan for history as it relates to mankind. What started out as a short series of messages delivered in Edinburgh, Scotland, has resulted in a worldwide ministry enabling me to proclaim the Lord and His coming earthly kingdom to this generation. As I delved deeper into the relationship of the European Union with the world around it, I began to see that for the first time in history, fulfillment of Daniel's prophecy regarding the final form of the Roman Empire was now feasible. What began as lessons from Daniel, turned into a time of finding answers to questions first formed while working as an engineer for an international company. Those questions involved far more than international business and, as I now understand, touch the lives of every human being. Today's EU alerted me and those who have studied this material to *"look up, and lift up your heads; for your redemption draweth nigh"* (Luke 21:28).

I would also like to thank my two editors, my wife, Pam, and Diane Valentine, who translated my engineering language writing skills into readable English. Their tireless work and patience as they sought to clarify and assist me to present my thoughts and concepts in clear and precise text went well beyond normal endurance. Their valuable inputs enabled me to convey God's great purpose of history in terms all can understand. I am most grateful to them for their assistance.

PREFACE

—⟋⟍⟍—

Is the European Union the embryo of mankind's fourth and final kingdom as foretold by the prophet Daniel?

Our world seems to be speeding down a one-way highway to its ultimate destruction. Global turmoil rules the day as both natural and manmade disasters take place in rapid succession filling hearts with fear. Institutions that once promoted stability and gave life purpose and meaning are being attacked and destroyed. Nothing that once was considered sacred has gone unchallenged, from marriage and the family to the Bible and even the existence of God Himself.

It is as if a giant were kicking away the props of our world to prepare humanity to accept a new global order. According to the Bible, this is just what will happen prior to the return of Jesus Christ to the earth. Satan, as ruler of this present world, will orchestrate his ultimate rebellion against God by establishing a kingdom that will encompass the whole earth, subdue it, and divide it into ten regions ruled by his man, the Antichrist. He will accomplish this through the alliance of a worldwide supra-government united with a supra-religion.

The very real possibility that the European Union is the start of this kingdom is thoroughly explored after first establishing the necessary Biblical foundation that is essential to understanding and identifying that final kingdom.

PROLOGUE

—⟩⟩⟩—

The entire world's a stage,
And all the men and women merely players;
They all have their exits and their entrances,[1]

Today's "stage" is far different from the 16th century "stage" William Shakespeare wrote about in his play, *As You Like It.* Men and women are still players and with a mere press of a button on a remote control, the world stage is presented before our eyes through the medium of the Plasma TV with Surround Sound.

Today as Americans, we are participating less and less as players because we fail to grasp fully the significance of the events television communicates to us. The sound bites and spectacular pictures seem to have little relevance to our own personal lives. Added to this is the tendency of American news channels to offer only news that is "American-centric." Because Americans only passively observe the world stage, they fail to see that it is being altered in a way that may soon directly touch the lives of every living American.

Though they are only hours away by air, Europe and the Middle East are perceived as distant lands of little significance to the average American citizen. Yet in Europe there are plans underway that could disrupt American government and business—no, not terrorism, but plans just as devastating to our way of life. Waiting in the "wings" of the world's theater is the looming potential loss of religious freedom, the hindering of the gospel of salvation, and the end of world missions.

Following World War I, the world began to be rearranged for what may be the final act of human history as prophesied by the prophet Daniel and Apostle John. A European empire is forming and may soon take center stage of the world. Certainly, history has witnessed the rise and fall of many empires and their cultures: empires such as Babylon, Mede/Persia, Greece, and as famously described by Gibbon, the Roman Empire. What makes the recent rise of the European empire significant is that it appears to satisfy the description given in Daniel 7:23 of being *"diverse."* Additionally, while the idea of the European Union was first conceived in the 1920s, the actual founding of its forerunner, the Council of Europe, occurred within days of an equally significant change to the world theater, the re-birth of the nation of Israel in May of 1948.

Unfortunately, the possible significance of these two events has gone unnoticed. Why? Because Americans have not been engaged in the world beyond the shores of the U.S. Specifically, for American Christians, the answer could be that many decline serious study of the prophets of the Old Testament and, therefore, fail to see the correlation between the European Union and what the Bible foretells as the final world empire.

During World War II, Christians became disillusioned and wary of prophetic teaching because many had set dates for Christ's return. Similarly, the "prophecy craze" of the 1970s with its emphasis on date setting and sensationalism seriously discredited the subject. Consequently, many well-meaning Christians have avoided studying the prophets and as a result, they ignore significant portions of the Scriptures. Furthermore, many churches discourage prophetic study, viewing it as divisive, inconclusive, and too controversial to be worth contending for. Finally, the doctrine of Replacement Theology, the teaching that the Christian Church has permanently replaced Israel in God's plan, has convinced many believers that Israel has no place in future events and that most of the Old Testament prophecies are to be taken allegorically or spiritually rather than literally. Such a position prevents them from recognizing that the "stage is being set" in our times. Yet, considering the United Nations' decision to re-establish Israel as a nation and recognizing the present centrality of Israel in world affairs, it is clear that the "dry bones" spoken of by Ezekiel as representing that nation are ready to "take on flesh" for the "final act" of mankind's history that immediately precedes the Messiah's return.

Jean Monnet, the true founder of the European Union, introduced the world stage for the final empire when he stated in his memoirs:

> The sovereign nations of the past can no longer solve the problems of the present: they cannot ensure their own progress or control their own future. And the Community itself is only a stage on the way to the organized world of tomorrow.[2]

His "world of tomorrow" and that foretold by the Bible share many common characteristics. This book seeks to demonstrate the commonality and how it uniquely relates to the nation of Israel.

This book is not intended to serve as a political commentary about world government and its threat to the American way of life. Its purpose is to alert Christians of all nations of the need and urgency to proclaim the truth of God's Word while there is still time and to realize that Bible events occurring today are very relevant.

In that vein, this book offers help for those who are seeking more information about the relevancy of world events to their lives. In particular, the reader can expect the following:

- A foundational explanation of God's plan and purpose for history, beginning with the creation of the universe and culminating in the Second Coming of the Lord Jesus Christ to rule and reign on the earth — As a result, the reader will be better able to understand world events and God's purposes in allowing evil to exist.

- An understanding of the feasibility of God's prophetic events taking place in our modern world when the books of Daniel and Revelation are considered in their literal sense

- A possible scenario of how God may be preparing the stage for the final act of history — Events once thought impossible by many are now possible in our modern world. It will be shown that the European Union could be the first kingdom in history that fulfills the prophecy spoken of in Daniel 7:23 regarding the characteristic of being "diverse."

- A presentation of evidence supporting the hypothesis that the European Union is the embryo of humanity's final kingdom — It will be shown that the EU has chosen symbolism that bears a striking resemblance to descriptions given in Revelation chapters 13, 17, and 19. It will be discussed just how the European Union is a resurgence of the Roman Empire and how a worldwide religion could be established that would be acceptable to all religions of the world.

How these factors relate to the nation of Israel and the Jewish people will also be addressed, for God's plan always has been and always will be centered on Israel.

This book is intended to be like the watchman making the cry in the night that there is imminent danger. It serves to alert Christians of the need to pay attention to world events, to get involved in sharing the Gospel, to correctly understand and study God's prophetic teaching, and to be ready for the coming of the Lord for His Bride, the Church. It does not ask the Christian to get involved in the political arena; rather, it suggests that the Christian grasp the eternal aspects of life and "redeem the time." May each reader come to understand God's plan and purpose of history and, through this understanding, seek to know the unique role God wants him or her to fill in that plan and purpose.

It is recognized that the scenario presented is just that, a possible scenario for setting the stage for the final act. This book offers its readers a thought out, logically presented and well documented study discussing how these events are now feasible. Since all men and women are players, not simply spectators upon the world stage, this book develops an awareness of what is happening today and what is to come.

Unlike Shakespeare's fictionalized entertainment, the real "play" is to be taken seriously for it is God's plan for this earth and its occupants. The events and choices made by those "players," will affect their eternal destinies. Through the understanding gained by this book, it is hoped that individuals will become motivated to get involved not just as passive spectators, but also as participants in God's plan— the greatest drama of history.

Act I – A Foundational Basis

—◁w▷—

ACT I – SCENE 1
GOD'S PLAN AND PURPOSE FOR HUMANITY

—◊◊◊—

Time: Eternity Past
Setting: Before the Foundation of the World
Enter: God

In the beginning God created the heaven and the earth.

Genesis 1:1

Hidden in the depths of eternal ages,[1] the uncreated Triune God purposed to begin an age to declare His glory. The "curtains" of the age opened, revealing the myriads of stars shining in a newly born universe:

The heavens declare the glory of God; and the firmament sheweth his handywork. Day unto day uttereth speech, and night unto night sheweth knowledge.

Psalms 19:1, 2

God's Glory

Like the psalmist we too can appreciate the immensity of the heavens with the vast and varied constellations of stars and spectacular show of twinkling lights. There is more to

25

be observed than just a beautiful sight—the heavens are the continual declarations of the glory of God.[2] No one else can speak a star into existence; much less place it in the heavens. He is the creator of the universe and we see an expression of His glory when we gaze at the night sky. The psalmist indicates that this handiwork of God does not merely serve as a backdrop for world history but reveals knowledge about God's glory.

"Glory" is "the exercise and display of what constitutes the distinctive excellence of the subject of which it is spoken."[3] What constitutes the "distinctive excellence" of God is the sum total of His divine attributes. These attributes are intrinsic in God.[4] Hence, the glory of God is the exercise and display of His divine attributes. This display of His attributes is not a need by God for self-gratification but a natural manifestation of His very being as God. Although human beings and angels appreciate and learn more about God from the display of His attributes, this revelation is a natural expression of God that radiates from His intrinsic being, independent of the need for or acknowledgement by an audience. When we recognize these attributes and speak of them, we join with all of creation in praise and worship, declaring His glory. When acknowledging these attributes, mankind glorifies God.[5] Three thousand years ago, King David of Israel wrote, *"Give unto the Lord the glory due unto His name; worship the Lord in the beauty of holiness"* (Ps. 29:2).

The heavens are not the only means by which God exercises and displays His glory or attributes. God's qualities or characteristics appear throughout the pages of Scripture. He exercises them during interactions with His creation, which includes the universe, the earth and all it contains, as well as human beings and angels. God purposely placed human beings as well as angels on His world "stage." As history unfolds through the Bible, it becomes evident that God intentionally has been using His interactions with creation, angels, and humanity in order to progressively reveal Himself. Apart from His dealings with creation, some of His attributes cannot be demonstrated for the clear-cut reason that He is entirely divine, an utterly sinless Being. Within the Triunity, which is composed of God the Father, God the Son, and God the Holy Spirit, there is harmony and sinless perfection. The Westminster Confession of Faith says that God "is alone in and unto Himself all-sufficient, not standing in need of any creatures which He hath made, nor deriving any glory from them, but only manifesting His own glory in, by, unto, and upon them."[6]

God's Glory Manifested through Humanity

Certainly, the universe reflects God's infiniteness and power—His attributes of omnipresence and omnipotence. For instance, our need for and dependence upon the light and heat of the sun trumpet His sovereignty as well as His wisdom and omniscience. Though the universe with its intricate and grand design, awesome grandeur, and artistic beauty serves to "declare" some of God's attributes and glory, it cannot reveal them all. God's attributes such as grace, mercy, patience, and love have been characterized as "manifestative,"[7] meaning that a recipient is needed for the attribute to be expressed or manifested. One of these attributes is shown in the verse that states, *"God is love"* (1 John 4:8, 16). God's love, one of His manifestative attributes, requires a recipient for it to be expressed. In this manifestation of His love, God created man. How could mankind be the instrument by which God could express His manifestative attribute of love? First, human beings became the recipients or beneficiaries of God's love:

In this was manifested the love of God toward us,
because that God sent his only begotten Son into the

27

*world, that we might live through him. Herein is love,
not that we loved God, but that he loved us, and sent
his Son to be the propitiation for our sins.*
1 John 4:9-10

Second, when He took on human flesh and came to
earth to suffer and die as mankind's substitute, God the Son
became the channel through which God displayed His manifestative attributes or glory.

Who [the Son] *being the brightness of his glory, and
the express* [exact] *image of his* [God's] *person, and
upholding all things by the word of his power, when
he had by himself purged our sins, sat down on the
right hand of the Majesty on high;*
Hebrews 1:3

God's Glory Manifested through Kingdoms

God also has purposed to reveal Himself and His glory
through a succession of earthly kingdoms or governments.
This sequence began with God's first earthly kingdom in the
Garden of Eden and proceeds through successive kingdoms
of man. Earth's history will culminate with the final earthly
kingdom—ruled by God the Son, the Lord Jesus Christ, for
one thousand years (Rev. 20:4). Initially, it will be popu-
lated with citizens who have freely chosen to be a part of
it. Following this period of history, time ends and eternity
begins as God makes a new heaven and a new earth where
Christ will reign with His followers forever.

With the chronicling of the successive kingdoms, the
king of Babylon testified that the Most High God ultimately
superintends history and its governments. Nebuchadnezzar
proclaimed:

...that the most High ruleth in the kingdom of men, and giveth it to whomsoever he will, and setteth up over it the basest of men.

Daniel 4:17

A Kingdom

A clear understanding of the term "kingdom" is essential before considering how God displays His glory through them. There are three elements that compose a kingdom:

- An authorized ruler
- A realm with subjects
- An authorized ruler exercising rulership[8]

When these three elements are in place, the kingdom becomes a reality. A distinction also must be made between God the Father's universal kingdom and God the Son's earthly kingdom as well as who qualifies for citizenship.

The Kingdom of God

A sequential study of the Scriptures about the kingdom of God reveals the following two essential truths concerning God the Father's universal kingdom:

Truth 1 It includes all of creation with its "seat of government" located in the heavens: *"The LORD hath prepared his throne in the heavens; and his kingdom ruleth over all"* (Ps. 103: 19).

Truth 2 It will continue forever: *"The LORD is King for ever and ever"* (Ps. 10:16a). *"The LORD sitteth upon the flood; yea, the LORD sitteth King for ever"* (Ps. 29:10).

These Scriptures demonstrate that the realm of God's kingdom includes the entire universe; He is exercising His rule today and will continue to do so forever. Also, He is the authorized ruler of the universe because as God there is no one greater—He is the Most High God. Yet, the Scriptures also speak of a future and eternal earthly kingdom of God. It is one that will follow a prophesied series of human earthly kingdoms:

And in the days of these kings shall the God of heaven set up a kingdom, which shall never be destroyed: and the kingdom shall not be left to other people, but it shall break in pieces and consume all these kingdoms, and it shall stand for ever:

Daniel 2:44

This future kingdom will be within God the Father's universal kingdom, and its realm will be upon the earth. Its authorized ruler will be the *"LORD of Hosts,"* a name often used for God the Son, and He will rule (future tense) from an earthly throne in Jerusalem:

Then the moon shall be confounded, and the sun ashamed, when the LORD of hosts shall reign in mount Zion, and in Jerusalem, and before his ancients gloriously.

Isaiah 24:23

Additionally, God the Father (the Highest) will authorize God the Son as ruler on this throne:

He shall be great, and shall be called the Son of the Highest: and the Lord God shall give unto him the throne of his father David:

Luke 1:32

The exercise of rule in this future, earthly kingdom is found in the book of Daniel:

I saw in the night visions, and, behold, one like the Son of man [Jesus Christ] *came with the clouds of heaven, and came to the Ancient of days* [God the Father], *and they brought him near before him. And there was given him dominion, and glory, and a kingdom, that all people, nations, and languages, should serve him: his dominion is an everlasting dominion, which shall not pass away, and his kingdom that which shall not be destroyed.*

Daniel 7:13-14

The time of this coming, according to Daniel, is in the latter days and will follow the defeat of man's fourth and final kingdom. Jesus Christ's own prophetic words tell of His future coming *"with the clouds of heaven"* (referring to the Church, His Bride, and the angelic hosts) to rule the earth:

And then shall appear the sign of the Son of man in heaven: and then shall all the tribes [nations] *of the earth mourn, and they shall see the Son of man coming in the clouds of heaven with power and great glory.*

Matthew 24:30

Today Jesus Christ is Lord of the individuals who have called upon Him as Savior, and in the future, He will be both Lord and King of His earthly kingdom (Phil. 3:20; Rev. 19:16).

In summary, God the Father as King exercises His "rule" (present tense) over the universal kingdom that encompasses all of creation. Within that universal kingdom is a future earthly kingdom that God the Son, the Lord Jesus Christ, will rule. It is through this future earthly kingdom that God will present the fullness of His Being and Glory for Jesus Christ said, *"...he that hath seen me hath seen the Father..."* (John 14:9).

Citizens of the Kingdom

After considering God's plan for history, it is natural to wonder why God simply did not create the world with Jesus Christ as ruler from the beginning. It is during earth's history that God is interacting with mankind and allowing each individual to freely choose whom he or she will serve, God or Satan. When Adam chose to disobey God and to follow Satan by eating the forbidden fruit, the world became Satan's domain. Each person who has been born thereafter is born as a citizen of Satan's kingdom. The apostle Paul calls Satan the *"god of this age"* (literal translation) and from his position as ruler, he blinds the minds of its citizens so that they cannot understand the things of God (2 Cor. 4:4). John also called Satan the *"prince of this world"* (literally translated *"the earth and its system"*) (John 12:31, 14:30, and 16:11). Each individual must make a choice—to do nothing and remain a citizen of Satan's kingdom or to turn to God by trusting in His Son, Jesus Christ, as Savior and Lord. If a citizen of Satan's kingdom trusts Jesus Christ, then that individual's citizenship is transferred to God's kingdom (Phil. 3:20). Without God's intervention and plan of redemption, there could be no citizens for the Son's future earthly kingdom. Therefore, *"...when the fullness of the time was come, God sent forth his Son, made of a woman, made under the law"* (Gal. 4:4). At the appropriate point in history, God revealed His plan of redemption for mankind:

> *Who* [Jesus Christ] *verily was foreordained before the foundation of the world, but was manifest in these last times for you,*
>
> 1 Peter 1:20

Jesus Christ made this possible, during His first coming in history when He died, shed His blood, and rose again — providing redemption and salvation for "fallen" mankind (Matt. 1:21). The purpose of Christ's first advent was to display God's manifestative attributes of love, mercy, and grace when he came to die as a substitute for sinners:

But God, who is rich in mercy, for his great love wherewith he loved us, Even when we were dead in sins, hath quickened us together with Christ, (by grace ye are saved;)

Ephesians 2:4, 5

This act satisfied the wrath of a righteous, just, and holy God and provided the only way for human individuals to become God's citizens.

For the wrath of God is revealed from heaven against all ungodliness and unrighteousness of men, who hold the truth in unrighteousness;

Romans 1:18

Because God is holy and therefore pure, sin is an offense and a barrier between Him and fallen human beings. God's attributes of holiness and justice require that a penalty be paid for sin. That penalty is the death of the sinner — both physical and spiritual separation from God forever.

For the wages of sin is death; but the gift of God is eternal life through Jesus Christ our Lord.

Romans 6:23

The only alternative, according to God, is for a sacrificial offering to be made in the sinner's place that includes the shedding of blood from a pure, sinless, eternal being.

The Bible tells us that *"the life of the flesh is in the blood"* (Leviticus 17:11a) and that God requires it as the payment for sin.

As descendents of Adam, human individuals are born with fallen sin natures already present within them. Therefore, God provided the means to pay for sin and to cleanse the individual, making him or her pure and righteous in God's sight. He sent His sinless, eternal Son to shed His own blood on the cross to accomplish this and to manifest His love, mercy, and grace.

> *For he hath made him* [Jesus Christ] *to be sin for us, who knew no sin; that we might be made the righteousness of God in him.*
>
> 2 Corinthians 5:21

Not only did Jesus Christ pay the penalty of sin, but He also provided cleansing so that individuals can have fellowship with a holy and righteous God.

> *But if we walk in the light, as he is in the light, we have fellowship one with another, and the blood of Jesus Christ his Son cleanseth us from all sin.*
>
> 1 John 1:7

By simply placing faith and trust in what the Son, Jesus Christ, has done, individuals may now experience the love and peace of God as Father. The choice is clear—God's love, mercy, and grace or, His wrath:

> *He that believeth on the Son hath everlasting life: and he that believeth not the Son shall not see life; but the wrath of God abideth on him.*
>
> John 3:36

God's final kingdom, ruled by His Son, will bring lasting world peace. The Most High God will allow earth's history to progress to a climax of near destruction before ultimately revealing Jesus Christ in His glory as He descends to the earth to destroy God's enemies and to gloriously rule and reign (Matt. 24:21-22, 27). Until that time, God allows Satan with his followers to roam the earth promoting Satan's plan to be *"like the Most High."* He is also striving to keep individuals from turning to God through His Son, Jesus Christ, and exchanging their citizenship. God warns us to:

> *Be sober, be vigilant; because your adversary the devil, as a roaring lion, walketh about, seeking whom he may devour:*
>
> 1 Peter 5:8

Thankfully, God has provided the armor that we need to defeat Satan and to defend ourselves (Eph. 6:10-18).

God's plan for history will ultimately prevail. His attributes and glory will be fully revealed through His creation, human beings, angels, His Scriptures, earth's kingdoms, and ultimately, His Son—the Lord Jesus Christ.

Through a succession of man-inspired kingdoms, God has been demonstrating humanity's inability to solve earth's problems through government. He has been revealing that it is only through His Son that human individuals and the entire world can truly experience lasting peace.

But our concern is for man's fourth and final earthly kingdom, one that could well be in an embryonic form at this time. Whatever the case may be, one thing is certain—the world stage is being altered, quite possibly for the final act.

Suggested Reading:
Alva J. McClain. *The Greatness of the Kingdom.* (Winona Lake, IN: BMH Books, 1974), pp. 1-44.

ACT I – SCENE 2
SATAN'S COUNTER-PLAN AND PURPOSE FOR HUMANITY

—ɷ—

Time: Just after the Creation
Setting: Heaven
Enter: Satan, also called Lucifer

> *…I will be like the Most High.*
> Isaiah 14:14b

Satan's Manifesto for Global Rule

The approach of the new millennium in January 2000 generated widespread fear that the Y2K Millennium Bug would bring the world's computers to a halt and with it, the world as we know it. While much of the world was focusing on a non-existent "Bug," a pronouncement of far greater import received little attention. European Union Commission President, Romano Prodi, declared that the EU's strategic objectives would touch the world:

> What we are aiming at, therefore, is a new kind of global governance to manage the global economy and environment. Europe's model of integration, working successfully on a continental scale, is a

37

quarry from which ideas for global governance can and should be drawn.[1]

Commenting on Prodi's speech, Britain's *Sunday Telegraph* stated that there was "an unmistakable sense of 'today Europe, tomorrow the world.'"[2] Many men have dreamed of a global government and empire—men such as Alexander the Great, Napoleon Bonaparte, Adolf Hitler, and Karl Marx. Before exploring the idea that the European Union might possibly be the embryo of Satan's final attempt at a global kingdom under his rulership, Satan's intentions for the earth and its inhabitants need to be examined.

It was during an early act of history that Satan declared his "manifesto of global rule," which is recorded in the fourteenth chapter of Isaiah. It is also here that God declares that He will ultimately defeat Babylon, its king, and Satan. While Bible scholars disagree as to whether this chapter is referring to the Babylonian Empire of the past or to a future Babylon, many do agree that verses 12-15 refer to Satan and his goals as well as God's response to him. Satan and Babylon have been inseparably linked from the Bible's first use of the term *"kingdom"* found in Genesis 10:10 until man's last kingdom foretold in Daniel 2 and 7 and Revelation 18. For this reason, God speaks of the defeat of both Satan and Babylon in Isaiah 14. Satan's involvement with Babylon will be discussed later, but first, Satan's statement of his goal of history:

> *For thou hast said in thine heart, I will ascend into heaven, I will exalt my throne above the stars of God: I will sit also upon the mount of the congregation, in the sides of the north: I will ascend above the heights of the clouds; I will be like the Most High.*
> Isaiah 14:13, 14

In these two verses, Satan proclaimed his goal—"to be like the Most High." He is striving to achieve this goal by establishing his throne of government upon the earth and diverting mankind's worship from the true God to himself. Satan's use of the term *"Most High"* intentionally refers to God Almighty's position over His creation.

In the Bible, the names given to individuals are intended to convey "the intrinsic character of the one who bore the name."[3] The names of God "are intended to reveal the nature of God."[4] The choice of the title, *"Most High,"* points out the singularity of God and His self-sufficiency.[5] Since it indicates "the Being supreme over all, it follows that God cannot be elevated. Nothing is above Him, nothing beyond Him."[6] The psalmist praised God emphasizing His nature:

I will praise the LORD according to his righteousness: and will sing praise to the name of the LORD Most High.

Psalms 7:17

Satan initiated his challenge to the very nature of God and this title in heaven at the dawn of history just after God created the angels (Neh. 9:6).[7]

Angels are spirit beings that serve as God's ministers (Ps. 148:2, Heb. 1:13, 14). Their powers and abilities are vast, without many of man's physical limitations; yet angels are more limited than man spiritually for God did not provide salvation for angels (1 Peter 1:12). The Scriptures indicate that the myriads of angels are governmentally organized or ranked (Dan. 7:10; Luke 2:13). The highest-ranking angel is called Lucifer or "son of the morning" (a Hebrew idiom conveying the idea of the "morning star," a star so bright that it can even be seen in the light of dawn) (Isa. 14:12).[8] Lucifer's position was immediately under God and his fall from this elevated position began as a tremor deep in the unseen depths of his will and heart as Isaiah indicates: "For thou hast said in thine heart...**I will be like** the Most High." Once the inward desire had taken root, it was only a matter of time before his insubordinate defiance burst forth in rebellion against God (Ezek. 28:15). Following his revolt, Lucifer became the adversary of God and His purposes. The conflict of the ages began with this heavenly rebellion, creating a spiritual shockwave felt in the idyllic Garden and continuing to impact mankind to this day.

What Satan Cannot Do

Satan carefully chose his words in his declaration of intent. Notice, he did not say, "I will **become** the Most High." Satan knows that God is the only Uncreated One, having no point of beginning. God is both sovereign and powerful over all of His creation, which He made from nothing.[9] Additionally, He is the only source of life, He knows all things, and He is present everywhere. The very definition of God means that there is no other being or object of greater power or ability in existence.[10] Uniquely, God is the only Being Who is not limited by any power greater than He Himself.

Although Satan once possessed the highest rank of all the angels, he knows that he is only a created being, not God (Ezek. 28:14). He is fully aware that he can never become the Uncreated One, nor will he ever have the power to create life. Aware of his limitations, the best that Satan hopes to achieve is an imitation of God's Person in order to be "*like*" God.

When considering aspects of God that he can imitate, Satan also knows that God, as Sovereign, can limit him. The book of Job provides an excellent example of God's power to limit Satan. It records an occasion when Satan appeared before God in heaven and God asked him:

Hast thou considered my servant Job, that there is none like him in the earth, a perfect and an upright man, one that feareth God, and escheweth [shuns] *evil?*

Job 1:8

Satan immediately responded to God by suggesting that the "*hedge*" of protection and the blessings that God had given to Job were the motivating reasons for Job's devotion to Him (Job 1:10). The implication is that Satan had already sought to harm Job in an attempt to turn him from God and had failed because God had placed a protective boundary around Job— God had limited Satan. Only with God's permission could Satan pass through the "*hedge*" to harm Job and his family, but even then God established limits to what he could and could not do—he could afflict him but he could not kill Job (Job 1:12, 2:6). This interaction shows that Satan can be very powerful with respect to man, but God places restrictions on him. In spite of his opposition to God's purpose for history, God ultimately will reveal that Satan has unwittingly served and glorified Him. Satan's purpose and being are the antithesis of God's purpose and being. As a "foil" or contrast, he serves God by displaying God's glory more fully. This is not implying that God created Satan with this intention; rather, that God is able to turn Satan's evil designs to good.

This account in Job also reveals that despite Satan's fall, he still has access to heaven and he accuses true believers before God (Job 1:6). He will continue to do so until he is finally cast out of heaven at the mid-point of the Tribulation (Revelation 12:9, 10). Today Jesus Christ defends believers as He carries out His priestly function of intercessor and advocate, seated at God's right hand in heaven (1 Tim. 2:5; Heb. 7:25).

What Satan Can Do

Because God places limits on Satan as he strives to attain his goal of being "*like the Most High*," Satan strives to

41

achieve his purpose within those areas where he can successfully imitate God. Two such areas are the following:

- To rule and govern a kingdom
- To receive worship from the subjects of that
  kingdom

A brief study of Isaiah 14 confirms that these are Satan's two
primary goals for history—to usurp the earthly kingdom and
to receive worship from its citizens.

To be Like the Most High

In Isaiah 14:13, Satan declared his intention of being king
of a kingdom when he stated, "*I will ascend into heaven, I
will exalt my throne above the stars of God....*" Satan was
not referring to celestial stars in this verse. The passage that
equates Satan with the morning star has already been noted.
The book of Daniel applies the term "*stars*" as symbols for
earthly, human potentates or rulers, while in Job, the "*stars*"
represent heavenly principalities or angelic powers (Dan.
8:10; Job 38:7; see also Rev. 12:4).[11] Therefore, through
these scriptural examples it can be concluded that Satan
desires to have a throne and to exercise his rulership over
the "*stars*" or subjects of his realm that is to include both
angels and human beings. Interestingly, the European Union
frequently uses stars as symbols representing a united citizenship under a perfect government. This will be discussed
in a later scene.

The stars were intended to glorify God (Ps. 19:1). Satan,
however, uses the stars of our universe to divert men from
God. Through astrology, stars become another means used
by Satan to control or govern mankind. Anticipating this,
God warned the ancient Israelites:

*And lest thou lift up thine eyes unto heaven, and
when thou seest the sun, and the moon, and the stars,
even all the host of heaven, shouldest be driven to
worship them, and serve them, which the LORD thy
God hath divided* [given] *unto all nations under the
whole heaven.*

Deuteronomy 4:19

God did not create the stars to be rulers of men. Rather,
He planned for them to be a revelation for *"all nations"*
of His creative power and greatness as well as indicators
marking days, years, and seasons, causing men to turn to
Him in praise and worship (Gen. 1:14). Job confirms this
when he defended the integrity of his walk with God. He
declared that if he had worshipped the sun, moon, and stars,
God would have been just in punishing him, for such worship
is worthy of God's judgment (Job 31:26). Despite God's
warnings, man still turns to the stars in the belief that they
determine his destiny, and Satan employs them as one of his
many "tools" in achieving his rule over earth's citizens.

The Bible refers to Satan's other devious methods as
being his "wiles" or, literally, "'schemes sought out' to
deceive."[12] These are seen best in scriptural descriptions of
Satan and include his ability to disguise himself as an angel
of light, his ability to slander, to murder and lie, to deceive,
to destroy, and to tempt (Isa. 14:12; 2 Cor. 11:14; 1 Peter 5:8;
John 8:44; Rev. 20:10; Rev. 9:11; Matt. 4:3). Therefore, any
individual seeking a defense against him must be equipped
to defend himself:

*Put on the whole armour of God, that ye may be able
to stand against the wiles of the devil.*

Ephesians 6:11

Satan's Organization - Angels and Mankind

All conflicts have a beginning offensive. Satan initiated his opposition to God within the angelic realm. At creation, it was God, also called the *Lord of Hosts*, Who gave Satan the highest rank and authority over the angelic realm. The Biblical term, *"Lord of Hosts"* means *"Lord of angelic armies."* The term, *"hosts,"* refers to angels.[13]

As Lord of Hosts, God organized His angels into ranks under Him (1 Kings 22:19; Ps. 103:19-22; Rm. 8:38; Eph. 1:21). These ranks consisted of the archangel, cherubim, seraphim, and princes. Additionally, the New Testament refers to angelic thrones, principalities, authorities, powers, and dominions.[14]

For Satan to be like God, he also needed organized, ranked angelic subjects or *"hosts"* to serve him just as they serve God. Ephesians 6:12 describes them as principalities, powers, and rulers of darkness. Following Satan's rebellious leadership, at least one-third of God's angels defected, choosing to be under Satan's command rather than to serve under God.[15] Angelic subjects alone, however, did not satisfy Satan in his desire to be "like God"—he needed human subjects as well.

In his "manifesto," Satan had also proclaimed his aspiration to *"sit also upon the mount of the congregation."* The word *"sit"* indicates his desire to sit upon a throne and to rule. Biblically, the one who sits upon the throne is the one who has the power to rule (1 Kings 1:30; Ps. 132:12; Jer. 13:13). The word *"congregation"* refers to governed humanity. Simply stated—Satan wants to "be king of the hill," ruling mankind.

A Throne and its Location

Satan is continually seeking the means by which he can achieve leadership and control of the *"congregation"* or mankind. The words, *"in the sides of the north,"* give more information regarding the location of this *"mount of the congregation."*

> *I will sit also upon the mount of the congregation, in the sides of the north: I will ascend above the heights of the clouds.*
>
> Isaiah 14:13

The phrase, *"the sides of the north,"* is found in only one other place in the Bible.

> *Beautiful for situation, the joy of the whole earth, is mount Zion, on the sides of the north, the city of the great King.*
>
> Psalms 48:2

This verse is speaking of the coming earthly kingdom of Jesus Christ that will be centered in Jerusalem. The location of Christ's throne will be *"mount Zion, on the sides of the north."* Thus, Satan's manifesto proclaims his intention: to usurp Christ's throne and to rule the *"congregation,"* the earth's entire population *"on the sides of the north,"* or from mount Zion in Jerusalem. Satan is directly challenging the promise that God gave to Israel's King David in the Davidic Covenant (2 Sam. 7:8-16; Isa. 9:7). In this Covenant God promised David that his throne would continue forever. David's descendant, the Messiah, will one day occupy David's throne in Jerusalem (*"on the sides of the north"*) for eternity. That Messiah will ultimately be the triumphal Lord Jesus Christ, ruler of the earthly kingdom.

In Isaiah's day, the expression, *"in the sides of the north"* also had a pagan interpretation that would have been familiar to Isaiah's listeners. The Babylonians believed that their gods met on a high mountain in the north of Babylon. Northern "meeting places" were common centers of worship in the ancient East—the Greeks worshiped at northern Olympus, the Persians worshiped at the north of the Caucasus Mountains,[16] and the Hindus worshiped in the Himalayan Mountains to the north.[17] Pagan people of the ancient world believed that the term, *"sides of the north,"* depicted a triangular mountain with the earth as its base and its sides converging at an extreme summit.[18] They believed that high place to be the location from which their gods ruled. The Targum, an Aramaic paraphrase of the Hebrew Scriptures, explains that this expression speaks of "extremes." Because pagan religions do not trust in the one true God, Satan has been misleading individuals throughout history in his attempt to usurp Christ's future throne of David on Mount Zion by causing them to focus on other false gods in high places.

In response to Satan's declaration, Isaiah assures future readers that God ultimately will bring his rebellion to an end, *"Yet thou shalt be brought down to hell, to the **sides of the pit** (Isa. 14:15)."* Instead of attaining an exalted throne high on the earth, an angel will bind Satan and throw him into the bottomless pit, the lowest place in the earth, during Christ's one thousand year reign (Rev. 20:1-3).[19] Following this time in the pit, he will be cast alive into the Lake of Fire for all eternity (Rev. 20:10).

In Satan's "manifesto," he further challenged God, *"I will ascend above the heights of the clouds."* The Hebrew text literally says *"the cloud,"* alluding to the cloud that led the nation of Israel during the Exodus (Ex. 13:21, 22). Students of the Bible recognize that this *"cloud"* was a manifestation of the Shekinah Glory of God. The Shekinah Glory was the finite manifestation of the infinite God upon the earth and demonstrated to all observers that God was dwelling or residing with His people, leading them, and blessing them.[20] It was the Shekinah Glory that led Israel during the forty years in the wilderness and on into the Promised Land. In this context, Satan's declaration was directly challenging God's right to rule and to lead the citizens of the earth.

Worship — Challenging "the Cloud"

In addition to guiding the nation of Israel, the Shekinah Glory also received Israel's worship each year on the Day of Atonement when the High Priest entered the Holy of Holies where the Shekinah Glory resided. He entered with blood to atone for the sins of the nation. This day marked the height of worship as well as recognition of the worshippers' dependence upon God. Therefore, Satan's declaration encompassed a challenge to God's earthly manifestation of Himself as *"the cloud"* for the right to rule, to lead, and to receive worship from the people of the earth.

Satan's ultimate challenge to *"the cloud"* of the Shekinah Glory will take place in the future when he seats his counterpart to Christ, the Antichrist, in the Temple in Jerusalem:

> *Who* [the Antichrist] *opposeth and exalteth himself above all that is called God, or that is worshipped; so that he as God sitteth in the temple of God, shewing himself that he is God.*
>
> 2 Thessalonians 2:4

In reality, the Antichrist never can replace God, being only a man empowered by Satan, but this act reflects Satan's desire to *"make myself* [himself] *like,"* or *"to act like"*[21] the Most High (the literal Hebrew use of the phrase).

The Conflict of the Ages

In order to rule the earthly kingdom and receive worship from mankind, Satan knew that he first had to seize ownership of the earth and its citizens. When God's first earthly representative, Adam, willingly chose to disobey Him and believe Satan's lie—that eating the forbidden fruit was not fatal and would, in fact, cause him and Eve to be *"as gods, knowing good and evil"* (Gen. 3:4, 5), the authorized ruler-ship of the earth and its citizens was forfeited to Satan. God then implemented the consequences of Adam's choice when He cursed the idyllic earth, causing it to grow thorns and thistles (Gen. 3:18). All of God's natural earthly creation began to suffer as it became subject to corruption and decay (Rom. 8:21, 22). Satan and his followers were included in the curse that God placed on Satan's "mouthpiece," the serpent (Rev. 20:2). God then began to unfold His promise—His ultimate plan to redeem mankind, to restore the earth, and to prepare an earthly kingdom for God the Son, the "seed of the woman."

> *And I will put enmity between thee and the woman, and between thy seed and her seed; it shall bruise thy head, and thou shalt bruise his heel.*
>
> Genesis 3:15

The promise declared that the Deliverer or Messiah would come through Eve's *"seed."* God said that her *"seed"* would *"bruise his* [Satan's] *head"*—destroying his works and power with a permanent, crushing wound (Heb. 2:14; 1 John 3:8). The serpent's *"seed"* would only bruise the *"heel"* of Eve's "seed"—inflicting a temporary, painful wound. The *"bruising of his heel"* occurred during the Messiah's first advent when Satan appeared to have succeeded in over-coming the promised Messiah when he orchestrated Jesus Christ's crucifixion. However, Jesus Christ's resurrection proclaimed Him the victor. His substitutionary, sacrificial death satisfied God's holiness that requires a just payment for sin and provided redemption for individuals who willingly choose to become members of His coming, eternal kingdom. Because of His death and resurrection, Christ will one day deliver the earth from its bondage of corruption (Rom. 8:21-

22). The mortal wounding of Satan is still in the future. Christ has yet to return to the earth to deliver the destructive blow when he will have Satan bound and placed in the bottomless pit and eventually in the Lake of Fire. In the interim, God is allowing Satan to roam freely while Christ is building and preparing the Church, His Bride, composed of individuals who freely choose to serve and obey Him rather than Satan.

The promise of the *"woman and her seed"* alerted Satan to be "on the lookout" for her as well as for her offspring. From the day that God promised a *"seed"* until Christ's resurrection, both the Old and New Testaments record how Satan sought to corrupt or destroy the righteous line of Adam and Eve's descendents through whom the Messiah was to come. God identified that line of descendents in Genesis when He declared that the Messiah would be of Abraham's seed (Gen. 12:3; Gal. 3:16). God then focused in upon Abraham's son, Isaac, and then Isaac's son, Jacob—whom God renamed Israel (Gen. 35:9-12). Clearly, God chose the nation of Israel to bring forth the Messiah. Of Jacob's twelve sons, God singled out Judah to father the kingly line of Israel and through it the King-Messiah (Gen. 49:10). God promised Judah's descendant, King David, that his kingdom would endure forever and that his throne, the "throne of David," will one day be occupied by David's descendant, the Messiah-King (2 Samuel 7:12-16).

Once the seed was identified, Satan knew that he must either destroy or spiritually corrupt the nation of Israel and the Jewish people in order to prevent the Messiah's earthly advent; otherwise, he would lose possession of his usurped earthly kingdom. The Old Testament records Satan's many attempts to annihilate or corrupt the nation of Israel. Even at Jesus' birth, Satan used Herod in his effort to destroy the Messiah, but God's intervention protected Him (Matt. 2:16). At Jesus' birth, God began the fulfillment of His promise to Adam and Eve, Abraham, Isaac, Jacob, Judah, David, and the Jewish people (Matt. 1:21, Luke 2:11). Before Jesus Christ could take David's throne in Israel, however, it was necessary for Him to redeem fallen mankind. The purpose of Christ's first coming was to open a way for sinful men to change or transfer their citizenship from the bondage of Satan's kingdom to Christ's coming kingdom (Matt. 1:21; Col. 1:13; John 1:12; Rom. 6). The cross provided the way of redemption — the physical and spiritual pain and suffering that Christ endured was the *"bruise"* inflicted by Satan's *"seed"* on Eve's *"seed."*

> *Who gave himself for our sins, that he might deliver us from this present evil world* [age], *according to the will of God and our Father:*
>
> Galatians 1:4

Christ's death upon the cross satisfied God's demand for justice and enabled Him to offer His grace and forgiveness of sins to all who willingly accept the substitutionary payment made by Jesus Christ.

Having failed in his attempt to stop the Messiah from opening the way to citizenship in His coming earthly kingdom, Satan is now striving to prevent Christ from returning to destroy him, reclaim the earth, and set up His glorious millennial kingdom that is to be followed by an eternal kingdom (Dan. 7:9-14). Meanwhile, God is continuing to work through His beloved nation of Israel in order to complete His plan of history (Gen. 12:3). God predicated Christ's return to reclaim His kingdom upon the nation of Israel's sorrow and repentance for their national rejection of their Messiah at His first coming (Lev. 26:40-42, Deut. 30:1-6, Jer. 3:11-18, Hosea 5:15, Zech. 12:10, 13:1, Matt. 23:37-39).[22] Therefore, to prevent the loss of his kingdom and his own destruction, Satan's only option is to destroy the nation of Israel and every Jewish person on earth. Without a nation of Israel, their national repentance could not take place and God's word about Israel's repentance would be rendered impossible to fulfill. Then God could not send the Messiah back to reclaim the earth and to rule from His throne in Jerusalem.

Just as Satan challenged God's word in the Garden of Eden, he has continued to do so through the ages. Ever since his failed attempt to destroy the seed, he has continued striving to annihilate God's chosen people. His motives give plausibility to the existence of anti-Semitism and why so many nations have sought to annihilate the tiny nation of Israel. Leaders of nations are under the subtle influence of the god of this world, Satan, and his followers (Eph. 6:12). However, God loves and protects Israel because He chose this nation to play a special part in His plan of history, which began with the promise made to Adam and Eve in the Garden regarding the "seed of the woman," the Messiah. It was through the nation of Israel that He came. Satan's supreme victory would be to cause God's word to fail by thwarting the fulfillment of the prophecies concerning Israel's repentance and the Messiah's return. The conflict of the ages is an ongoing spiritual battle between God's goal of history and Satan's goal of history.

While the spiritual battle wages between God and His followers and Satan and his followers, the implications offer an expanded perspective about world issues as well as Biblical answers to many questions—questions such as:

- Why is our world in a continual state of tension and conflict?
- Will humanity ever find lasting peace through man-inspired forms of governments such as the European Union?
- Why are Jewish people and born-again Christians under attack today?

By knowing God's plan of history and Satan's opposing plan, answers to these and other questions can be found.

Beginning in heaven, Satan has continued to wage his conflict against God upon the earth. During the millennia of earth's history, the earth has been the "stage" upon which Satan has challenged God and His plan. When God has accomplished His purposes, Christ will destroy Satan as He gloriously returns to the earth as its rightful ruler and King to sit upon the throne of David in Jerusalem.

Suggested Reading:
Renald Showers. *What on Earth is God Doing? Satan's Conflict with God.* (Bellmawr, NJ: The Friends of Israel Gospel Ministry, Inc., 2005).

ACT I – SCENE 3
GOD'S FIRST EARTHLY KINGDOM

—∿∿—

Time: Creation
Setting: Garden of Eden
Enter: Adam and Eve

When God raised the curtain of history, He created the universe. He placed a spotlight on one breathtakingly beautiful orb suspended among the other celestial spheres—planet earth. *Genesis*, literally the book of beginnings or firsts, records the origin of God's grand creation, which includes the stars and galaxies, the first man and woman, the first garden, the first sin, the first city, the first kingdom, and most importantly to future generations—the first promise of salvation. While not often recognized as a capital, the Garden of Eden was undisputedly the center of God's first kingdom upon the earth. It was the place where He introduced the players on the world's stage and established a pattern for man's kingdoms that were to follow in His plan for history:

> *And the LORD God took the man, and put him into the Garden of Eden to dress it and to keep it.*
> Genesis 2:15

The Garden Before the Fall

In the green, lush, fragrant garden somewhere in the Middle East, God structured His first earthly kingdom when He authorized the first man, Adam, as its ruler. This kingdom was to extend over the entire earth.

And God said, Let us make man in our image, after our likeness: and let them have dominion over the fish of the sea, and over the fowl of the air, and over the cattle, and over all the earth, and over every creeping thing that creepeth upon the earth.

Genesis 1:26

As the first authorized ruler, man was formed in God's own image and likeness, both male and female (Gen.1:27). Though he reflected God, the first man, Adam, was neither God nor a duplicate of Him. Only the last Adam, the Lord from heaven, Jesus Christ, is the *express* [exact] *image* of God (Heb. 1:3). Additionally, God completed Adam when He created Eve, who was formed from him and was to assist in his rule (Gen. 2:18). For without her, he was incomplete and unable to fulfill his responsibilities. Adam and Eve were *"one flesh"* (Gen. 2:24); together they were to co rule the earth just as Christ and His Bride, the Church, will do one day. They were the first "picture" of Christ and His Bride. Just as the Bride of Christ is to look to Him as "head," so too, was Eve to look to Adam. It is the presence of sin and its influences in the hearts of both men and women that makes this difficult to accept apart from God's help.

God gave to both Adam and Eve something that He had not given to any of earth's creatures—souls that live forever (Gen. 2:7; 1 Cor. 15:45). He also gave them, along with the angels, the power of volition or the freedom to make choices that included whether or not to obey Him.

God not only made Adam in his image but He also made a declaration about his responsibilities. In Genesis 1:26 the word *"Dominion"* means "to rule, subjugate, or reign"[1] and clearly refers to governmental aspects or duties. Adam was to be over all living things upon the earth, as "...God's representative, clothed with authority and rule as visible head and monarch of the world."[2] Thus, the realm that God gave to Adam was *"all the earth."*

God declared how Adam and Eve together were to accomplish this exercise of rulership when He said:

> *...Be fruitful, and multiply, and replenish the earth and subdue it: and have dominion over the fish of the sea, and over the fowl of the air, and over every living thing that moveth upon the earth.*
>
> Genesis 1:28

A close study of the Hebrew indicates that *"replenish"* means, "to fill."[3] Through Adam's exercise of rule, God intended to fill the realm with human beings. This is seen as God's command because the words, *"be fruitful and multiply,"* immediately precede and grammatically link with the word *"replenish,"* to fill the earth. Through Adam and Eve, God purposed to populate the entire earthly realm. Under God's authority, Adam's exercise of rulership included two aspects:

- to have dominion over the earth and its creatures
- to spread out and fill the entire earth with righteous citizens

At its creation, this first kingdom was one of harmony, peace, and prosperity (Gen. 1:31). There was unity and fellowship between Adam and Eve and their Creator as well. They walked and talked with God face to face. God had given

Adam and Eve the freedom of choice because He desired to have fellowship with them that was willingly given.

After the Fall of Adam
The Lord God spoke the following words to Adam:

> *...Of every tree of the garden thou mayest freely eat:*
> *But of the tree of the knowledge of good and evil,*
> *thou shalt not eat of it: for in the day that thou eatest*
> *thereof thou shalt surely die.*
>
> Genesis 2:16-17

The one and only command of God, to refrain from eating the forbidden fruit of the tree of knowledge of good and evil, provided a clear and simple means of demonstrating obedience and submission to God as Sovereign. Although the Scriptures recount that it was Eve who first tasted the forbidden fruit, it was Adam, as God's authorized ruler, who was the first to sin. Eve was deceived by Satan while Adam consciously and deliberately chose to disobey God (1 Tim. 2:14). Because Adam was the authorized ruler, his sin resulted in both physical and spiritual death for all of humanity as well as for himself. God's spoken words of a sure death had come true—Adam's soul experienced spiritual death (separation from God) and his physical body became subject to decay, sickness, and ultimate death (Gen. 3:9-10).

A consequence of this spiritual death was that all individuals to come would be born spiritually dead and separated from God (Rom. 5:14; Eph. 2:1-2). When Adam, as authorized ruler, chose to obey Satan rather than God, he placed himself and his descendents under Satan's authority, thereby allowing Satan to become the "god" of earth's realm. No longer was the world harmonious and peaceful; prosperity became difficult.

And unto Adam he [God] *said, Because thou hast hearkened unto the voice of thy wife, and hast eaten of the tree, of which I commanded thee, saying, Thou shalt not eat of it: cursed is the ground for thy sake; in sorrow shalt thou eat of it all the days of thy life; Thorns also and thistles shall it bring forth to thee; and thou shalt eat the herb of the field; In the sweat of thy face shalt thou eat bread, till thou return unto the ground; for out of it wast thou taken: for dust thou art, and unto dust shalt thou return.*

Genesis 3:17-19

Even after Adam's fall, however, mankind was to continue to have dominion over the earth. God reissued the command to "*be fruitful and multiply and replenish the earth*" on two more occasions (Gen. 8:16-17; 9:1). God continued His plan for history using individual men and women through whom He would bring about a chosen people, the nation of Israel, and eventually the promised "seed of the woman," the Messiah (Gen. 35:11; Jer. 23:3). Mankind continued to rule earthly kingdoms but the consequence of Adam's fall and the inherited sin nature resulted in unjust and unrighteous rulership. Fallen mankind, in concert with Satan and his goal of history, create a divided world riddled with wars, rivalries, and conflicts.

Ever since Satan rebelled against God and mankind agreed with the rebellion, the world has continually suffered under his evil leadership and its consequences. He has persisted in steering the world's population toward rebellion against God. In spite of failed attempts, he relentlessly works to glorify himself, imitate God's dominion, and receive worship by using mankind's governments and false religions. Kingdoms and empires have succeeded each other in mankind's relentless search to return the earth to Eden-like conditions and to regain the lost harmony, peace, and prosperity. All of the schemes of fallen mankind to bring about world peace apart from God fail because Satan blinds the minds of men and women, causing their wisdom to be foolish or vain (1Cor. 3:19-20).

God has permitted the world to experience disharmony and chaos. He allows it, to reveal more of Himself and His attributes. As the world is allowed to go awry, it is obvious that mankind's efforts are futile in seeking solutions apart from God. When human beings make these vain attempts, their inherent rebellion toward God their Creator is exposed. While these rebellious actions do not glorify God, they serve God's purpose by uncovering the focus of the disobedience, the sinful nature of the heart, thereby revealing His attribute of truthfulness for He said:

> *The heart is deceitful above all things, and desperately wicked: who can know it?*
>
> Jeremiah 17:9

With Adam's sin, God's first earthly kingdom ended, and Satan appeared to be the victor as he usurped the earthly realm as its ruler. When Satan's "new age" began, the world fell into spiritual darkness as he proceeded to use the realm of earth and fallen men and women to carry out his plan for history. Paul reminds those who have trusted in Christ that they are in a battle with Satan and his manifesto:

> *For we wrestle not against flesh and blood, but against principalities, against powers, against the rulers of the darkness of this world* [literally: age], *against spiritual wickedness in high places.*
>
> Ephesians 6:12

While the battle is being waged with individual Christians, it encompasses far more; for Satan embraces and uses governments and false religions to further his ends. Ultimately, he will use a supra-government allied with a supra-religion in his final challenge to be *"like the Most High."* He has done it before through man's first kingdom on the earth, Babel. The next scene will unfold the methodology he uses and provide the basis for understanding how Satan may possibly use the European Union in his last grand attempt to defy God.

Suggested Reading:
John J. Davis. *Paradise to Prison* (Grand Rapids: Baker Book House, 1975)

ACT I – SCENE 4
SATAN'S FIRST EARTHLY KINGDOM

—〜〜—

Time: After Noah's Flood
Setting: The Plain of Shinar
Enter: Nimrod

When Adam and Eve were expelled from the Garden of Eden, their environment was totally changed. They lived in separation from God in a world influenced by Satan. The earth became a very wicked place as its citizens rejected God's ways and followed the leading of their own sinful hearts, establishing a godless civilization that was "characterized by polygamy and violence,"[1] reaching its apogee under Lamech.[2] Lamech was a descendent of Cain who followed in his murderous footsteps and should not be confused with Noah's father who had the same name (Gen. 4:23). Parallel to this increasing violence was the development of cities, first initiated by Cain (Gen. 4:17). These cities served to localize and unite mankind, facilitating unification in rebellion against God. This is evidenced by mankind living in wickedness just prior to the worldwide Noahidic Flood.

During the period of history between the fall of man and the great flood, two "ruling factors"[3] restrained or governed men and women. One factor was the conscience of the individual. Paul comments on the purpose of conscience when he discusses its workings within the hearts of the Gentiles who were without the Law of Moses:

For when the Gentiles which have not the law, do by nature the things contained in the law, these, having not the law, are a law unto themselves: Which show the work of the law written in their hearts, their conscience also bearing witness, and their thoughts the mean while accusing or else excusing one another.

Romans 2:14-15

The second ruling factor during this period was the influence of the Holy Spirit to restrain evil. In Genesis 6:3 God declared that His Spirit will not *"always strive with man."* The word *"strive"* means to rule or judge.[4] Humankind, though living separated from God, had the ruling influence of the Holy Spirit. However, even with the presence of the third Person of the Godhead striving to restrain evil, humanity generally was quenching or resisting God's influence and He would not allow this to continue indefinitely.

As the earth's population increased in numbers, the Bible reveals that *"the wickedness of man was great in the earth and that every imagination of the thoughts of his heart was only evil continually"* (Gen. 6:5). God had commanded mankind to *"be fruitful and multiply."* It is apparent that the problem was not the population's growth but rather its wickedness. Mankind, made in the image of God, was not reflecting His image. During this time men and women reflected their "own self-determination, modified and corrupted by sin."[5] With the passage of time only one man, Noah, *"walked with God"* and remained righteous before Him. The Scriptures record only two men about whom it was said that they *"walked with God,"* Noah and Enoch. As seventh in the generations from Adam through the line of Seth, Enoch had "the closest communion with the personal God, a walking as it were by the side of God."[6] In contrast to Enoch, the seventh generation from Adam through the line of Cain produced a murderer, Lamech. These two lines descending from Adam contrast the righteous and unrighteous and aptly illustrate the conflict occurring during this period of time.

As previously discussed, God had promised that the Messiah/Deliverer would come one day through the woman's Seed and destroy Satan's power and kingdom (Gen. 3:15) would come the Deliverer, Messiah Who would one day destroy Satan's power and kingdom. In opposition to God's promised Seed was Satan's seed, manifested in fallen humanity, through which Satan was ever seeking to solidify his earthly kingdom by destroying the line of the Deliverer. Two prevailing trends in the history of mankind demonstrate this conflict: marriage between the godly and ungodly was one trend that Satan promoted in his attempt to corrupt the Messianic line (Gen. 6:1-4); the other was murder, the destruction of human life made in God's image (Gen. 4:16-24; 6:11-13). The human race became perverted with apostasy that was revealed in violence, murder, and all manner of wickedness.

Responding to these trends of history, God displayed His attributes of mercy and grace by delivering Noah, his family, and two of every kind of living thing (Gen. 6: 8, 19). With Noah's preservation, the line of Seth continued, ultimately bringing forth the Messiah. At the same time, the flood destroyed all ungodly members of Satan's kingdom (2 Peter 2:5), with an estimated population of over one billion people.[7] "This gave the human race an opportunity for a new beginning with God."[8]

God Establishes Government

Following the flood, God re-issued the command to replenish or fill the earth (Gen. 9:1, 7). In consideration of the evil trends of the pre-flood days and the fact that the human race had been influenced by a murderer, God "instituted capital punishment for the purpose of hindering the development of perversion again after the flood."[9] In order to properly administrate this new restraint upon mankind, God instituted government as a means to externally restrain mankind's "tendency to perversion."[10]

Whoso sheddeth man's blood, by man shall his blood be shed: for in the image of God made he man.
Genesis 9:6

A foundational concept underlying the purpose of government is to protect human life.[11] Because God created human beings in His own image, those who destroy the life that bears that image should be required to forfeit their own (Gen. 9:6). Through this command given to Noah, God established civil government[12] and unmistakably made clear an important restraint upon inherently sinful human beings who consider committing murder.

God added this third deterrent of government to the two previous deterrents, conscience and the restraining influence of Holy Spirit, as a means of assuring the fulfillment of His command to multiply and fill the earth, as well as to continue the line which would bring forth the Seed of the woman, the Deliverer.

God intends for this deterrent to be applied by "divinely appointed rulers" of government, thereby precluding personal vengeance, and laying "the foundation for a well-ordered civil development in humanity"[13] (Rom. 13:1-6). These rulers are ordained "to discharge their duties 'for good' to mankind in general and to 'execute wrath' upon those who do evil" (Rom. 13:1-6).[14] The check on this leadership is their accountability to God, for ultimately, individuals as well as governments will answer to God for their actions (Ps.

67:4, Micah 4:3). Clearly, God instituted government "for only one reason—the protection, conservation, fostering, and improvement of human life."[15]

It seems probable that the world had degenerated before the Flood largely because of marriages between godly and ungodly individuals[16] as well as the violence associated with murder (Gen. 6:2). The biblical record of this period begins with the murder of Abel by Cain and ends with the record of another murderer, Lamech (Gen. 4:23. 24).

God's grace allowed Cain to live, despite the fact that he had murdered his brother. God sent Cain from His presence with "a mark" upon him that protected him from any possible human judgment or *lex talionis*, a life for a life (Gen. 4:15). Protected from society's revenge, Cain moved to the land east of Eden called Nod. He began a family and established the Bible's first named city, Enoch (Gen. 4:17).[17] While Genesis does not provide a direct link between Cain and Satan, the Lord Jesus' own words offer a connection when He said that Satan *"was a murderer from the beginning"* (John 8:44). Most likely, Jesus Christ was referring to the first murder of Abel by Cain.[18] Just as Satan had initiated rebellion in heaven earlier, Cain demonstrated a similar rebellion against God. This rebellion was revealed when Cain became enraged because God had found Abel's offering to be proper and acceptable but his to be improper and unacceptable (Gen. 4:5; Heb. 11:4). Abel's offering reflected his godliness and Cain's reflected his ungodliness. At that point, Satan tempted Cain by appealing to his wounded pride. Cain's rebellion and pride caused him to commit the first murder.

Unlike Adam and Eve who acknowledged their sin when confronted by God, Cain boldly denied it (Gen. 4:9).[19] Because he refused to seek God's forgiveness through confession and repentance, he became disqualified to bring forth the Deliverer. This is precisely what Satan desired. With this murder, no deliverer could come forth to reclaim the earthly kingdom from Satan's control since only a righteous line could bring forth God's promised "Seed of the woman." However, when Adam and Eve had a third son, Seth, the potential for a Deliverer resumed. Once again, two lines proceeded from Adam and Eve, one righteous and one unrighteous. For each descendent, a decision was required— either choose to be righteous and follow the example of Seth or choose to be unrighteous and follow Cain's example.

Choosing Cain's way of sin, the world's population degenerated to such a state that God's attributes of holiness, justice, and wrath required Him to destroy it. His attribute of long-suffering or patience, may have permitted this situation to develop in order to demonstrate mankind's need for the added restraint of government (2 Peter 3:9). Satan, in his determination to defy God, challenged this new constraint.

Nimrod: Satan's Authorized Ruler

In the far distant past, on the Middle Eastern plain of Shinar, Satan's first attempt to unify mankind through worldwide government and religion began with a mighty hunter called Nimrod:

> *And Cush begat Nimrod; he began to be a mighty one in the earth. He was a mighty hunter before the Lord; wherefore it is said, Even as Nimrod the mighty hunter before the Lord.*
>
> Genesis 10:8-9

With acclaim came power over others, some by consent and some by force.[20] Because no mention is made of Nimrod acknowledging God's leading in his life, it is possible that his success was the result of Satan's influence prompting him. Nimrod apparently ignored the influence of God's Spirit. Just as he had succeeded with Cain, Satan may have found a ready entry into Nimrod's heart and mind through his pride by offering him rulership of a kingdom. The gospel of Luke relates how Satan tempted the Lord Jesus Christ with the offer of the *"kingdoms of the world."* Satan told Christ that He could avoid the cross and become the authorized ruler of earth's kingdoms simply by worshiping him (Luke4:5-8). It is reasonable to consider that Satan may have subtly suggested this to Nimrod with the intention of forming an alliance with him. His intention was to counter God's command to Noah to fill the entire earth with people, a command which certainly entailed a dispersion of people worldwide (Gen. 8:17).

The dispersal of mankind throughout the earth would be a threat for Satan because unlike God, Who is omnipresent, Satan is a finite, created being and cannot be everywhere at the same time. Prior to modern technology, simple logistics limited his sphere of control to a relatively small region of the earth. Therefore, through a designated leader like Nimrod, Satan could influence earth's people. Under the control of this figurehead, they would not follow God's command to scatter throughout the world. Clearly, the Bible indicates that Nimrod did not want the people to be scattered (Gen. 11:4). It seems that Satan was successful in tempting him with the promise of a kingdom because he began to use Nimrod as his instrument in uniting mankind in a single location.

And it came to pass, as they journeyed from the east, that they found a plain in the land of Shinar; and they dwelt there.

Genesis 11:2

Satan may have influenced Nimrod to choose this idyllic river valley as the location for his kingdom because its luxurious gardens and abundant water supply made it reminiscent of the Garden of Eden. Although the Flood greatly altered the world's topography making it impossible to arrive at any definite conclusion, it is conceivable that the site Nimrod selected was in or near the pre-flood location of Eden.[21] Surely, Satan knew its location and could guide Nimrod. The book of Genesis mentions two rivers that were in the Garden — the Hiddekel (Tigris), and the Euphrates (Gen. 2:14).

If these two rivers are indeed the same ones that exist today, archeological findings show that the past kingdom of Babylon and today's Iraq share this same site. The ancient Jewish historian, Josephus, records that following the Flood, some people sought protection in the newly formed mountains. However, under the leadership of Nimrod, men moved down to the plains to begin great cities:[22] Just as they had done before the Flood, the citizens of the earth continued to reject God's ways and to follow the inclination of their own sinful hearts.

Mankind's First Worldwide Government

And the beginning of his kingdom was Babel, and Erech, and Accad, and Calneh, in the land of Shinar [later named Babylonia or Chaldea].

Genesis 10:10

Nimrod was not just creating a few cities, however. He dreamed of a kingdom that would reach to heaven. Not only would this be humanity's first attempt at a kingdom, but also it would be Nimrod's foundational work or "first" in a series.[23] His ultimate goal was to expand his kingdom until it became mankind's first empire with Babel at its center.[24] A study of history confirms that this is precisely what Nimrod accomplished as the world's first conqueror.[25] From the land of Shinar, his conquests expanded to include Assyria where he founded the city of Nineveh (Gen. 10:11).[26] Estimates have placed the extent of Babel to be five to ten times greater in size than London.[27]

*And they said one to another, Go to, let us make
brick, and burn them thoroughly. And they had brick
for stone, and slime had they for mortar. And they
said, Go to, let us build us a city and a tower, whose
top may reach unto heaven; and let us make us a
name, lest we be scattered abroad upon the face of
the whole earth.*

Genesis 11:3, 4

Like many world leaders throughout history, Nimrod
recognized the value of a symbol in picturing his greatness and uniting humanity under his government. He chose
to authorize a building project that would accomplish both
of these aims—the construction of a magnificent tower
that would *"reach unto heaven."* The plain of Shinar was
the ideal location or setting for this tower and there was
ample clay and water for the construction project as well.
As a motivating factor, Nimrod appealed to mankind's pride
by saying, *"let us make us a name."* By appealing to the
prideful sin nature of human beings, this alliance between
Satan and Nimrod succeeded in concentrating humanity's
effort "into one common center which would have led to
universal despotism and universal idolatry...."[28] In blatant
arrogance, this union under Nimrod had the potential of
becoming the "world center for the human race...[with] the
monumental tower [serving]...as a physical and spectacular
symbol of world unification."[29] Through Babel's government, Satan offered united humanity a false security from
God's judgment.

Mankind's First Worldwide Religion

The Tower of Babel symbolized more than fallen
mankind's unified opposition to God, however. It also represented the first alliance between a false worship system and
government. With this exceedingly high tower, Satan hoped

to achieve his goal of being *"like the Most High,"* seated upon *"the mount of the congregation in the sides of the north"* (Isaiah 14:13). Explorations of the area support these Biblical proclamations about Satan and his expectations.

Archeological findings have revealed that a similar tower existed as far back as the 3rd millennium BC in the ancient Sumerian holy City of Eridu.[30] Eridu, which actually may have been Babel, was the religious and political center of its day.[31] The name of the tower, *Etemenanki,* means "the Building of the Foundation-platform of Heaven and Earth."[32] Other ancient records indicate that this tower or "ziggurat" was associated with the worship of the false god, Marduk ("solar calf")[33] and was declared to be "the building whose top is (in heaven)."[34] Possibly these tower-like designs originated with Nimrod's prototype at Babel. Because evidence shows that ancient ziggurats were symbols of mankind's unification through the alliance of religion and government, it would seem likely that this was the purpose of the original tower at Babel.

According to ancient tradition, Nimrod had a wife named Semiramis, a former prostitute.[35] Tradition further indicates that she is the one responsible for initiating Babel's false religion.[36] Although details regarding this religion's form of worship vary, there is consistency when it comes to her role as a mother-goddess who miraculously gave birth to a son called Tammuz.[37] If the basis for these accounts is accurate, it would seem even more realistic that Satan first attempted to present a counterfeit "woman" with her "seed" to the people at Babel.[38] Satan's unrighteous influence contrasts God's righteous influence and how like him to use an ungodly prostitute while God's plan was for a godly, chaste virgin! Of course, Satan could never bring about a miraculous virgin birth; instead, he appealed to the baser instincts of fallen mankind by presenting a prostitute. Many false religious systems throughout history have included prostitution and sexual perversion in their worship.[39] Satan consistently uses this approach in dealing with humanity, taking advantage of mankind's fallen nature to gain his desired ends.

It is reasonable to wonder if intelligent people actually believed that a tower could be built *"whose top may reach unto heaven."* It seems unlikely that its builders really thought that they could construct a tower that would attain heaven's height. More likely, the building of a tower expressed their religious intent to make contact with the "gods of the heaven." In a similar fashion, men of more recent ages have constructed soaring cathedral spires in the belief that these structures direct the thoughts and prayers of people heavenward.[40]

Thus, it is consistent with Satan's efforts to receive worship that this tower could be considered the forerunner of mankind's *"high places,"* (Lev. 26:30; Num. 22:41; Micah 1:3) and reflect Satan's desire to be on the *"mount of the congregation."* God has the final word on the matter, however, for Isaiah wrote:

> *But your iniquities have separated between you and your God, and your sins have hid his face from you, that he will not hear.*
>
> Isaiah 59:2

Humanity's first kingdom, with its center at Babel, was Satan's initial attempt to achieve his goal of uniting humanity through religion and government. It was a legitimate kingdom for it satisfied the three characteristics of a kingdom:

- Authorized ruler: Nimrod
- Realm: the earth
- Exercise of rule: concentrating humanity in one location

The Tower of Babel is a symbol of the alliance of government and religion in opposition to God. God, as sovereign, demonstrated His wisdom by introducing a new constraint.

God Creates a "Fence"

The completion of the Tower of Babel through Nimrod would have symbolized Satan's success in achieving the alliance of world government with religion—a major step in his plan. Had God allowed this Tower to be completed, the earth's population would have quickly fallen into absolute rebellion against God, for the Bible says:

> *Behold, the people is one, and **they have all one language**; and this they begin to do: and now nothing will be **restrained** from them, which they have imagined* [devised or planned][41] *to do.*
>
> Genesis 11:6

Because the earth's population had *"all one language,"* a project such as the Tower of Babel could easily be coordinated and carried out. Apparently God thought that the design could be accomplished apart from His interposition. The word *"restrained"* in this verse means to "fence in." Without a restraining fence, Satan would have been free to use fallen humanity to achieve every imaginable evil, including his goal of being like the Most High. This outcome would be the expected result because the inherent fallen natures of both men and women blind their minds and hearts causing them to devise plans that are contrary to God's will, for the Scripture says, *"the imagination* [plan] *of man's heart is evil from his youth"* (Genesis 8:21). Only when an individual transfers citizenship from Satan's realm to God's through faith in the His Son, the Lord Jesus Christ, is he or she able to begin to discern, through the Bible and with the help of the Holy Spirit, what is good or evil, truth or error.

Howbeit, when he, the Spirit of truth is come, he will guide you into all truth: for he shall not speak of himself; but whatsoever he shall hear, that shall he speak: and he will show you things to come.

John 16:13

God redirected humanity by erecting the "fence" of national languages. He caused family groups to speak in many different "tongues," bringing about confusion and frustration at the Tower's building site. Because people were unable to understand one another, they could not coordinate their efforts to build the massive structure. Instead of union based upon the alliance of government and religion, families united into groups based upon common languages and dispersed throughout the world, founding nations. Instead of being an evil, differences of speech became a positive "fence," designed by a loving God to protect mankind from further self-destructive rebellion. What humanity refused to do, God accomplished through the different languages.

At Babel, Satan had taken God's positive constraint of government and redirected it to his rebellious purposes through the willingness of Nimrod. Ever since that day, he has used man-devised governments and false religions in his attempts to return to Babel and to regain the success that he very nearly attained there. When his attempt was foiled at Babel, Satan with his finite limitations knew that the earth's growing population would expand into areas beyond his direct command. Consequently, he knew that he would need to rely more and more upon the fallen angels or demons to assist him as his organized army. The Bible uses the terms *"principalities"* and *"powers"* to designate the fallen angels who rule over the nations of the world (Matt. 25:41, Eph. 6:12). They sway the minds of world leaders through their sin natures much as Satan did with Nimrod. Conflicts, wars, mass killings, abortion, and euthanasia are all the result of

Satan and his followers appealing to the selfishness, pride, greed, and cruelty within humanity's fallen nature. This is how he attempts to minimize the earth's population and to destroy human beings that bear God's image. Meanwhile, Satan continues to direct the world's religions toward false worship and the eventual unification of religion with government, a union through which he hopes to achieve his goal.

The Tower of Babel continues to be the biblical symbol of the alliance of government and religion for world unification. Notably, the symbolic representation of the Tower has emerged again on the earth in the design of the European Union's parliament building in a modern form. The European Union, as a growing entity of nations, may be an embryonic form of the fourth and last kingdom of humanity—the one that Daniel called "diverse." The book of Daniel describes four kingdoms of mankind that follow one another during earth's history. Not only will this fourth kingdom be unique among all of earth's previous kingdoms, but also it will be the one Satan uses in his ultimate and definitive attempt to achieve his goal of being *"like the Most High."* Israel's significant involvement with this fourth kingdom, as well as with the previous three, needs to be understood before considering how the European Union may be "setting the stage for the final act."

ACT II – The Kingdoms of Scripture

—◊◊◊—

ACT II – SCENE 1
THE KINGDOM OF ISRAEL

—∿∿—

Time: Approximately 2165 BC
Setting: Babylon
Enter: Abraham

From the time in Eden until the call of Abram the spotlight was focused on one particular geographic region on the world stage—commonly called the "cradle of civilization." Notably, this is the same site of the once mighty nation of Babylon, today's Iraq. It may also be the location of the Garden of Eden. Following humanity's dispersal from Babel, in the land of Sumer, stretching from the tip of the Persian Gulf to the land between the Tigris and Euphrates Rivers, was situated the Chaldean city-state of Ur (Gen. 10:9-10).[1] In this fertile land of commerce, the Sumerians had developed a "high degree of culture"[2] and the oldest form of pagan religion on record.

In the midst of this highly cultured and pagan society, God "called" a seemingly obscure citizen, Abram, for He desired to use this man as his instrument, blessing him and giving him a unique role in His plan for the earth. Abram and his descendents were destined by God to shift the focal point of history from the eastern extremity of the Fertile Crescent to its western fringe area, now known as the Middle East. From this point on in the Biblical record, the two nations

77

of Babylon[3] and Israel have shared the spotlight while other nations and empires continued humanity's expansion throughout the earth. Today, thousands of years later; current events, world leaders, and the news media continue to focus on the dramatic clash between these two nations.

As humanity approaches the time that God spoke of as being *"the latter days,"* or the days immediately preceding the return of Jesus Christ to restore His earthly kingdom, the Bible states that Babylon and Israel will be central to world events. Therefore, insightful understanding of these future events calls for a foundational knowledge of the origin of the nation of Israel and the Jewish people as well as the Arab nations and its peoples. The roots of the conflict between the two can be traced to events that took place in the land of Ur of the Chaldees, for God's call to Abram of Ur has a direct connection to the Arab/Israeli conflict in our present world.

Ur of the Chaldees

The Sumerian city of Ur was situated on a large plain between present day Baghdad and the Persian Gulf, approximately 140 miles south of ancient Babylon.[4] By the end of Ur's third dynasty, the Babylonians had overcome the Sumerians and were ruling and occupying it.[5] Babylon's King Ur-Nammu instituted a system of centralized control that enabled him to develop a highly organized empire. This led to Ur developing into the center of this celebrated dynasty.[6] It was during Ur's third dynasty (2113-2006 BC)[7] that many temples were constructed to the moon god, Nannar, including the largest and most beautiful of them all known as the "Ziggurat."[8] From this religiously centered and prosperous metropolis, Abram, the son of Terah, moved to center stage in history (Gen. 11:31). The Bible relates very little information concerning Abram's early life in Ur. Years later, Joshua recorded the little that is known:

And Joshua said unto all the people, Thus saith the LORD *God of Israel, Your fathers dwelt on the other side of the flood* [Euphrates River] *in old time, even Terah, the father of Abraham, and the father of Nachor: and they served other gods. And I took your father Abraham from the other side of the flood, and led him throughout all the land of Canaan, and multiplied his seed, and gave him Isaac.*

Joshua 24: 2, 3

The World of Abram

The ancient Chaldeans worshipped a pantheon of gods, but each city-state tended to recognize one particular god as their own protector or tutelary deity.[9] Ur's guardian was the moon-god, Nanna and his wife was Ningal (lit. Great Lady).[10] Since Ur was the main seaport for the entire Mesopotamian region, Nanna and Ningal's fame spread throughout the known world.[11] In the center of Ur was a ziggurat with a base measuring two hundred feet by one hundred fifty feet, supporting a structure that rose seventy feet. At its pinnacle was a shrine and temple to Nanna.[12] The worship of Nanna and Ningal actually predates the Chaldeans to the time of the Sumerians, the earliest occupants of Ur.

Legend indicates that Ningal's daughter was called Innin (Lady of Heaven)[13] in the Sumerian era and that she was the goddess of the city of Erech (Gen. 10:10), part of Nimrod's kingdom. Hence, it appears that the worship of Innin began in the days of Babel. The origin of this "Lady of Heaven" began with Semiramis, Nimrod's wife. Innin continued to be an influence in Israel's later history under the name of Ishtar. Act III - Scene 5 discusses the guise of the Lady of Heaven that has continued even to this day and just how she will be involved in latter day events.

As the passage from Joshua points out, Abram and his family *"served"* or worshipped these false gods. In His

79

mercy and grace, God called Abram to come *"forth out of Ur"* and to separate himself from what was likely the pagan world of Satan.

God's Call to Abram (Abraham)

God commanded Abram to separate himself from his pagan roots and go to a land where God would bless him mightily. Not only did he prosper, but according to God's promise, his name is also remembered and honored to this day in three major religions of the world: Judaism, Christianity, and Islam (Gen. 12:2). God memorialized His promise to Abram by changing his name from Abram (exalted father) to Abraham (father of a multitude).[14]

> *Thou art the LORD the God, who didst choose Abram, and broughtest him forth out of Ur of the Chaldees, and gavest him the name of Abraham; And foundest his heart faithful before thee, and madest a covenant with him to give the land of the Canaanites, the Hittites, the Amorites, and the Perizzites, and the Jebusites, and the Girgashites, to give, I say, to his seed, and hast performed thy words; for thou art righteous:*
> Nehemiah 9:7, 8

This brief summary of Abraham and his life brings out the following four important points:

1. God chose and called Abraham. Abraham's story is not of a man searching for God and then fabricating a new religion; rather, it is the account of God reaching out and calling an ordinary man in order that he might know the true and living God. Unlike man-made religions, which suggest that God may be found only through human effort and hard work, God gives true

faith. He calls individuals to him, those who through no merit or effort of their own, are brought to know-ledge of God through God Himself.[15] God the Son, the Lord Jesus Christ, is God's ultimate revelation of Himself (I Cor. 4:4; Heb. 1:1-3).

2. God instructed Abraham. He told him to leave Ur and go to a place of God's choosing:

> *Now the LORD had said unto Abram, Get thee out of thy country, and from thy kindred, and from thy father's house, unto a land that I will shew thee.*
>
> Genesis 12:1

3. God changed Abram's name. He became Abraham, father of a multitude, a name that would serve as a memorial or reminder of God's promise to Abraham and his descendents.

4. God established a lasting covenant or promise with Abraham. It is known as the *Abrahamic Covenant* and is found in Genesis 12:1-3, 7:

> *Now the LORD had said unto Abram, Get thee out of thy country, and from thy kindred, and from thy father's house, unto a land that I will show thee: And I will make of thee a great nation, and I will bless thee, and make thy name great; and thou shalt be a blessing: And I will bless them that bless thee, and curse him that curseth thee: and in thee shall all families of the earth be blessed. ...And the Lord appeared unto Abram and said, Unto thy seed will I give this land: and there builded*

he an altar unto the LORD, who appeared unto him.

Genesis 12:2-3, 7

Abraham was no longer an obscure citizen of Ur who possibly might raise a noble family. Abram (exalted father) was to become a father of nations as Abraham (father of a multitude). This promise, however, constituted far more than just a large family with many descendents. It included:

- Abraham founding a great nation
- God's blessing upon Abraham
- God making Abraham famous
- God's blessing upon those that bless Abraham and His curse upon those who curse Abraham
- God's blessing upon all the families of the earth through Abraham
- The land of Canaan as a possession forever

Eventually Abraham journeyed around the Fertile Crescent to its western fringe and lived in the land of Canaan, ultimately called Israel. Once in the land, God began fulfilling His covenant or promise to Abraham. The fulfillment of this promise takes into account the restoration of the earth and its kingdom to God the Son, but that comes later in Act III - Scene 5.

Why God Chose Abraham

Prior to Abraham's call, God had revealed Himself and His glory through individuals. Some of these individuals included Abel, Enoch, and Noah; men whose lives and testimonies honored and glorified God (Heb. 11:4. 5; Jude 14; Heb. 11:7). As the timeline of history progressed to Abraham, God enlarged His ways of revealing Himself — He chose to reveal Himself to the world not only through individuals but also through a single nation. That nation served to reveal the glory of God and was the instrument through which Jesus Christ, the ultimate revelation of God, would enter earth's history for the first time. Israel is the nation for which He will return at His second advent when He comes to save it from annihilation by the satanically blinded nations of this world (Jer. 32:37-40; Ezek. 39:21-29; Joel 3:16; Rev. 19:11-21).

It is clear from Jesus Christ's own words that Abraham understood that the Messiah was to come through his line of descendents for He said, *"Your father Abraham rejoiced to see my day: and he saw it, and was glad"* (John 8:56). The Messiah came through Abraham, bringing salvation not only to Israel but also to *"all the families of the earth"* (Gal. 3:14).[16]

It is difficult for many to understand why God chose Abraham and the nation of Israel to be the channel through which He would send the Messiah. Moses answered this mystery when he spoke to the Israelites in the wilderness:

For thou art a holy [separated] *people unto the LORD thy God: the LORD thy God hath chosen thee to be a special people unto himself, above all people that are upon the face of the earth. The LORD did not set his love upon you, nor choose you, because ye were more in number than any people; for ye were the fewest of all people: But because the LORD loved you, and because he would keep the oath which he had sworn unto your fathers...*
Deuteronomy 7:6-8a

God chose to set Abraham and the nation of Israel apart simply because he loved them. There was nothing noteworthy or admirable about them, it was simply His choice. This is the very same reason that God sent His Son into the world to die, *"for God so loved the world...."* This reveals God's attribute of love:

In this was manifested the love of God toward us, because that God sent his only begotten Son into the world, that we might live through him.

1 John 4:9

The attribute of God's love was channeled through the nation of Israel that brought forth the Messiah, Jesus Christ. His love is extended to any individual who responds to His offer of salvation.

The distinguishing or singling out of Abraham and Israel, however, reflected a significant differentiation in God's definition of the world's peoples and nations—they were now either Jewish or Gentile, an important demarcation. From this time forward, individuals were distinguished by genealogy as either Jews or Gentiles rather than by nationality or place of origin. It is as if humanity had been driving down a single lane road and came to a fork; the Gentile nations followed one road and the Jewish nation of Israel the other. Important to these two roads is the fact that salvation is available on only one road, that of (literally "out of") the Jews (John 4:22). This did not mean that this road was without opposition. Satan knew when this fork appeared that he must pursue Abraham and his descendents along that road in an attempt to destroy them before they could fulfill their God-given purpose.

Genesis 13 amplifies God's promise of Genesis 12 by indicating the extent of the land that He would give to Abraham as well as the number of his descendents:

And the LORD said unto Abram, after that Lot was separated from him, Lift up now thine eyes, and look from the place where thou art northward, and southward, and eastward, and westward: For all the land which thou seest, to thee will I give it, and to thy seed for ever. And I will make thy seed as the dust of the earth: so that if a man can number the dust of the earth, then shall thy seed also be numbered.

Genesis 13:14-16

Here God presented to Abraham and his *"seed"* the title deed of this land forever. This deed is significant for two reasons. First, in Ur the gods were believed to own the land so Abraham could not have owned any land back in Ur.[17] Second, the deed is still in effect even in the 21st century, for it was to pass down through Abraham's descendents "for ever."

Having been promised the land, Abraham now needed a male descendent, his *"seed,"* in order for this second aspect of the covenant to be fulfilled. However, he and his wife, Sarah, were childless. In the ancient world, a man longed for a son and heir to whom he could pass on both his position as well as his possessions as an inheritance. Since God had promised to give the land to Abraham and his *"seed,"* he awaited the birth of the promised son. As time progressed and no son was born to him and his wife, he began to consider alternative means by which he could pass on his inheritance.

Looking within his own household, Abraham considered "legal heirship," a customary option of his day. Typically, a wealthy man of that time could designate an heir by adoption in order to continue his line and pass on his inheritance. Therefore, Abraham considered adopting his steward, Eliezer, making him his legal heir (Gen. 15:2). God immediately stopped Abraham from this action by declaring, *"This shall not be thine heir; but he that shall come forth out of the own bowels shall be thine heir"* (v.4). God's plan to make a nation from Abraham himself had been determined and God would not allow him to alter the line of his descendents by giving it to anyone less than a true biological son (v. 2). God reassured Abraham by repeating His promise to him:

And he brought him forth abroad, and said, Look now toward heaven, and tell the stars, if thou be able to number them: and he said unto him, So shall thy seed be. And he believed in the LORD; and he counted it to him for righteousness.

Genesis 15:4-6

Abraham's faith was demonstrated when he believed what the LORD promised him, causing God to declare him righteous.

The Birth of the Arab Nations

Despite the assurance from God, time and difficulties clouded Abraham's recollection. Ten years later, he and Sarah were still childless. Blinded by the pressure of the "now," Abraham responded to a "solution" to what he considered to be an insurmountable problem. Sarah suggested that they "help God out" by giving her Egyptian handmaiden, Hagar, to Abraham. If this maiden became pregnant, she would have a surrogate child, one that would be considered Sarah's as well as Abraham's. Having a surrogate was an accepted practice in the pagan culture of their day. In retrospect of this situation, Satan used deception with Sarah just as he had with Eve. Deception is one of the methods he employs to thwart God's plan and purpose. Sarah urged Abraham to do it "man's way" instead of waiting for God's way. Listening to his wife rather than God, 86 year-old Abraham fathered a child with Hagar. She gave birth to a son whom God had told her to name Ishmael. The Arab nations would come from the line of the child of this Egyptian handmaiden.

Nevertheless, Ishmael was not of the line through which God planned for the Messiah to be born. God does not forbid or condemn intermarriage between individuals of divergent cultures or races but His plan was for Abraham and Sarah to have a child, for they were of the same line. Abraham's relationship with Hagar was an attempt by Satan to divert Abraham's line of descendents.

The Birth of the Nation of Israel

Thirteen years after Ishmael was born, when one hundred year old Abraham and ninety-year-old Sarah were well past the age to have children, God performed a miracle enabling Sarah to conceive (Gen. 17:17, 24-25). She gave birth to Abraham's long-promised *"seed"* or heir (Gen. 21:2). Because this was a miraculous conception it appears that Sarah prefigured the young virgin, Mary, who would have a miraculous conception and give birth to the Son of God.[18] Abraham's son was a child of promise, a conception depending upon an act of God rather than man.[19] Through an aged woman and man past childbearing years, Sarah and Abraham glorified God in the birth of their son, for it demonstrated God's attribute of omnipotence or power over His creation.

The year before the baby's birth, God had restated his promise to give Abraham and Sarah a son. At the same time He also declared that the covenant given to Abraham was to continue through that son's line. God told him to name the child Isaac, (laughter), for his birth would bring great joy.

And Abraham said unto God, O that Ishmael might live before thee! And God said, Sarah thy wife shall bear thee a son indeed; and thou shalt call his name Isaac: and I will establish my covenant with him for an everlasting covenant, and with his seed after him. And as for Ishmael, I have heard thee: Behold, I have blessed him, and will make him fruitful, and

*will multiply him exceedingly; twelve princes shall
he beget, and I will make him a great nation. But
my covenant will I establish with Isaac, which Sarah
shall bear unto thee at this set time in the next year.*
Genesis 17:18-21

Because Abraham loved Ishmael, he petitioned God,
asking that this son be allowed to receive the promise. God
did not abandon Ishmael and in fact promised to richly bless
him and make a great nation of him. Furthermore, God told
Abraham that twelve princes would come forth from Ishmael.
Nevertheless, the covenant or promise given to Abraham at
least twenty-three years earlier applied to Isaac and to his
seed forever. Ishmael also was to share the blessings that
God had promised to the *"families of the earth,"* through
Abraham's promised descendent, the Messiah. These blessings were to come through Isaac, not Ishmael.

The Family Conflict Begins

It was at this point in history that the Middle East
Crisis began and continues to this day. Because the Arabs
are descendents of Ishmael and the Jews are descendents
of Isaac (both children of Abraham), it is a family feud
over the promise of God. Ishmael's descendents, like older
siblings, do not want to only "share" the possessions of the
younger siblings (Isaac's descendents), who are perceived
as favored. They cannot understand why God chose to bless
the younger rather than the elder and are enraged with jeal-
ousy and anger. It was simply God's choice to call Abraham
and Sarah because both were from the pagan center of Ur,
a location that history has revealed to be highly prized by
Satan, possibly because it may be the original location of
Eden. This choice demonstrated God's grace as He used this
husband and wife as instruments in His plan to redeem the
world and its citizens from this stronghold of Satan.

Satan used Ishmael and his descendents in an attempt to destroy the line of the Messiah before He could be born. Today he is using them again, either wittingly or unwittingly, to destroy the nation of Israel before He returns in the future. Satan has persisted in such endeavors ever since the Garden when he used Cain in an attempt to stop the line of the Deliverer. Prior to the flood, Cain's descendents were instruments used by Satan as he tried to corrupt all of humanity and the line of descent again. At Babel, Satan sought to combine false religion and government in another attempt to mislead all of humanity, which included the Messianic line.

God called Abraham with his wife Sarah to come out from a nation that practiced a pagan religion in order to form a new nation through which the Deliverer would come. That Deliverer would redeem those turning to Him for salvation, making them righteous citizens of His restored earthly kingdom. God's offer of salvation is for whoever chooses to accept it, including modern-day descendents of Ishmael, the Arabs:

> *For I am not ashamed of the gospel of Christ: for it is the power of God unto salvation to every one that believeth; to the Jew first, and also to the Greek* [Gentiles, including Ishmael's descendents] *For therein is the righteousness of God revealed from faith to faith: as it is written, the just shall live by faith.*
>
> Romans 1:16, 17

The Family Conflict Continues

While salvation is open to all, the promises of the Abrahamic Covenant were to continue through Isaac:

> *Sojourn in this land, and I will be with thee* [Isaac], *and will bless thee; for unto thee, and unto thy seed,*

89

*I will give all these countries, and I will perform the
oath which I sware unto Abraham thy father; And I
will make thy seed to multiply as the stars of heaven,
and will give unto thy seed all these countries; and in
thy seed shall all the nations of the earth be blessed;
because that Abraham obeyed my voice, and kept my
charge, my commandments, my statutes, and my laws.*

Genesis 26:3-5

Isaac and his wife, Rebekah, had twin sons. The firstborn
was named Esau and the second, Jacob. Because these two
babies had been literally wrestling with each other within the
womb, God told Isaac and Rebekah that two nations were
struggling within her (Gen. 25:22, 23). He also had said that
the elder would serve the younger. Because Esau, the elder,
was a carnal man, he despised the Abrahamic Covenant, his
birthright, and sold it to Jacob in a moment of fleshly weakness for a bowl of "stew." Although Jacob at this time was
a rascal and "schemer," later stealing even Esau's blessing,
he eventually repented and was blessed by God (Gen. 28:13-
15; 35:9-12; 48:3-4).

*...I am the LORD God of Abraham thy father, and
the God of Isaac: the land whereon thou liest, to thee
will I give it, and to thy seed; And thy seed shall be
as the dust of the earth, and thou shalt spread abroad
to the west, and to the east, and to the north, and to
the south: and in thee and in thy seed shall all the
families of the earth be blessed. And, behold, I am
with thee, and will keep thee in all places whither
thou goest, and will bring thee again into this land;
for I will not leave thee, until I have done that which
I have spoken to thee of.*

Genesis 28:13-15

Esau, angered at the loss of his blessing, determined to kill Jacob. He might have succeeded had Rebekah not encouraged Jacob to flee to her brother's home in Haran. There he married cousins of his own bloodline, Leah and her sister, Rachel. Esau, however, married two Canaanite women and later, Ishmael's daughter. This marriage alliance joined the lines of Esau and Ishmael and further cemented the growing conflict between their descendents and the descendents of Isaac and Jacob.

Esau fathered the nation of Edom, the country that later challenged and refused the Israelites passage on their journey to the Promised Land. Centuries later, King Herod, an Edomite, sought to kill the infant Jesus.[20] Consequently, the Middle East conflict, which has been ongoing for over four thousand years, has roots going back to Abraham and his children (Ishmael and Isaac), and Isaac's children (Esau and Jacob). Rather than accepting God's plan, their descendents continue to quarrel and fight.

God Defines the Line of the Messiah

Because God is truthful and trustworthy, He kept His word to Abraham. As God had promised, He blessed him with many descendents and made him father of many nations. The line for the promised Deliverer passed from Abraham to Isaac and then to Jacob.

God renamed Jacob, changing his name to "Israel" (Prince with God), indicating that He would form the nation of Israel from Jacob's line (Gen. 32:27-28). Ultimately, Jacob fathered twelve sons and each became the progenitor of one of Israel's twelve tribes. Later, God brought them down into Egypt where they lived for four hundred years, eventually becoming slaves. However, they learned many skills and greatly increased in number so that by the time of their exodus from Egypt, these twelve tribes numbered at least two million people.[21]

From these twelve tribes God selected the tribe of Judah to carry on the promise. Prior to his death, Jacob called his sons together to give each of them a prophecy concerning events that would befall their descendents *"in the last days"* (Gen. 49:1). The prophecy that Jacob gave to Judah predicted that his descendents would possess the *"scepter"* or rule Israel.

> *Judah, thou art he whom thy brethren shall praise: thy hand shall be in the neck of thine enemies; thy father's children shall bow down before thee. Judah is a lion's whelp: from the prey, my son, thou art gone up: he stooped down, he couched as a lion, and as an old lion; who shall rouse him up? The scepter shall not depart from Judah, nor a lawgiver from between his feet, until Shiloh* [Messiah] *come* [to whom it belongs][22]; *and unto him shall the gathering of the people be.*
>
> Genesis 49:8-10

Through this prophecy, Jacob indicated that the scepter would remain with Judah until claimed by his descendent and earth's final ruler, Jesus Christ.

For a period of time following Jacob's death, God Himself ruled Israel through judges. When the people of Israel began to desire to be like other nations that were ruled by visible kings, God granted their wish by appointing an outwardly impressive man named Saul as Israel's first ruler (1 Sam. 9). After bringing much grief and servitude to Israel, Saul was succeeded by Judah's descendent, a humble shepherd named David.

God's Promise to King David

David was a man who loved and honored God. Because he desired to build a permanent house of worship or a temple for God in Jerusalem, God blessed David with a promise or covenant. This Davidic Covenant relates to the coming earthly kingdom of the Messiah (2 Sam. 23:5; 2 Chr. 7:18; 21:7; Ps. 89:3-4, 28-29, 34-37; Jer. 33:19-26).[23]

> *Now therefore so shalt thou say unto my servant David, Thus saith the LORD of hosts, I took thee from the sheepcote, from following the sheep, to be ruler over my people, over Israel: And I was with thee whithersoever thou wentest, and have cut off all thine enemies out of thy sight, and have made thee a great name, like unto the name of the great men that are in the earth.*
>
> *Moreover I will appoint a place for my people Israel, and will plant them, that they may dwell in a place of their own, and move no more; neither shall the children of wickedness afflict them any more, as beforetime, And as since the time that I commanded judges to be over my people Israel, and have caused thee to rest from all thine enemies. Also the LORD telleth thee that he will make thee an house. And when thy days be fulfilled, and thou shalt sleep with thy fathers, I will set up thy seed* [singular] *after thee, which shall proceed out of thy bowels, and I will establish his kingdom. ...and thine house and thy kingdom shall be established forever before thee: thy throne shall be established for ever.*
>
> 2 Samuel 7:8-12, 16a

In David's day, the term *"house"* referred to descendents. God promised David that one of his descendents, *"thy seed,"* would have a kingdom and would rule and reign forever.[24] The word *"Kingdom"* could mean only one thing to David, rulership over Israel.[25] Obviously, David was mortal and eventually died. God intended that the Davidic rule over

Israel should continue through his descendents,[26] never being transferred to another family line.[27] Approximately one thousand years later, the angel Gabriel announced God's intention to Mary by proclaiming:

> *And, behold, thou shalt conceive in thy womb, and bring forth a son, and shalt call his name, Jesus. He shall be great, and shall be called the Son of the Highest: and the Lord God shall give unto him the throne of his father David: and he shall reign over the house of Jacob for ever; and of his kingdom there shall be no end.*
>
> Luke 1:31-33

Mary, as a daughter of Eve, was the "woman" whose seed God prophesied of back in the Garden of Eden. As a descendent of King David, she gave birth to God's Son, Jesus Christ, in fulfillment of His promise to David as well.

Israel's Kingdom Divided

During the period of history in which kings ruled Israel, God used this nation and people to illustrate two truths: obedience to God brings happiness and blessing and disobedience to God brings unhappiness and chastening. In a very real sense this tiny nation with its people was a microcosm of the world and humanity, serving as a warning of how God will deal with nations and individuals. Israel also was the instrument God used to reveal Himself as He actively dealt with this nation. His attributes were exercised when He either loved and blessed them for their obedience or admonished and chastened them for their disobedience. In some passages of scripture God likens Israel to a son whom a loving father disciplines while in other passages He likens Israel to a wife whom He loves in spite of unfaithfulness. It was to this nation that He entrusted His word, the Scriptures.

Following King David's reign (1011-971 BC), his son, Solomon, ruled. Although Solomon was gifted by God with wisdom and initially was a wise ruler, Satan was successful in drawing him away from God through idol worship, introduced to him by his many wives and concubines (I Kings 11:4). Because of this sin, the nation was divided when Solomon died in 931 BC. Ten of Israel's tribes became known as "Israel," the northern kingdom, while the two tribes of Benjamin and Judah composed "Judah," the southern kingdom.

Each kingdom had its own succession of kings, but only Judah's kings descended from David. Some kings were godly and obedient, some were ungodly and disobedient, and some were a combination of good and evil. Although God sent prophets to warn them, their words were ignored. Ultimately, idol worship brought the spiritual states of both Israel and Judah to such a decline that God was compelled to judge and chasten them by using ungodly nations as his instruments of discipline. The northern kingdom of Israel was the first to merit God's judgment and for this He used the Assyrian Empire.

It was during this time that the Assyrian Empire was developing and rising to power in the northern part of the Fertile Crescent. Nimrod and his descendents were the original founders of Assyria's capital, Nineveh (Gen. 10:11, 12).[28] When Israel succumbed to the sin of idolatry, God allowed Assyria's King Sargon II to destroy its capital of Samaria in 721 BC.[29] The Assyrians began a deportation of Israelites lasting 65 years. The conquered Israelites re-settled in Assyrian territories of the eastern Fertile Crescent,[30] while the remaining, scattered Israelites assimilated into the Assyrian culture (2 Kings 18:10, 11). This ended Israel's northern kingdom. However, it is important to understand that God permitted this to happen as a demonstration of His holy and just nature; God is almighty and capable of defending His

people. A list of 20 reasons for God's judgment is found in
2 Kings 17 verses 7-18. God summarized the reasons for the
northern kingdom's captivity when He said:

> *Because they obeyed not the voice of the LORD their*
> *God, but transgressed his covenant, and all that*
> *Moses the servant of the Lord commanded, and*
> *would not hear them, nor do them.*
>
> 2 Kings 18:12

The southern kingdom of Judah remained faithful to
God for about one hundred more years before turning
away from Him and declining spiritually. During this
time Assyria captured the city of Babylon and controlled
much of the region. The Assyrian Empire was overcome
by the Neo-Babylonian Empire in approximately 612-609
BC. Nabopolassar and his son Nebuchadnezzar II led this
assault.[31] Fearing the power of the Neo-Babylonians, the
kings of Judah turned to the Egyptians for protection rather
than to God. Judah's King Jehoiakim reflected the attitude
of the nation's people toward God when "he took a scroll
of Jeremiah's sermons, calmly cut it into pieces, and threw
it into the fire after hearing only three or four columns read
(Jer. 36:20-26)."[32] In 605 BC, the Egyptians initiated a
confrontation with the powerful Babylonians whose army
was led by Nebuchadnezzar. The prophet Jeremiah declared
that not only would the Babylonians win the battle, but that
they also would take Judah captive, controlling it for a period
of 70 years (Jer. 25:1-11; cf. Hab. 1:1-17). That same year
Nebuchadnezzar also became king of Babylon and by 587
BC he had captured Judah's capital, Jerusalem.[33] God had
allowed this defeat of Judah for the same reasons that He
allowed it to happen to Israel – they had not listened to the
Lord (Jer. 25:3).

The Babylonians took "certain of the children of Israel, and of the king's seed, and of the princes" back to the city of Babylon and taught them the ways of the Babylonians (Dan. 1:3). These young men were to serve as liaisons, favoring Babylon in dealings concerning the Jews. Again, this was an apparent attempt by Satan to corrupt those who might be of the promised line of the Messiah through the tribe of Judah. One of these young princes was Daniel (Dan. 1:3, 6).

From Genesis to the book of Daniel, the spotlight on the world stage followed Abraham from Ur in Babylon to the western portion of the Fertile Crescent, Israel. In the book of Daniel, the spotlight shifted back to Babylon in the land of Shinar, the place where Nebuchadnezzar's god, Marduk, was worshiped. Marduk was simply another name for Nannar of Ur and Satan desired to use this false god to corrupt Judah's seed. Through a godly young man named Daniel, God would reveal the future of Babylon and the Gentile kingdoms that would follow during a time of earth's history known as "the times of the Gentiles" (Luke 21:24).

Suggested Reading:
John J. Davis and John C. Whitcomb. *Israel: From Conquest to Exile*. (Winona Lake, IN: BMH Books, 1989).

ACT II – SCENE 2
GOD REVEALS EARTH'S FUTURE KINGDOMS

—〜〜—

Time: During the Babylonian Captivity
Setting: Babylon, the King's Palace
Enter: King Nebuchadnezzar

As the curtain rises, Babylon's King Nebuchadnezzar has just been given a perplexing dream from God, one that greatly troubled him. Bible scholars debate as to whether or not he could recall his own dream, but clearly the distress it gave him caused Nebuchadnezzar to desire its immediate interpretation (Dan. 2:5). Calling his wise men together, he gave what seemed to be an unreasonable request—he demanded that they not only tell him his dream's meaning but also the dream itself! Whether he had forgotten the dream or merely feigned forgetfulness in order to test his wise men is uncertain. It is certain, however, that their lives were at risk, for he told them that failure to comply with his demand would mean their deaths as well as the deaths of all wise men throughout the Kingdom of Babylon.

It is at this point in the event that four young captives of Israel, Daniel and his three companions, enter the picture. Through them, the one and only true God was exalted for His wisdom and might (Dan. 2:20). They had remained faithful to God by refusing to eat food that most likely was connected with worship of the Babylonian's false god,

Marduk. As a result, God rewarded them with *"knowledge and skill in all learning and wisdom,"* and Daniel was given the additional ability to understand all visions and dreams (Dan.1:17). In answer to the prayers of these four young men for mercy, God showed and explained the dream's meaning to Daniel through a vision. Their lives and the lives of all of the wise men were spared. As he stood before King Nebuchadnezzar, Daniel was careful to give God the praise and credit for the dream's interpretation, and eventually this pagan King acknowledged the *"most High God"* (Dan. 2:28, 4:34). Surely, God was glorified when He enabled Daniel to fulfill this Gentile King's unreasonable request by revealing the secrets of history through a dream.

Daniel's interpretation of Nebuchadnezzar's dream began with a proclamation declaring God to be the One Who ultimately controls the progression of earth's kingdoms and that He alone both establishes and removes kings. Also, it is God Who reveals the future, *"the deep and secret things:"*

Blessed be the name of God for ever and ever: for wisdom and might are His: and he changeth the times and the seasons: he removeth kings, and setteth up kings:...He revealeth the deep and secret things:
Daniel 2:20-22

Then he told Nebuchadnezzar his dream: There was an awesome and gigantic image of a man. The various body parts of this image were composed of distinctly different materials: it had a head of gold, arms and breast of silver, belly and thighs of brass, legs of iron, and feet of both clay and iron (Dan. 2:32, 33). Suddenly, a stone *"that was cut out without hands"* came and struck the feet of the image, causing the entire figure to disintegrate and blow away. Then the stone grew, becoming a mountain that filled the entire earth (Dan. 2:34, 35). The chart below indicates the symbols in the dream, the materials they were made of, and the king-doms each represented:

INTERPRETATION	NEBUCHADNEZZAR'S DREAM DANIEL 2:31-45	
KINGDOM	SYMBOL	MATERIAL
FIRST BABYLONIAN	HEAD v. 32	GOLD
SECOND MEDE/PERSIAN	BREAST & ARMS v. 32	SILVER
THIRD GREEK	BELLY AND THIGHS v. 32	BRONZE
FOURTH STAGE 1	LEGS v. 33	IRON
FOURTH STAGE 2	FEET & TOES vv. 33, 41	IRON & CLAY
FIFTH MILLENNIAL	STONE CUT w/OUT HANDS v. 34	STONE

This dream, found in the second chapter of Daniel, is the key to understanding God's plan for the Gentile king-doms during the time that Jerusalem is trodden down by the Gentile nations (Luke 21:24, Rm. 11:25). This timeframe began with Nebuchadnezzar's kingdom of Babylon and Judah's captivity and progresses forward in time through three successive Gentile kingdoms to the period of time called "*the latter days*" (Dan. 2:28). These are the days immediately preceding the Second Coming of Christ. This dream was a revelation from God regarding the relationship of four Gentile kingdoms and the nation of Israel. It will culminate with the period of history immediately preceding Christ's return.

The chart below shows the progression of earth's kingdoms and where these four kingdoms fit in.

PROGRESSION OF EARTHLY KINGDOMS

Garden of Eden	Tower Of Babel	Kingdoms Exodus - Malachi		Babylonian Kingdom #1	Mede Persian Kingdom #2	Greek Kingdom #3	Unnamed King- dom #4	Fifth & Final Kingdom
		King- dom of Israel	Divided King- dom of Israel & Judah	Gentiles are Dominant world powers Jerusalem trampled underfoot by Gentiles				Restored Earthly Kingdom Jewish & Gentile
		Israel Kingdom Era		Times of the Gentiles				Millen- nium
God's King- dom		Satan's Kingdoms						Christ's Kingdom

Nebuchadnezzar's dream was an image of a man that revealed the future. Daniel also had a revelation of the future in a dream and vision, but the symbols in his dream were animals. Nebuchadnezzar's perspective was typical of the world's view of events. He saw the kingdoms from man's viewpoint, glorifying man, while Daniel saw them from God's viewpoint, as unruly beasts.[1]

Daniel 7 and 8 discloses that Daniel himself had both a dream and a vision about the same future Gentile kingdoms from God's viewpoint. In the dream of chapter 7, Daniel saw a lion with eagle's wings, a lopsided bear with three ribs in his mouth, a four-headed leopard with four wings, and an indescribably terrible beast having iron teeth and ten horns. Later, a little horn, having eyes and mouth of a man, replaced three of the ten horns and spoke "great things." Then thrones (kingdoms) were cast down and One called the Ancient of days (God the Father) appeared on His throne. The Son of man (God the Son) came with the clouds of heaven, stood before Him, and was given an everlasting kingdom, the fifth kingdom of Daniel.

In Daniel's vision of chapter 8, he saw a ram with two horns, one being higher than the other. A male goat appeared next, first having one great horn, then four horns, and finally one *"notable"* little horn that grew very large. Both Daniel's dream and vision expand our understanding of the kingdoms. The vision actually identifies the second and third kingdom by name.

The aspects of Nebuchadnezzar's dream and Daniel's dream and visions are presented in parallel form in the chart below. When put side-by-side in this manner, the linkages become obvious and the identities of three of the kingdoms are clear. In successive order they are the Babylonian Kingdom (Dan. 2:38), the Mede-Persian Kingdom (Dan. 8:20), and the Greek Kingdom (Dan. 8:21). The fourth kingdom remains unnamed.

Interpretation	Nebuchadnezzar's Dream Dan. 2:31-45		Daniel's Dream Dan. 7:3-7	Daniel's Vision Dan. 8:3-10
Kingdom	*Symbol*	*Material*	*Symbol*	*Symbol*
First Babylonian	Head v. 32	Gold	Lion with Eagle's Wings v. 4	
Second Mede/Persian	Breast & Arms v. 32	Silver	Bear with one side Raised Higher v. 5	Ram with Two Horns--one higher than the other vv. 3, 4
Third Greek	Belly and Thighs v. 32	Bronze	Leopard with Four wings upon its Back v. 6	He Goat with single Notable Horn vv. 5-8
Fourth Stage 1	Legs v. 33	Iron	Dreadful and Terrible Beast v. 7	
Fourth Stage 2	Feet & Toes vv. 33, 41	Iron & Clay	Dreadful and Terrible Beast with ten Horns, then a little horn v. 7	
Fifth Millennial	Stone Cut without Hands v. 34	Stone	Son of Man with Clouds of Heaven vv. 13-14	

Kings and kingdoms are separate in the 21st century experience, but that was not so in Nebuchadnezzar's day. Kings and kingdoms were viewed synonymously.[2] For example, when giving the interpretation of the great image and the head of "fine gold," Daniel said to King Nebuchadnezzar in Daniel 2:38, *"thou art this head of gold"* which we would understand as referring to his position as king. Yet, in verses

39 and 40, Daniel used king and kingdom interchangeably when speaking of the kingdoms that would follow King Nebuchadnezzar.

The First Kingdom Identified
Daniel interpreted *"the head of gold"* (Dan.2: 38) as King Nebuchadnezzar of Babylon, the first kingdom of the dream. The head of the image aptly represented its preeminence. Gold was commonly used in Babylon not only as currency but also to adorn objects. The lion with eagle's wings described in Daniel's dream (Dan. 7: 4) also was an excellent representation for Babylon since the lion has always been regarded as the "king" of beasts and the eagle the most exalted of birds. The eagle wings indicated the swiftness with which Nebuchadnezzar gained his power.

Dreams and Vision in Daniel 2, 7, and 8

Interpretation		Nebuchadnezzar's Dream Dan. 2:31-45		Daniel's Dream Dan. 7:3-7	Daniel's Vision Dan. 8:3-10
Kingdom	*Scriptural Identification*	*Symbol*	*Material*	*Symbol*	*Symbol*
First	Babylonian empire Dan. 2:38	Head v. 32	Gold	Lion with Eagle's Wings v. 4	

Babylon was a highly developed and prosperous kingdom. Because Nebuchadnezzar's kingdom was portrayed as having preeminence with the value and quality of gold, Nebuchadnezzar became prideful. Daniel attempted to humble Nebuchadnezzar when he told him that it was *"the God of heaven"* Who gave him his power, strength, and glory (Dan. 2:36-37). Daniel's terms, *"the God of heaven"* and later, *"the most high God"* (Dan. 5:18) remind the reader, that while Satan sought to be like *"the most High"* through these earthly kingdoms of men, the Son of the Most High God, the "*stone*," ultimately will destroy them. His kingdom will grow as the stone did filling the entire earth (Dan. 2: 34, 35).

This first kingdom identification signifies God's prophetic word and the future of the "*times of the Gentiles.*" When Daniel wrote his prophecy, the only world empire was Babylon. Only the omniscient, sovereign God could have revealed the identities of the next two kingdoms that were yet in the future.

The Second Kingdom Identified

The image's two arms and breast of silver aptly picture the kingdom that conquered and followed Babylon, the Mede/Persian kingdom; for the arms, joined at the breast, represent their co-rule. By uniting in 550 BC, these two nations were successful in overcoming and capturing Babylon in 539 BC and destroying King Belshazzar who had succeeded Nebuchadnezzar (Dan. 5). Historical record reveals that silver was the medium of exchange for these two nations and it was "collected through an extensive tax system (Ezra 4:13; Dan. 11:2)."[3] This was the next Gentile kingdom that maintained its control over the land of Israel, treading Jerusalem under its feet. The lopsided bear in Daniel's dream also represents this Mede/Persian alliance because the Persians ultimately dominated the Medes.[4] The three ribs in the bear's mouth most likely represent the three nations they conquered, Babylon, Lydia, and Egypt.[5]

Daniel's vision confirms this identification, for the angel Gabriel told Daniel, "*The ram which thou sawest having two horns are the kings of Media and Persia*" (Dan. 8:20). The use of the image of the ram is also quite appropriate because the guardian spirit of the Persian kingdom was believed by the Persians to appear in the form of a horned ram, and the Persian king led his army wearing the head of a ram.[6] The observation that the ram's two horns were of unequal height foretold the dominance of the Persians over the Medes just as the lopsided bear had indicated. Knowledge of a culture and its symbols is helpful to gaining an understanding of the Biblical revelation, but in this instance, God provided an indisputable confirmation of the symbols through the angel Gabriel.

Dreams and Vision in Daniel 2, 7, and 8

Interpretation		Nebuchadnezzar's Dream Dan. 2:31-45		Daniel's Dream Dan. 7:3-7	Daniel's Vision Dan. 8:3-10
Kingdom	*Scriptural Identification*	*Symbol*	*Material*	*Symbol*	*Symbol*
First	Babylonian empire Dan. 2:38	Head v. 32	Gold	Lion with Eagle's Wings v. 4	
Second	Mede-Persian Empire Dan. 8:20	Breast & Arms v. 32	Silver	Bear with one Side Raised Higher v. 5	Ram with Two Horns one higher than the other vv. 3, 4

Daniel's dream and vision occurred about fifty years after Nebuchadnezzar's dream, during King Belshazzar's reign. With Belshazzar's death and the capture of Babylon, the Mede/Persian Empire became the dominant world power. The expansion of the empire encompassed Israel in addition to Asia Minor and Egypt. However, the strength of the Medes and Persians was no match for the leader of the next kingdom, Alexander the Great.

The Third Kingdom Identified

Young Alexander of Greece was the amazingly gifted general who swiftly conquered and replaced the Mede/Persian Empire with that of Greece. Once again, God clearly identified this kingdom that was symbolized in Nebuchadnezzar's dream as the image's belly and thighs of bronze. The Greeks used this metal alloy extensively to make their tools and weapons of war. Most likely, the image's belly represented Alexander himself while the two thighs signified Seleucus and Ptolemy, two of his four generals that succeeded him and who played significant roles in history as rulers of Syria and Egypt.

In Daniel's dream, the Greek Empire was represented by a leopard having four wings and heads while in his vision, it was portrayed by a male goat with feet that did not touch the ground and one prominent horn that was later replaced by four. The leopard's four wings and the goat's feet that did not touch earth both represented Alexander's swiftness in conquering the Mede/Persians.

And the rough goat is the king of Greece: and the great horn that is between his eyes is the first king.
                                                        Daniel 8:21

It was God who revealed the identity of this empire to Daniel through the vision. He also used it to demonstrate that what He promises will come true, for He sovereignly controls history and His word or prophecy is sure or certain (Daniel 2:45). Long before Alexander was born or Greece was a significant country, God not only indicated that Alexander's Grecian Empire would replace the Mede/Persian Empire on the world stage, but that four kings would share power following Alexander's death as the leopard's four heads and the goat's four horns indicate (Dan. 8:22).

Historical record confirms this prophecy, for Alexander came to power, thrusting Greece into dominance as a world empire by conquering the Mede/Persians. When Alexander died at the age of 32 in Babylon, his four generals (Cassander, Lysimacus, Seleucus, and Ptolemy),[7] divided the Greek Empire into four regions or nations (Dan. 8:22) that were individually ruled but united as one empire. This prophecy truly reveals the attribute of God's trustworthiness in that what He showed in dreams and visions centuries ago is completely accurate from the historical perspective.

Dreams and Vision in Daniel 2, 7, and 8

Interpretation		Nebuchadnezzar's Dream Dan. 2:31-45		Daniel's Dream Dan. 7:3-7	Daniel's Vision Dan. 8:3-10
Kingdom	Scriptural Identification	Symbol	Material	Symbol	Symbol
First	Babylonian empire Dan. 2:38	Head v. 32	Gold	Lion with Eagle's Wings v. 4	
Second	Mede-Persian Empire Dan. 8:20	Breast & Arms v. 32	Silver	Bear with one Side Raised Higher v. 5	Ram with Two Horns one higher than the other vv. 3, 4
Third	Greek Empire Dan. 8:21	Belly and Thighs v. 32	Bronze	Leopard with Four Wings upon its Back v. 6	He Goat with Single Notable Horn vv. 5-8

The Fourth Kingdom Identified

Unlike the previous three kingdoms, God does not identify the fourth kingdom by name. Its identification is derived from descriptions found in the two dreams. In Nebuchadnezzar's dream it is described as the image's two legs of iron with feet and toes of iron and clay. In Daniel's dream, the fourth beast is not a common, identifiable earthly creature but is merely described as being *"diverse"* (different, unique) from all the beasts that were before it. It is *"dreadful, terrible, and exceedingly strong"* with teeth of iron and stamping, crushing feet. Next, this beast is described as having ten horns, three of which are later replaced by a little horn having the eyes and mouth of a man — a mouth speaking great or pompous words.

As previously shown, Daniel identified three of the four empire/kingdoms that precede Jesus Christ's earthly kingdom by name. Many scholars speculate that Daniel's fourth, unnamed empire is the Roman Empire.[8] They base their conclusion on the historical pattern established by the three identified empires of Daniel. They note that the second empire, Mede-Persia, conquered the first empire, Babylon, and that in a similar manner, the third empire, Greece, conquered the second empire, Mede-Persia. Extrapolation of this pattern requires that the fourth empire must be the conqueror of the third empire, Greece. This makes the Roman Empire the only viable historical candidate for the fourth kingdom.

This conclusion is strengthened by the identification of *"iron"* as the metal that composes the image's legs (Dan. 2:33; 7:7). The Roman legions used iron weapons of war and "were noted for their ability to crush all resistance with an iron heel."[9] Certainly, history records the Roman army's ability to break conquered nations into pieces (literally: to "crush and demolish").[10] The image's two legs indicate the two regional divisions of the Roman Empire; the Eastern, with its center in Constantinople and the Western, centered in Rome. Only liberal scholars who oppose the prophetic nature of Daniel reject the Roman Empire as Daniel's fourth empire.[11] Nebuchadnezzar's dream also suggests that there are two phases to the fourth empire while Daniel's dream divides it even more finely into three.

The idea that there are two main phases to the Roman Empire is based upon the image's anatomical and compositional distinctions regarding the fourth kingdom—the legs of iron are distinguished from the feet and toes of iron and clay. This would appear to suggest that there are two distinct phases to the fourth empire. Bible teachers traditionally view the iron legs as the first phase, representing the ancient Roman Empire; while the feet and toes suggest a second phase—a latter day, revived Roman Empire.

The beast of Daniel's dream suggests a three-phased Roman Empire: In the first phase, the beast is called dreadful and terrible with teeth of iron and stamping feet. In the second phase, it is portrayed as having ten horns. In the third phase, a little horn with the eyes and mouth of a man comes up and replaces three of the ten horns and speaks *"great things"*

(Dan. 7:8). Renald Showers defines the three-phased Roman Empire as:

- Phase 1—The Conquering or Beast phase, symbolized by the iron and its destructive power
- Phase 2—The Ten Horn/Ten Kingdom phase, symbolized by the ten toes and the ten horns
- Phase 3—The Little Horn/Antichrist phase, symbolized by the little horn of Daniel 7[12]

He believes that Phase 1 was the ancient Roman Empire while Phase 2 represents a latter-day revived Roman Empire consisting of ten nations or regions. Phase 3, he says, will occur during the Tribulation period with the rise to power of the Antichrist (the little horn) from within the ten-nation empire of Phase 2.[13] This concept simply divides the second phase into two parts—the revived Roman Empire *before* and the revived Roman Empire *after* the Antichrist rises to power.

According to this interpretation, phase 1 of the ancient Roman Empire ended and a gap or interim period of time occurs before Phase 2. The concept of a gap is justified by the fact that Daniel "passes over the present [Church] age, the period between the first and second coming of Christ, or, more specifically, the period between Pentecost and the rapture of the church."[14] Such gaps or skips do occur in the Old Testament with respect to the first and second coming of Christ.[15] The Old Testament prophets portray Christ as being both a suffering Savior as well as a conquering King. At His first advent He came as a suffering Savior to redeem both humanity and creation; in the future He will return as a conquering King. The gap in time was not recognized by many in Israel and contributed to the rejection of their Messiah. Therefore, the gap concept is a possibility with regard to the Roman Empire. According to this scenario, the ancient Roman Empire will "revive" in the modern era as the

0009001003 55

Sell your books at
World of Books!
Go to sell.worldofbooks.com
and get an instant price
quote. We even pay the
shipping - see what your old
books are worth today!

ten-toe/ten-horn stage. This revived empire will include the former territories of the ancient Roman Empire and possibly those western hemisphere nations that trace their ancestry back to lands within the ancient Roman Empire. Certainly, this explanation satisfies the demands of the dreams and vision found in the book of Daniel.

The Fifth Kingdom Identified

The *"stone...cut without hands"* symbolizes the fifth and final kingdom that will crush the preceding four Gentile kingdoms, for Jesus Christ as the Son of God was not made with hands and is the *"stone"* that the builders (Israel) rejected (Dan. 2:34; Psalm 118: 22, Matt. 21: 42). His earthly kingdom will be established by the *"God of heaven"* beginning with Christ's Millennial Kingdom, which will be centered in Jerusalem on Mount Zion and continue forever in a new heaven and earth (Dan 2:44; Is. 28:16; Zech. 14; Rev. 20:4, 21:1).

The Legacy of Humanity's Four Gentile Kingdoms

In this fleeting review of history, it is apparent that God's word is certain and He truly does establish as well as bring down kings and kingdoms (Dan. 2:21). It is also important to understand that the ancient kingdoms of Babylon, Mede-Persia, and Greece are gone, yet not entirely. When viewed sequentially, it is apparent that each succeeding empire/kingdom assimilated historically, culturally, and religiously the preceding conquered empire.[16]

- Under Cyrus, the Mede/Persian Empire fully accepted and absorbed the Babylonian religion and culture and integrated them into the Persian world beginning in 539 BC.
- Under Alexander the Great, the Greeks began to absorb the Mede/Persian culture in 331 BC, with

a resulting amalgam of cultures later known as Hellenism.

- With Roman conquests, starting in 63 BC, the Romans "did not annihilate the religious, philosophic and cultural aspects of the various Greek and Hellenistic kingdoms but incorporated them into the multifaceted empire called Rome."[17]

This means that when the first three empires ceased to rule, their cultures and religions did not also cease to exist; rather, they merged with the succeeding empire, "so that elements of each still exist in the final phase of the Roman Empire."[18]

God used Daniel in a mighty way to give "wisdom unto the wise and knowledge to them that know understanding." It is available to those who genuinely desire to seek it out. Through these dreams and vision He has revealed his outline for human history regarding mankind's kingdoms and the coming kingdom of His own Son. As He promised, *"the dream is certain, and the interpretation thereof sure."*

Dreams and Vision in Daniel 2, 7, and 8

Interpretation		Nebuchadnezzar's Dream Dan. 2:31-45		Daniel's Dream Dan. 7:3-7	Daniel's Vision Dan. 8:3-10
Kingdom	Scriptural Identification	Symbol	Material	Symbol	Symbol
First	Babylonian empire Dan. 2:38	Head v. 32	Gold	Lion with Eagle's Wings v. 4	
Second	Mede-Persian Empire Dan. 8:20	Breast & Arms v. 32	Silver	Bear with one Side Raised Higher v. 5	Ram with Two Horns one higher than the other vv. 3, 4
Third	Greek Empire Dan. 8:21	Belly and Thighs v. 32	Bronze	Leopard with Four wings upon its Back v. 6	He Goat with single notable Horn vv. 5-8
Fourth Stage 1	Not Identified most probably Roman Empire	Legs v. 33	Iron	Dreadful and Terrible Beast v. 7	
Fourth Stage 2	Not Identified most probably a reformed Roman Empire	Feet & Toes vv. 33, 41	Iron & Clay	Dreadful and Terrible Beast with ten Horns v. 7	
Fifth	Christ's Earthly Millennial Kingdom Rev. 20	Stone Cut w/o Hands v. 34	Stone	Son of Man with Clouds of Heaven vv. 13-14	

Suggested Reading:

Renald E. Showers. *The Most High God.* (Bellmawr, NJ: The Friends of Israel Gospel Ministry, Inc., 1982)

John F. Walvoord. *Daniel-the Key to Prophetic Revelation.* (Chicago: Moody Press, 1971).

John C. Whitcomb. *Daniel – Everyman's Bible Commentary.* (Chicago: Moody Press, 1985).

Act III — The Kingdoms Of Our World Today

—⁓—

ACT III – SCENE 1
THE GRAND DREAM OF HUMANITY'S LAST KINGDOM

—๛—

Time: May 1948
Setting: The Hague, Netherlands
Enter: Winston Churchill

The revival of what possibly may be humanity's final earthly kingdom began on a bright spring day in a most unlikely setting—an 18th century Knight's Hall in the land of tulips.[1] Over 800 delegates from all over war-torn and ravished Europe gathered at this first meeting of the Congress of Europe following World War II. Reflecting the state of Europe in 1948, an eyewitness to the proceedings noted, "The vast majority of all the delegates were shabby; frayed cuffs and soiled collars were conspicuous."[2] Rising to speak, dressed in a long frock coat, a style discarded by most politicians at the start of World War I, Winston Churchill addressed the delegation. "He reminded delegates that the unity of Europe was not something they had to invent but to rediscover."[3]

> Ladies and gentlemen...there are many famous names associated with the revival and presentation of this idea. But we may all, I think, yield our pretensions to King Henry of Navarre, Henry IV of France,

who with his great minister, Monsieur Sully, between the years of 1600 and 1607 labored to set up a permanent committee representing the 15—now we are 16—leading Christian states of Europe. ...This he called the Grand Design.[4]

Rediscovering the European dream

The "Grand Design" of King Henry IV (1553-1610) is also what many others have called the "European Dream"—the re-establishment of a united Christian Europe.[5] In the wake of World War II, the battle-weary and impoverished leaders of Europe were earnestly seeking a means of dealing with religious conflicts, national frontier disputes, and internal disturbances, as well as the perceived danger from the eastern Islamic country of Turkey.[6] The meeting in Holland took place May 7-11 and represented twenty European countries as well as American and Canadian observers.[7] They came together with one purpose: to promote political unity by creating a European council whose prime goal would be to break "down national sovereignty by concrete practical action in the political and economic spheres."[8] The Council of Europe emerged out of the Congress of Europe. This council not only marked the revival of the European Dream but was instrumental in forging the first link in a sequence of events leading to the formation of the European Union and possibly initiated the fulfillment of Daniel's 2500 year old prophecy regarding the fourth and final Gentile kingdom. Today, the European Union has moved to the center of the world's stage in an attempt to restore Europe to its former greatness, first achieved with the ancient Roman Empire.

On May 14th, only three days later, the free and independent Jewish state of Israel was re-born as the prophet Ezekiel had foretold. Jews from all over the world rejoiced.

After many days thou shalt be visited: In the latter years thou shalt come into the land that is brought back from the sword, and is gathered out of many people, against the mountains of Israel, which have been always waste: but it is brought forth out of the nations, and they shall dwell safely all of them.

Ezekiel 38:8

Just as Europe had a Grand Design or Dream, so too, the Jewish people dreamed of the re-establishment of the nation of Israel with Jerusalem as its governmental and spiritual capital. This Dream had begun nearly 1900 years earlier with the destruction of Jerusalem and its Temple in AD 70 by the Roman legions.

When viewed in light of God's Word and His providence, the synchronized revival of the Grand Design and Jewish Dream is especially meaningful. The greatest battle of all time will be fought between the Gentile nations of the world and the Lord Jesus Christ as He comes to rescue His beloved nation of Israel. These two nearly simultaneous resurrections were the result of the same earth-shaking war, for the devastation it left in its wake prompted Europeans to seek permanent peace through unity at whatever the cost. So too, the annihilation of almost half the world's Jewish population during this same war evoked the world's sympathy, creating a brief "window of opportunity" during which Israel was re-established as a nation. The inseparable linkage between the Roman Empire and Israel in ancient times seemingly was "forged" again in 1948, and it appears that this prophetic connection will continue to hold significance in the 21st Century. It is quite possible that the attainment of these two dreams may be setting the stage for the final act of world history where the two protagonists, God and Satan, will have the ultimate "show-down" in the latter days.

A Tower - Symbol of the Dream

The full implication regarding the two dreams can only be understood and the "dots connected" by applying the Biblical principles and truths that were presented in the previous two acts of this book. Then the realization of these two dreams does not appear to be in any way serendipitous but the possible fulfillment of Daniel's prophecy regarding humanity's fourth and final kingdom. It was in Babylon, today's Iraq, where Satan first attempted to achieve his goal of being "like the Most High." Here he used Nimrod to unite fallen humanity at Babel by constructing a Tower. Ever since God intervened by creating language barriers and nations, Satan has desired to lure fallen humanity back to the unity of Babel in his attempt to achieve his desired ends. Significantly, the European Union has chosen a comparable symbol to represent the European Dream of unity.

Front of the EU's Parliament building, the "Louise Weiss Building"—Strasbourg

This dream of unity is reflected in the design of the European Union's Louise Weiss Building, meeting place of its Parliament. Situated on a point of land created by the merging of France's Ill River and Germany's Rhine River, this strategic location in the ancient border city of Strasbourg, has witnessed numerous battles between these two nations.

"Louise Weiss Building"—the "Hemicycle" where Parliament meets

The site was specifically chosen to reflect the peaceful merging of these two ancient enemies while the building itself represents the near completion of mankind's dream of a united Europe living in peace and harmony. Its tower of glass and steel provides not only the meeting place of the European Union's parliament;[9] but also, offices for its bureaucracy. Anyone familiar with the famous work of the Tower of Babel by Renaissance painter Brueghel is struck by the modern building's resemblance to Brueghel's tower. The Babylonian symbolism from the painting is further re-enforced by hanging gardens in the upper stories of the building and by the use of multi-lingual phrases on the exterior glass surfaces of its posterior side where Parliament meets.

"2006 - EU Parliament Building — Strasbourg"

The structure's naked, steel beams that stretch skyward give it an unfinished appearance and were intentionally designed to depict a state of incompleteness. At its dedication in December of 1999, an EU spokesman declared that the building symbolized the European Union as being "perpetually unfinished, always an imperfect unity, which we must strive to improve."[10] This designed "incompleteness" was inspired by the world-famous Swiss-born architect, Le Corbusier, who came into prominence in the 1920's achieving fame for his many unique designs of concrete, glass, and steel. He, along with Frank Lloyd Wright, is one of the two best-known architects of that era and was greatly influenced by the visionary thinking of the time. He is remembered and revered by architects even today and was emulated by those who designed the EU building. In light of the fact that individuals of the past have contributed to shaping our present world, it would be helpful at this point to briefly review history in order to retrace and recognize key individuals and events leading up to the formation of the European Union.

Dreamers of the Past

Following World War I, the 1920's was an era when men dreamed of lasting peace and prosperity. Emerging from the ashes of the "war to end all wars," individual visionaries sought the means to fulfilling these dreams. In Europe, government leaders were more than ready to pursue the European Dream. Their nightmares and recent memories were filled with the devastation of war. The crescendo of that war was the year long battle of Verdun. It was here that France and Germany battled "each other to destruction in the most intense and prolonged concentration of violence the world [had] ever seen...The number of dead and wounded on both sides exceeded 700,000."[11] In the 75 years preceding the war, those two nations battled on three occasions, each time with terrible loss of human life. All of Europe cried "never again!"

In the 1920's the newly formed Congress of Europe defined the European Dream with five goals:

- "A united Europe, throughout whose area the free movement of persons, ideas, and goods is restored."

- "A Charter of Human Rights guaranteeing liberty of thought, assembly and expression as well as the right to form a political opposition."

- "A Court of justice with adequate sanctions for the implementation of the Charter."

- "A European Assembly where the live forces of all our nations will be represented."

- All to pledge to "give our fullest support to all persons and governments working for this lofty cause, which offer the last chance of peace and the one promise of a great future for this generation and those that will succeed it."[12]

The Congress of Europe was merely restating aspirations voiced in the past; for nearly 150 years earlier, Napoleon (1769-1821) had made a similar pledge. In this pledge he had sought a single European system of government to administer a single code of law under a single judiciary. He declared that there would be "but one people throughout Europe."[13] Actually, Napoleon was merely repeating the words of the poet and statesman, Dante (1265-1321), who called for an "'empire' above them all...."[14] Dante believed the national governments of Europe needed to be constrained by a single authority, independent and above national governments—a **supranational** authority. Added to these voices of the past were those of the dominant Roman Catholic Church whose leaders suggested that only through a renewed alliance of church and state, as in the days of Roman Emperor Constantine, could the Dream of lasting peace be realized. Napoleon, also believed this principle; he formed a church-state agreement with the Vatican in 1801.

Recalling Churchill's words to the Congress of Europe's 1948 meeting emphasizing the need for a "Christian Europe," it is apparent Protestant Britain of post World War II echoed this same sentiment. To the majority in Europe, however, "Christian" would be interpreted as referring to the Roman

Catholic Church. The significant role the Church of Rome has played in the birthing of the European Union and even in the designing of its flag is discussed in Act III Scene 4.

All of these historical influences inspired the leaders of war-torn Europe to seek peace in 1919 through the League of Nations. Many hoped the League would fulfill the European Dream by establishing peace and prosperity for a united Christian Europe. Before the League of Nations could achieve the Dream, however, it had to resolve the causes as well as the consequences of the previous conflict. With little resolution and a great deal of retribution, the League struggled in the 1920's to re-unite Europe, particularly by diffusing the strong antagonism between France and Germany. The monetary reparations imposed on Germany for damages caused by the War, however, were more than that nation could bear. Believing the League could never unite Europe, two men seized the opportunity to fulfill the Dream in their own way by choosing the route of dictatorship in the early 1930's.

Standing in St. Peter's Square of the Vatican during the election of Pope Pius XI in 1922 was an atheistic Italian agitator who remarked, "Look at this multitude of every country! How is it that the politicians who govern the nations do not realize the immense value of this international force, of this universal spiritual Power?"[15] In 1923, Cardinal Vannutelli, Head of the Sacred College of Cardinals, declared that this atheistic agitator, Mussolini, "had been chosen (by God) to save the nation and to restore her fortune."[16] On December 20, 1926, the Pope "declared to all nations that 'Mussolini is the man sent by Providence.'"[17] In October of that same year, Pope Pius XI and Mussolini signed the Lateran Treaty, which recognized the Vatican as an independent sovereign state.[18] By the 1930's these two men had formed an alliance with the intent of utilizing that "spiritual Power." Benito Mussolini rose to the height of authority with the prime goal of restoring the Roman Empire with himself as emperor, united with the Roman Catholic Church.

Simultaneously, Germany's Adolph Hitler was forging the Third Reich (third kingdom) with the same goal of uniting Europe. Allied by this common aim; Germany, Italy, and the Vatican planned to form Europe into the ultimate super-state empire. In 1933, Hitler duplicated Napoleon's church-state agreement of 1801 with the Vatican,[19] and in 1936, Mussolini officially declared this trilateral alliance as the resurrection of the Roman Empire.[20] There is no need to recount the havoc and devastation of the succeeding nine years. Countless millions died, including six million Jews in Europe alone, in a world war that swept nearly every continent into its vortex. On the European front, Hitler's advance into Russia repeated Napoleon's ill-fated campaign and was the beginning of the end for this alliance. Peace finally came to a ravished and desolate Europe in 1945. Ironically, since the fall of Rome nearly 1600 years before, those seeking the Dream of Union had only succeeded in generating wars, instability, and economic failure in Europe. While some leaders genuinely sought betterment for their people, the vast majority, like Napoleon, Mussolini, and Hitler sought power, wealth, and notoriety. One seeking its betterment was Jean Monnet.

Jean Monnet — From Brandy Salesman to Statesman

Behind the scenes of world events and politics was a quiet but influential brandy salesman, turned bureaucrat, by the name of Jean Monnet (1888-1979). Like many people of the 1920's, he was deeply affected by the events of the First World War. Born into the family's international brandy business in Cognac, France, Monnet had been exposed to international business from his youth. He learned English and beginning at the age of nineteen, sold "cognac abroad for the family firm"[21] until the outbreak of the War. After a visit to the United States, Monnet developed a key principle, one that he would apply to his dream of a European union. He noted, "Here I encountered a new way of looking at a thing: individual initiative could be accepted as a contribution to the general good. ...Everywhere, I had the same impression: that where physical space was unlimited, confidence was unlimited too. Where change was accepted, expansion was assured."[22] He gained political knowledge and expertise because his family's international status necessitated a knowledge of and dependence upon politics. The Monnets often entertained envoys (government officials) as well as foreign customers who came from Britain, Germany, Scandinavia and America.[23] One such visitor was France's Minister of Commerce and Posts, Etienne Clementel.

Because he was physically unable to serve in the army at the outbreak of World War I, Monnet accepted a position under Clemental, as *chef de cabinet*. It was during this time in 1917 that he, along with his close friend and English civil servant, Arthur Salter, initiated what is considered to be the first prototype of the European Union.[24] Aided by Salter, Monnet coordinated "requisitioning merchant shipping for the Admiralty."[25] In this position, he proposed the first supranational organization designed to dictate all Allied shipping.[26] Following the war, Monnet became a deputy secretary general of the League of Nations. His superior, Sir Eric Drummond, reflected Monnet's idea that the League's Secretariat should not "consist of national delegates but of international servants whose first loyalty was to the League."[27] Monnet strongly believed the League of Nations was "a means to organize peace."[28] The League's lack of success in achieving these aspirations was a great disappointment to him. Reflecting upon the reasons for the League's failure, he concluded that Europeans had lacked the foresight necessary to foresee the eventual consequences of the League's decisions regarding Europe. Monnet wrote, "It was to take many years, and much suffering, before

Europeans began to realize that they must choose either unity or decline."[29] A second reason he gave for the failure of the League was the member veto. Any single nation could prevent a decision by the League through a single negative vote; thus unanimous agreement was required for all decisions of the League. Monnet considered these two reasons as the root causes for the failure to achieve lasting peace. He summarized this by writing, "The veto is the profound cause and at the same time the symbol of the impossibility of overcoming national egoism."[30] "...I was impressed with the power of a nation that can say no to an international body that has no supranational power. Goodwill between men, between nations, is not enough. One must also have international laws and institutions."[31] Monnet believed the veto resulted from national loyalties and only a supranational form of government could prevent such regionalism. Monnet would not forget the conclusion that a supranational government and its laws should not be subject to veto by its peoples and national governments. His experience, gained through the League's failure, prompted him to conceive the idea of a united Europe ruled by just such a supranational government (see Act III, Scene 3).

Monnet's associate, Arthur Salter, agreed, stating he believed the League could only succeed if the leadership "...would be above the power of national ministers, run by people who no longer owed any national loyalty."[32] He also concluded the way to erode nationalism would be to "split up its member states into regions."[33] The Great Depression of the 1930's put all such plans temporarily on hold.

By 1939, however, Monnet had defined the European Dream more specifically as the re-unification of Europe as it once was under Rome. It was to include a single code of laws, a single judiciary, and a single passport permitting freedom of travel within Europe, as well as free trade, and prosperity for the people. The authority governing this union was to be

free of national loyalties, national prejudices, national rivalries, and national pride, seeking only the good of each individual, regardless of nationality. Monnet's dream again was
sidetracked when World War II broke out.

When the war ended, Germany was ruined, Italy was
devastated, and Europe prayed for no more dictatorial
solutions to the Dream. The Vatican published the Pope's
views; he believed Europe "must seek religious unity
if it is to advance beyond political division, and he [had]
prayed for 'all the Christians of the East and West, that they
become united in Christ and expand the Kingdom of Christ
throughout the world.'"[34] Resolved to learn from the failures
of the League of Nations, representatives of fifty countries
gathered in San Francisco in April of 1945 to bring peace to
the world through the United Nations, an intergovernmental
co-operative. Its goal was "to promote peace and prevent
another world war."[35]

Many of the people involved with the United Nations had
roots reaching back to the League of Nations. The famous
UN building in New York was designed by Le Corbusier,
the architect described as the "...most Utopian of all 1920's
architects."[36] His rectangular tower was the forerunner of
the EU Parliament's Babel-like tower. In his many writings about social reform achieved through architecture, Le
Corbusier envisioned a "Radiant City" for people to live
in. He philosophized that if people were merely given the
right leadership, incentives, and a better environment that
included better housing, conflicts and strife would cease.[37]
This city would be a "...perfectly planned world created by
efficient technocrats..."[38] These ideas echoed those of Jean
Monnet who dreamed of a "supranational government of
the future, run by technocrats rising above all the messy
complications of nationalism and democracy."[39] As the
United Nations was taking shape, a movement motivated by
visionaries with similar ideals was taking place in Europe.

As discussed previously, the Congress of Europe met in The Hague in 1948 to promote the realization of the European Dream[40] by creating the Council of Europe.

The Dream becomes Reality — The Council of Europe

By 1949 The Council of Europe was a union of ten countries: Belgium, France, Luxembourg, the Netherlands, the United Kingdom, Ireland, Italy, Denmark, Norway, and Sweden.[41] Primarily, representatives to the Council were selected by the parliaments of member nations and sent to the seat of the Council in Strasbourg. Today the Council of Europe represents over 800 million people from 46 European countries. Its greatest function is to administer the European Court of Human Rights and support the work of its offspring, the European Union. The Court of Human Rights dominates Europe with its decisions because its rulings always override those of the courts of its member nations. Therefore, it holds substantial judicial power over all 46-member states. Its declared mission is "to preserve and to promote human rights, democracy and the rule of law."[42]

The Council of Europe's greatest weakness is its dependence upon national authorities to recognize and enforce its decisions. Influential European leader, Prime Minister Jean-Claude Juncker of Luxembourg, conducted a study and recommended that the European Union become a member of the Council of Europe by 2010. He said the EU's membership would be "necessary for the democratic security of people of our continent."[43] Through the European Union's membership, the Council of Europe would gain both legal and political power to enforce its decisions on human rights. This decision could gravely affect the freedom of religion and the proclamation of the Gospel within the EU, a concern discussed further in Act III, Scene 2. From a purely human perspective, however, the EU's membership in the Council of Europe seems logical and beneficial.

During a recent visit to the impressive COE head-quarters, the author found it quite difficult to gain admittance or to obtain any specific information relating to the Council's functions. Noticeably, the visitors most welcomed to the Council were groups of schoolchildren from all over Europe. Clearly, the observed intention is to influence and gain support from the next generation.

The EU's Beginning

When West Germany became self-governing as a federation of eleven land regions in 1949, the resurgence of its economic strength caused fear in neighboring France. This fear was grounded in the belief that both world wars were the result of disputes regarding the coal and steel industries of the Ruhr, a region in the heartland of Germany. Reaching a crisis point, the United States' Secretary of State, Dean Acheson, proposed a foreign ministers' meeting to resolve growing tensions.

In the wings, Jean Monnet had been waiting for just such an opportunity to take center stage and propose a solution he had devised back in 1941.[44] He recommended the pooling of coal and steel as the "first step of a Franco-German Union."[45] The experience he had gained at The League of Nations led him to believe that nationalistic rivalries in this instance could only be overcome by setting up a supranational governing authority over these two industries. The man Monnet chose to publicly represent his view was Robert Schuman, chief assistant to France's foreign minister.

Born in Luxembourg of a German mother, Schuman's ties to both France and Germany gave him an understanding of both nations and made him an ideal choice for the position. At the foreign ministers' meeting held in May of 1950, he offered Monnet's solution, later titled the "Schuman Plan." Its acceptance placed the coal and steel industries of France and Germany under an independent supranational governing authority called the "High Authority." This declaration was the embryo "of a common economic system for Europe."[46] After much behind the scenes negotiating, an agreement was reached on May 9, 1950, establishing the European Coal and Steel Community. The European Union regards this date as its birthday and celebrates it each year as "Europe Day." Monnet noted that with this event his "silent revolution had started."[47]

The acceptance of the Schuman Plan and the "High Authority," later renamed and replaced by the more innocuous-sounding "Commission," marked the beginning of the European transfer of sovereign rights to an independent authority. It was a trade-off, the relinquishing of the sovereign right to determine coal and steel policies in exchange for peace and prosperity (see Act III, Scene 3). German Chancellor Conrad Adenauer declared the Coal and Steel Community to be the "salvation of Europe and the salvation of Germany."[48] The Grand Dream had become reality.

The Dream Gears Up for the World

What few understand is that the Coal and Steel Community was the first cog or gear in Monnet's machine that was to promote the European dream of union. No other man did more to achieve the European Dream than he did. With time, Monnet's method of ongoing, relentless pressure to expand and increase supranational powers became known as the "Monnet method," *engrenage* (gearing up), as he called it.[49] *Engrenage* was "a blanket word to describe all those various techniques whereby the 'project' could advance what was really its only underlying agenda: a steady, relentless pressure to extend the Commission's supranational powers."[50] It got this name because "each new advance it [supranationalism] made would merely be regarded as a means of gearing up for the next."[51] Monnet's method was to propose a seemingly minor treaty or agreement. Within that treaty was hidden a principal or precedent, which once made law, opened the door to a much larger application and expansion of the granted power. "Thus, brick by brick,...the great supranational structure [would] be assembled. Above all, it would be vital never to define too clearly what was the 'project's' ultimate goal, for fear this would arouse the countervailing forces which might seek to sabotage it before it was complete."[52] He believed that a "lack of vision [by the populace] is the key to...strength."[53]

Monnet's method of establishing seemingly insignificant precedents through treaties has enabled the EU to grow in power and influence. The history of today's European Union can be traced through a series of six treaties beginning with the original Coal and Steel treaty of 1950. Each new treaty established a precedent that opened the door to include more powerful clauses in the next treaty. This explanation may help to explain a common misunderstanding regarding the EU's constitution.

Unlike the Constitution of the United States that establishes and clearly spells out the duties and responsibilities of the three branches of government, forming a check and balance system as well as establishing a bill of human rights, the European Union's constitution is merely an expansion of its six treaties. In 2005, a ponderous 250-page document, newly labeled the "European Union Constitution" was offered to the people of Europe. For the most part, this document was a re-worded version of the six previous treaties with the addition of some new powers, especially in the area of immigration and open borders. This constitution was not intended to replace the previous six treaties; rather, it built upon them by increasing the supra-authority's power while decreasing the sovereignty of individual member nations. The original Coal and Steel Community treaty had removed sovereignty of only two nations over only two industries. Monnet's "gearing up" method has been so effective that today the EU controls sovereignty over legal, economic, environmental, and policy decisions of twenty-seven nations. The rejection of this constitution by the people of France and the Netherlands did not sound a "death knell" for the European Union as many uninformed individuals believed. The general populace of these two countries had simply objected to the new clauses introduced in the constitution. The EU will continue to function under its approved compilation of treaties until a more acceptable constitution can be drafted. Approval by general election is not required; some countries have allowed government representatives to ratify it.

Monnet's *engrenage* method has enabled the European Union to grow into an organization gaining more and more control over Europe. His conviction that the peoples' lack of vision is the key to strength or success has seemingly paid off. His method of keeping the general populace in the dark concerning the EU's ultimate goal may lead not only to a united Europe but, eventually, to a united one-world government. By gradually and subtly gearing-up the world like a well-oiled machine, such a plan could succeed. This principle continues to this day as noted by Luxembourg's Prime Minister Jean-Claude Juncker: "We decide on something, leave it lying around, and wait and see what happens. If no one kicks up a fuss, because most people don't know what has been decided, we continue step by step until there is no turning back."[54]

Monnet succeeded in uniting nations at variance by exploiting the fear of conflict in Europe. What is to keep the world at large from being united by exploiting the same fear of conflict, terrorism, or even global warming? The Schuman Declaration of 1950 launched the European "project" by stating as a prime principle: "Europe will not be made all at once, or according to a single general plan. It will be built through concrete achievements, which first create a *de facto* solidarity."[55] This same strategy could be applied and extended to the world; plans, policies, and agreements already are being put in place that may do just that.

ACT III – SCENE 2
THE EUROPEAN UNION'S NEIGHBORHOOD

—ᘉᘉ—

Time: 2000 and beyond
Setting: EU Neighborhood
Enter: Jean Monnet

"**P**lease, won't you be my neighbor?" was a familiar question asked by a cheery and popular children's television host, the late Fred Rogers. His program's appeal rested upon the ageless and universal desire of human beings for peace and security at home and in their surroundings. From caves and castle walls, to timber forts of the American Wild West and chainlink fences of modern suburbia, individuals throughout history have sought peace and safety. It goes without saying that contentious neighbors are undesirable and unwelcome in any neighborhood, for they disrupt the peace and tranquility and threaten the quality of life for the entire neighborhood. Most people want to have amiable neighbors who are friendly and helpful or at least do not impose in any way on their lives. Even today, the European Union is seeking this peace and safety not only for itself but also for the countries in its surrounding "neighborhood." Like Fred Rogers, the EU is asking nations to be its neighbors.

The European Neighborhood Policy

The European Union is striving to maintain peace and prosperity for its own citizens by eliminating any threats posed by its neighbors, particularly those in the Balkans and the Middle East. Through the European Neighborhood Policy (ENP), the EU hopes to "share the enlarged EU's peace, stability, and prosperity with [its] neighbors"[1] by offering its "'ring of friends' a new, special relationship."[2] The European Union's own website proclaims that its "neighborhood watch" can eliminate potential world problems for itself as well as for its neighbors:

> The European Neighborhood Policy is a new policy that invites our neighbors to the East and to the South to share in the peace, stability and prosperity that we enjoy in the European Union and which aims to create a ring of friends around the borders of the new enlarged EU.[3]

As noble as this policy sounds, the European Union's definition of "neighborhood" raises concern among many in the world community since the EU's neighborhood is quite large, encompassing all the nations surrounding the Mediterranean Sea. Within this zone are peoples of many nationalities and three major religions.

While bringing peace to this region is a commendable goal, a closer examination of this policy reveals a future neighborhood that may be even greater than most people imagine. In the light of the prophecies of Daniel and John, the Neighborhood Policy may provide the means through which mankind's final global empire comes into existence. The EU's stated reasons for forming the ENP suggest such a goal:

The implementation of the European Neighborhood Policy itself brings with it the perspective of moving towards a **significant degree of integration**...by which partner countries can participate **progressively** in key aspects of EU policies and programmes [author's emphasis].[4]

The above quote demonstrates how the European Union's use of the term "integration" is equated with the gradual process of absorption into the union, particularly as participation in the ENP is considered by discerning observers to be "one step below full membership in the EU."[5]

Once introduced, integration into the EU progresses along a predictable path. It begins with a proposal for an economic relationship that is established upon a free trade treaty between the EU and a non-member nation. An independent authority usually administers the treaty. Once this new governing authority has become firmly established and effectively operative, it then suggests that the treaty expand to include open borders, common passports, and a shared monetary system (the Euro). Those involved usually find that the convenience of these shared community benefits outweighs what appears to be only a slight loss of national sovereignty. Eventually, those promoting integration seize upon some crisis affecting the greater community and use it as an opportunity for furthering closer integration. Terrorism, drug crime, and environmental issues in today's world present many so-called "crisis" opportunities that necessitate the community's intervention. The EU advantageously offers to intervene, to aid in bringing about a better quality of life. Eventually, the EU community is looked to as the best authority to establish a judicial system and to define human rights. In time, the community judiciary supersedes the national judiciary through community laws, community policing, and community courts. National laws are often replaced or simply made obsolete. Building upon fears such as the threat of war from outside the community, a foreign policy is formed through a new "community diplomatic corps" instead of national departments of state. Individual member nations are not permitted to formulate foreign policy apart from the community's defined policy.

The stated goal of each step of this integration process is to foster peace and prosperity within the community, independent of the concerns of any individual nation within it. Integration is established on the concept of strength through union—"united we stand, divided we fall." Ultimately, the community's governing authority controls the entire community, doing away with national distinctions and self-determination. The European Union has historically followed this technique, growing from its original six to the current twenty-seven nations. Its influence or connection with many economic/free trade treaties around the world is giving rise to speculation regarding even further EU enlargement.

The ultimate result of integration will be attained when its members recognize the EU as the final authority for determining human rights as well as policies for social progress within the "community." The community courts will deal with people within the EU who are not like-minded or who are resistive to the authority and its established goals. The result of the progressive encroachment of this supra-authority over national sovereignty is the dissolution of individual nations and the formation of a single homogenized union.

The Monnet Method of engrenage or gearing-up has enabled the European Union to grow in size and power through a five-step progressive sequence as illustrated below:

The Monnet Method: Five Progressive Steps from Economic Treaty to Supra-Authority Government

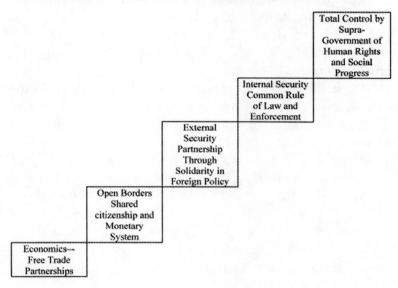

To date, the European Union has made progress in many of these steps; though as yet, it has not succeeded in fully implementing them. A significant advancement in these steps will be secured when a European Union Constitution is ratified. Meanwhile, the EU is using its Neighborhood Policy to get its "foot in the door" of its neighbors with the intention of initiating the process.

Israel is a Neighbor

Currently, Israel is the EU's biggest trading partner; 40% of Israeli imports come from the EU while 30% of Israeli exports go to the EU.[6] Israel's technologically advanced economy meets many of the technical needs of Europe. Israel is a prosperous land, slightly smaller than the state of New Jersey, with annual exports of $40 billion and a population of 6.3 million.[7] It is home to one-half of the world's Jewish population.[8] The future of Israel has a direct influence on the European Union, making it one of its most important neighbors. Not surprisingly, the unrest in the Middle East is a great concern to the neighborhood. The EU's Europa website "FAQ" notes, "A solution to this conflict is of highest priority to the EU."[9]

Through its Neighborhood Policy, the European Union formalized a three-year Action Plan with Israel in December of 2004. At the time, the EU Commissioner for External Relations noted:

> There are moments in political life when your instinct tells you that a fundamental shift has occurred. Sometimes the feeling is no more distinct than a faint breeze; sometimes it is as clear as a sudden break in the clouds. My instinct tells me that such a shift has just taken place in the European Union's relationship with Israel.[10]

The stated intent of this Action Plan is to "deepen [Israel's] political cooperation and [Israel's] economic **integration** with us [the EU] in return for working together on issues of mutual concern" (author's emphasis).[11] The European Union's Action Plan with Israel is a natural outcome of a shared history that emerged out of World War II. The parallel developments of both have progressed along intertwining paths and now are intersecting through the establishment of sub-committees that provide forums to discuss politics, business markets, research, energy and transport, and matters of justice. True to the Monnet methodology, the first goal of the Action Plan was to establish a free trade zone for services. All of the sub-committee's actions are under the auspices of the parent of the ENP, the Euro-Mediterranean Partnership (Euromed) of the European Union.

As recently as 1995, Euromed was established as a partnership between the European Union and twelve Mediterranean countries: Turkey, Cyprus, Malta, Morocco, Algeria, Tunisia, Egypt, Israel, the Palestinian Authority, Lebanon, Syria, and Jordan. Libya holds observer status and can partake in discussions but has no voting privileges. Following the Monnet Method discussed above, the Euromed trade partnership resulted in the absorption of Cyprus and Malta by the EU when they were granted full membership in 2004. Turkey is now undergoing the initial steps to membership.

Although not yet a member of the EU, Israel's Foreign Minister Silvan Shalom expressed the desirability of Israel joining the European Union in May 2003 when he stated that "Israel and Europe share similar economies and democratic values."[12] Israel views this partnership as a means of obtaining peace and prosperity in its neighborhood and also believes that EU membership could be the means to ending "the regional isolation it suffers and [of obtaining] a strong security guarantee, along with all the economic advantages of the vast EU market."[13] In light of all that has been discussed concerning Monnet's ongoing *engrenage* method, perhaps the EU envisions ultimate control of Israel through absorption. This Action Plan should trigger Bible students around the world to consider the possibility that its implementation could lead to Satan's latter-day action plan found in the books of Ezekiel and Daniel.

Latter Day Action Plan

Satan's ultimate action plan will be the formation of a seven-year covenant or agreement with Israel. When Israel and the Antichrist enter into this agreement, it will mark the beginning of what the Bible refers to as the Great Tribulation. Several requirements for the introduction of this covenant or "action plan" are outlined in Daniel 9:27 and Ezekiel 38:8, 11 and specify circumstances that distinguish that future plan from the current three-year Action Plan Israel has with the EU.

Chapter 9 of Daniel introduces a prophecy about a period of seventy *"weeks."*

Seventy weeks are determined upon thy people and upon thy holy city

Daniel 9:24

The term *"weeks"* in Daniel's time was understood to mean a time period of years, a seven-year time frame. To his first readers, this reference about seventy weeks was understood to be seventy sevens of years or 490 years and was familiar language.[14] Consequently, in verses 24 to 27, Gabriel was giving Daniel foreknowledge about a series of events that were to take place over a period of 490 years.

The beginning and the end of the first period of time described as the 69 weeks or 483 years, related in verses 24 to 26, are defined or bracketed in the prophecy by the following two historical events: It begins with the issuing of a decree by the Persian king, Artaxerxes; and it ends with the presentation of the Messiah as Israel's king just prior to His being *"cut-off"* or crucified. As is shown in the table below, the one remaining week or seven years, known as the 70th week, is yet in the future. A gap of an unknown length of time between the 69th Week and the 70th Week is implied. This prophetic account of a timeline is the second occasion in the book of Daniel where a gap in time is indicated; the first was discussed in Acts II, Scene 2 where the fourth kingdom's history is depicted in the images of *"legs and feet"* and the fourth beast's ten-horns.

Daniel's 70 Weeks Prophecy[15]		
69 Weeks	Gap	70th Week
Artaxerxes decree to rebuild Jerusalem March 14, 445 BC to April 6, 32 AD, the presentation of the Messiah to the people of Israel (Palm Sunday)	From the "cutting off" of the Messiah to at least the Present	The start of the covenant (Satan's Action Plan) which begins the Tribulation period, just prior to the Millennial Kingdom
483 years = 69 X 7	Unknown Length of Time	7 years = 1 week

Know therefore and understand, that from the going forth of the commandment to restore and to build Jerusalem unto the Messiah the Prince shall be seven weeks, and threescore and two weeks: the street shall be built again, and the wall, even in troublous times.

Daniel 9:25

The prophetic explanation concerns two princes. The first clearly is the Messiah. Verse 26 introduces a second, unidentified and future prince.

And after threescore and two weeks shall Messiah be cut off, but not for himself: and the people of the prince that shall come shall destroy the city and the sanctuary; and the end thereof shall be with a flood, and unto the end of the war desolations are determined.

Daniel 9:26

In the original language, the phrase, *"the prince that shall come,"* is more accurately translated "a prince the one coming"[16] or "the coming prince." The actions described in verse 27 coincide with those already expressed in the little horn's actions, which arises in the Fourth Kingdom (Dan. 9:25). For that reason, Bible students identify the coming prince as the Antichrist.[17] The "people" of verse 26 are the ancient Romans who destroyed Jerusalem in 70 AD. The implication is that the "little horn" or "the coming prince" will be a descendent of these people.

And he shall confirm the covenant with many for one week: and in the midst of the week he shall cause the sacrifice and the oblation to cease, and for the overspreading of abominations he shall make it desolate, even until the consummation, and that determined shall be poured upon the desolate.

Daniel 9:27

The angel Gabriel is speaking to Daniel in verse 27 and states that a prince will *"confirm"* a covenant for one *"week"* or seven years (the 70th Week [Dan. 9:21]).

The *"he"* in verse 27 cannot refer back to the Messiah-Prince of verse 25, because Jesus never "made a seven year covenant."[18] As explained, the Antichrist will be the ruler or *"prince"* leading the Fourth Kingdom and will be performing actions identical to those described in this prophetic Biblical passage. Further, the *"he"* in verse 27 is grammatically the closest antecedent to the *"prince that shall come"* in verse 26.[19] Therefore, the *"prince that shall come"* in verse 26 and the *"he"* in verse 27 are one and the same, the Antichrist.

The covenant in verse 27 is between the Antichrist, as ruler of the final phase of the Fourth Empire and Daniel's *"people," "the many"* (Dan. 9:24, 27). These people and the many are the same, the nation of Israel.[20] Renald Showers, a widely recognized theologian, believes that the confirmation of this seven-year covenant between the Antichrist and Israel will officially begin the seven-year Tribulation[21] referred to in the Scriptures.

If the European Union is the embryonic form or precursor of humanity's Fourth Kingdom, then a future EU leader, a descendent of the ancient Roman Empire, will arise and "confirm" this covenant or Satanic "Action Plan" with the restored nation of Israel. Considering Monnet's *engrenage* method, one sees the likelihood that this covenant could be based upon the precedent established by the 2004 EU Action Plan. Before rushing to any conclusion that the current EU Action Plan with Israel is the latter day Action Plan, it should be pointed out that the current Action Plan is a three-year rather than a seven-year agreement. While that is an obvious arithmetic issue, the book of Ezekiel adds another parameter in its description of conditions in Israel during the Tribulation, ones that are significantly different from those of present-day Israel.

Chapter 38 of Ezekiel indicates that a time is coming when an enemy of Israel, called "Gog," will attempt to destroy it (Ezek. 38:2). Allied with Gog are *"the chief prince* [Rosh] *of Meshech and Tubal"* (modern-day Russia),[22] the nation of Persia (Iran), Ethiopia (modern Sudan or part of Arabia), and Libya (land adjacent to Persia [Ezek. 38:5]).[23] Ezekiel indicates that this attack will come in the "latter years."

After many days thou shalt be visited: in the latter years thou shalt come into the land that is brought back from the sword, and is gathered out of many people, against the mountains of Israel, which have been always waste: but it is brought forth out of the nations, and they shall dwell safely all of them...And thou shalt say, I will go up to the land of unwalled villages; I will go to them that are at rest, that dwell safely, all of them dwelling without walls, and having neither bars nor gates,

Ezekiel 38:8, 11

An understanding of the term "latter years" and additional details in this passage greatly help in establishing the historical time period for Israel that is being referred to.

The Latter Days

To the Jewish people of Ezekiel's day, "latter days" was synonymous with "latter years" and was understood to refer to the period of time immediately prior to Israel's glorification, salvation, and blessing in the Kingdom Age, otherwise known as the Millennial Kingdom or "last days" (Isa. 2:2-4; Micah 4:1-7).[24] Since this period of time occurs just prior to the establishment of the Millennium, the words "latter days" or "latter years" could only refer to the time of the Great Tribulation. Since the Tribulation is seven years long (one Biblical week) and it begins with Israel signing a covenant with the Antichrist, Ezekiel's description of the attack upon Israel must occur during Daniel's 70th Week (Dan. 9:27).

		Latter Days	Last Days
69 Weeks	Gap	70th Week	Millennium Kingdom
Artaxerxes decree to rebuild Jerusalem March 14, 445 BC to April 6, 32 AD the presentation of the Messiah to the people of Israel (Palm Sunday)	From the "cutting off" of the Messiah to at least the Present	Signing of the Covenant (Satan's Action Plan) which begins the Tribulation period, just prior to the Second Coming of Christ	Second Coming of Christ, Israel's Glorification, Salvation, Blessing
483 years = 69 X 7	Unknown Length of Time	7 years = 1 week	1000 years Revelation 20:2-5

A further criterion in Ezekiel indicates that prior to the attack from Gog, Israel will "dwell in the midst of the land" (Ezek. 38:12). By placing the context of chapter 38 with the chapters before and after it, it is possible to determine the historical timeframe Ezekiel is referring to. Chapters 36 and 37 of Ezekiel are descriptive of a gradual re-gathering of the Jewish people from all over the earth to their homeland. Modern history confirms just such a re-gathering that began at the end of the 19th century and is ongoing with a heightened influx since the re-establishment of Israel as a nation in 1948. Today over half of the world's Jewish population is in the land. Following the attack on Israel in chapters 38 and 39, the prophet writes of the Millennium. It is reasonable to conclude that the attack in Ezekiel 38 will occur during the period of time between the present day re-gathering of Israel and the Millennium. This would be during the seven-year Tribulation or the 70th Week.

TIME RELATIONSHIP AND PROPHETIC PASSAGES			
EZEKIEL 36 & 37	DANIEL 9:27	EZEKIEL 38 & 39	EZEKIEL 40
Re-gathering of Jews to Israel	Satan's Action Plan (covenant)	Attack by Gog	Temple
Present Day	Triggers start of 7-years or 70th Week (The Tribulation)	During the 7-year or 70th Week	Millennium

The passage in Ezekiel 38 also indicates that during this time Israel will be a *"land of unwalled villages,"* having no bars or gates, and that the inhabitants will be enjoying rest and safety. In Ezekiel's lifetime this was unheard of because walls, bars, and gates were considered essential for security's sake. By this seemingly incredible prophecy, the ancient Hebrews understood that a time was coming when there would be no need for defense. These will be the very conditions Israel will experience through the covenant it makes with the Antichrist (Dan. 9). The events foretold in Ezekiel 38 and 39, as well as the Antichrist's Action Plan, must be in the future; for Israel today is experiencing neither rest nor safety.

The Jewish Dream Becomes Reality

From its birth in 1948, the small nation of Israel has fought for its right to exist. Wars and terrorism have marred the dream of the Jewish people for their homeland. The dream began when ancient Rome attacked and destroyed Jerusalem and the Temple in 70 AD. Since that time, the pages of history and literature have been filled with the image of the *wandering Jew*. In the late 19th century, men began to vocalize the Jewish Dream of a homeland as they remembered God's words, *"And yet for all that, when they are in the land of their enemies, I will not cast them away"* (Lev. 26:44). These words had offered hope during the 1,800 years of dispersion and persecution. Held close to the Jewish heart was Ezekiel's promise of a return to the land of Israel, *"For I will take you from among the nations, and gather you out of all countries, and will bring you into your own land"* (Ezek. 36:24). This was and is the Jewish Dream.

On August 29, 1897, Theodor Herzl, a Viennese journalist, called 200 leading Jewish and Zionist thinkers together at the First Zionist Congress in Basil, Switzerland.[25] The goal of the meeting was to demonstrate "to the world what Zionism is and what it wants."[26] It began a political movement focusing world attention to the need for a Jewish homeland in the Middle East. Since the Eastern Roman Empire's domination of the Middle East ended, Europe has sought ways to influence and control the region that included the land belonging to Israel. In 1917, Arthur James Balfour, the foreign secretary of Britain, advocated a national homeland for the Jewish people. His thoughts were memorialized in the Balfour Declaration, a British government policy statement of sympathy with the Zionist goals of a homeland. That statement proclaimed Britain's endorsement of a Jewish homeland in Palestine provided that it did not "prejudice the civil and religious rights of existing non-Jewish communities in Palestine."[27] In January 1919 at the Paris Peace Conference, the Arab delegates endorsed the Balfour Declaration.[28] At the time, King Hussein wrote:

> We saw the Jews...streaming to Palestine from Russia, Germany, Austria, Spain, America...The cause of causes could not escape those who had the gift of deeper insight; they know that the country was for its original sons, for all their differences, a sacred and beloved homeland.[29]

As part of the peace agreement, the British government was given a mandate to govern the land of Palestine beginning in 1922. Prior to its defeat in the war, Turkey, as part of the Ottoman Empire had governed (1516-1917) these lands that once were once within the Eastern Roman Empire. Britain divided the mandated governance into two territories: one became the state of Jordan (1928) that was jointly governed with King Abdullah ibn Hussein while the other remained unnamed and solely under British jurisdiction.[30] Britain gave Jordan complete sovereignty in 1946.

At the close of World War II, the world learned of the extermination of six million Jewish people under the Nazi regime and became ready to recognize a Jewish homeland. To the Jewish people, Israel would be their safe haven from persecution. Responding to world opinion, the United Nations voted (November 29, 1947) to divide Palestine into an independent Jewish and an independent Arab state. Jerusalem was to be under international (Gentile) control.[31] With the end of the British mandate on May 5, 1948, the British withdrew its governing forces and the Arabs of Palestine began to attack the Jewish people in the former British mandate. On May 14, the National Council of Israel declared independence and the nation was re-born after eighteen hundred years of dispersion. The Jewish Dream had become reality.

From that day to the present, Israel has been under constant threat of destruction from its Arab neighbors. In its quest for peace, Israel has turned to the European Union's Action Plan. The precedent established by the European Union's Action Plan with Israel could one day lead to steps toward making the covenant with the Antichrist, an event which will signal the beginning of the 70th week of Daniel or the start of the seven-year Tribulation. The Monnet Method of "gearing up" through precedents established by previous agreements clearly makes this a possibility since precedents have been shown as indicators to the EU's future actions.

The World is the EU's Neighborhood

While the Bible by and large focuses upon Israel, it does not limit the final phase of the Fourth Kingdom to Israel and the lands of the ancient Roman Empire alone. Before the *"little horn"* arises, there will be ten horns or kings who will rule over or *"devour the whole earth"* (Dan. 7:24).

Thus he said, The fourth beast shall be the fourth kingdom upon earth, which shall be diverse from all kingdoms, and shall devour [consume]^{32} *the whole earth, and shall tread it down, and break it in pieces. And the ten horns out of this kingdom are ten kings that shall arise: and another shall rise after them; and he shall be diverse from the first, and he shall subdue three kings.*

Daniel 7:23, 24

In the original language, *devour*, is associated with "an oppressor consuming its victims" as if they were food.^{33} So too, the Fourth Empire will consume independent states making them a part of itself, eradicating any visible national identities.

After considering the global aspect of this kingdom's description and recognizing that at no time in history did ancient Rome or any empire encompass or *"devour"* the entire earth,[34] the timing of this final phase is a period yet in the future.[35] It will be a time when a global form of the restored Fourth Kingdom will control a significant portion of the world, including both North and South America.[36] For the European Union to be this latter-day form of government, it must be global in nature and not limited to Europe.

Today the European Union is slowly "integrating" nations. It seeks to minimize their nationalistic identities and expand its own territorial influence, ultimately devouring nations. Past performance of the European Union's expansion and its current Neighborhood Policy clearly demonstrate that it is a viable candidate to act out the prophetic final phase of the Fourth Empire.

The Mediterranean is a Neighbor

By applying the Monnet Method of "gearing up," the EU hopes to achieve "the creation of a free trade zone between the two banks of the Mediterranean by 2010."[37] Labeled as "a turning point in Euro-Mediterranean relations,"[38] this partnership has achieved only limited success in its ten years of existence. The European Union believes its new Neighborhood Policy will increase its success and influence. The inclusion of the North African states would complete the encirclement of the Mediterranean and what was once Rome's Empire. Commenting on this aspect, a British EU minister said, "The Romans called the Mediterranean 'our sea' and there's no reason why we should not do the same."[39] Former president of the EU Commission, Romano Prodi stated, "It would be a grave mistake to neglect the

Mediterranean, the cradle of European civilization, as we build a new Europe."[40] Reflecting on the Roman name for the Mediterranean, *Mare Nostrum* (Our Sea), Prodi noted, "For the Romans the Mediterranean was a space to be shared with all peoples who live on its shores."[41]

In December 2004, the EU formally began accession talks with Turkey. On that occasion European Commission President Barroso said, "Tonight the EU has opened its door to Turkey."[42] By December of the following year, the EU had adopted the "partnership for accession."[43] Turkey is not only the bridge between both Western Europe and Asia but also the bridge between Christian Europe and the Islamic Middle East. With Turkey's accession, the door would truly open to expansion around the Mediterranean. That bridge will enable the expanded EU to have a greater influence in the Middle Eastern neighborhood.

In addition to Euromed, the European Union also has a contractual relationship or a Cooperation Agreement, "with the Gulf Cooperation Council consisting of six Gulf states as well as with Yemen—thus comprising the whole of the Arabian peninsula."[44] These countries include Saudi Arabia, Kuwait, Bahrain, Qatar, United Arab Emirates and Oman. "The EU is one of the main customers for Middle Eastern energy exports"[45] and as a result also maintains cooperative relations with Iraq and Iran.[46] The stated primary goal of the Gulf Cooperation Council is to establish an economic free-trade area that enhances mutual prosperity.[47]

Following Monnet's five-step method, the first step for admittance into the European Union is initiated through economics and later reinforced through political and security issues. The EU established a precedent known as the Barcelona process that paved the way for further involvement in Middle East politics. At the announcement of the Action Plan with Israel, "European officials were highlighting the foothold that the agreement gives Europe in the diplomatic process" of the Middle East.[48] The EU increases that foothold through its financial aid to these countries, including aid to the Palestinians of €250 million in 2005.[49] This relationship with the Palestinians could explain the EU's unwillingness to stand by Israel amid crises in the Middle East.

Today Europe...Tomorrow the World

Many in the western hemisphere of the Americas fail to grasp that the European Union is expanding and "devouring" nations simply by employing Monnet's *engrenage* method. The current European Union encompasses almost four million kilometers of land, about half the size of the United States. Its population, however, is 1.5 times that of the United States while economically, it is about equal with it.[50] Today the EU touches the nations surrounding the Mediterranean Sea; "tomorrow" it likely will cross the ocean to the western hemisphere. Unification with the western hemisphere could add significant gain to the EU's power and prestige.

While most American's pay little attention, Europe sees itself as a sleeping giant, awakening as "a new political entity and a new commercial force on the world scene."[51] Italy's current Prime Minister, Romano Prodi, believes the European Union's "goal is to establish 'a superpower on the European continent that stands equal to the United States.'"[52] Prodi and those like him are not foreseeing potential conflict between these two superpowers. Instead, they see them moving from "confrontation...to willingness to cooperate in the economic sphere and **then on to integration**" (author's emphasis).[53] In other words, rather than fighting, the European Union is employing Monnet's method by beginning with economics. This pattern paves the way for the EU eventually to "gear up" and assimilate the United States.

Wherever the European Union begins to offer free-trade zones, the Monnet Method is at work. First, the Euromed/ENP began by bringing the Mediterranean nations into the Union.

Next, it hopes to absorb the Latin American countries, which will be followed by North America. Mark Leonard, Director of Foreign Policy at the Centre for European Reform, notes that 80 countries are currently "umbilically linked to an EU that is their biggest trade partner and main source of credit, foreign investment and aid."[54] The term, "umbilically linked" refers to nations having historical roots to Europe and its history. Approximately one-third of the world's population is now within the Eurosphere, i.e., under European Union influence. In an ongoing *engrenage*, Europe will take advantage of "this dependence to sign agreements with each of these countries that bring them under the European legal and political umbrella."[55] The pattern is always faithfully followed, first trade and economics, then legal and political control.

Of great concern for Christians is the reality that all aid given to a country carries with it stipulations governing human rights[56] (one of the key means of controlling its citizenship's thinking and speech). This practice of stipulating human rights as defined by the EU could be a restrictive technique that potentially stifles the freedom to proclaim the Gospel. As will be seen later, the present European view of tolerance prohibits the exclusivity of Christianity's claim to be the only way to heaven through Jesus Christ. The verse, *"Neither is there salvation in any other: for there is none other name under heaven given among men, whereby we must be saved"* (Acts 4:12) is considered to be exclusive in the "extreme." The European Union's progenitor, the Council of Europe, is the primary human rights court over forty-six countries of the world. The United States, Canada, Japan, Mexico, and the Vatican are all observers in the Council of Europe, suggesting their interest in it and possible future membership. It is noteworthy that all new EU members have first been members of the Council of Europe.

This judicial system of forty-six nations has the power to either permit or severely restrict religious freedom for more than 800 million people. Many of its cases are brought by individuals as appeals to the rulings of their own national "supreme courts." In several cases, the national judiciary of a country has been overridden. If the Council of Europe's decisions continue to reflect the current European view of religion, Christian expression could be severely limited. For example, "In France, an official government publication labeled mainstream Protestant denominations as 'sects', and one French school textbook on life in England labels the Salvation Army a 'cult.'"[57] There have been several cases of harassment of Christians for street preaching in Britain.[58] As both the European Union and its co-partner in expansion, the Council of Europe, gain jurisdiction in more countries, true Christianity could be significantly affected and hindered from obeying Christ's command to evangelize the world.

South America is a Neighbor

The European Union's definition of "neighborhood" appears to know no bounds. The western hemisphere is considered part of its unofficial neighborhood. Through Mercosur, the Southern Common Market (*Mercado Común del Sur*), the South American countries of Argentina, Brazil, Paraguay, and Uruguay established an economic alliance with the European Union in 1991.[59] Mercosur provides a strong trading bloc in South America's dealings with the United States in free trade zone negotiations. For years, Mercosur was stagnant because of internal struggles. In 2005, Mercosur admitted powerful Venezuela into its free trade association in the hopes that this would strengthen and reinvigorate it. Upon acceptance, Venezuela's current president, Hugo Chavez, proclaimed his vision for Mercosur:

> I believe Mercosur must be more political. I believe it's a political project...We need a Mercosur that every day moves farther away from the old elitist

corporate models of integration that look for ...finan-
cial profits, but forget about workers, children, life,
and human dignity.[60]

His allusions to "elitist corporate models of integration"
can only be interpreted as a reference to the United States,
a nation Chavez has been challenging whenever possible.
Chavez is no friend of the United States and its competitive
corporate models.

The political structure of Mercosur is loosely patterned
after that of the European Union.[61] In September of 2005,
a commission of EU representatives met with Mercosur
ministers with the goal of establishing "the first ever region-
to-region **political** strategic partnership. Mercosur is **a key
partner for the EU** in Latin America [author's emphasis]."[62]
The European Union has offered full technical and institu-
tional support to Mercosur, thereby influencing its organization and goals.[63] What started as a trade association in Latin
American could potentially become the world's largest free
trade area, encompassing almost 700 million people. The
aim of the meeting in September 2005 was to establish a
"comprehensive political and economic partnership between
the two regions."[64] An analysis, by the author, of the European
Union's discussion of its relationship to Mercosur covering
the years 1991 to 2004 reveals a reversal of emphasis: in 1991
the word "economic" routinely appeared before the word
"political;" by 2004, "political" preceded "economic."[65]

The United States is a Neighbor

In June of 2005, the US Senate endorsed a free trade
agreement between the United States and six Latin American
nations.[66] The Central America Free Trade Agreement
(CAFTA) affects Costa Rica, El Salvador, Guatemala,
Honduras, the Dominican Republic, and Nicaragua. In July
of the same year, the House of Representatives approved

CAFTA.[67] A similar agreement was established with Canada and Mexico through the auspices of the North American Free Trade Agreement (NAFTA).

Following the Monnet Method, the United States may be "gearing up" for an EU-like union in North America. Using the NAFTA office of the Department of Commerce, working groups have been formed to implement the Security and Prosperity Partnership (SPP) agreed to by President Bush, President Fox of Mexico, and Canadian Prime Minister Martin.[68] The SPP appears to be seeking a North American union by following a blueprint devised by a Council on Foreign Relations task force.[69] It is reported that this blueprint calls for "a union that would merge the U.S., Canada and Mexico into a new governmental form."[70] The CFR website calls this union "a North American economic and security community."[71] At its inception, the EU was a "community." This is the same CFR that extensively supported Monnet's attempts to create a European Union in the 1940's and 50's. In words right out of the EU's manuals, the task force states its duty: "to provide specific advice on how the partnership can be pursued and realized....The Task Force proposes the creation by 2010 of a North American community to enhance security, prosperity, and opportunity. ...Its boundaries will be defined by a common external tariff and an outer security perimeter within which the movement of people, products, and capital will be legal, orderly, and safe. Its goal will be to guarantee a free, secure, just, and prosperous North America."[72] Additionally, the Task Force proposes a North American judicial court, inter-parliamentary group, executive commission, military defense command, customs office, and development bank.[73] These goals are identical with those of the EU.

Linking the European Union and the United States together, an EU-US summit in Goteborg, Sweden in June of 2001 issued the following statement: "...when the EU and US work hand-in-hand ...we can be an engine for positive global change."[74] In 1995, the EU defined the New Transatlantic Agenda (NTA) between itself and the United States as "a partnership of global significance."[75] The EU often uses this phrase and ploy when discussing trade agreements. The EU offers the United States a "solid and coherent partner in all areas, beyond trade matters."[76]

It is this connection with Latin America's Mercosur that establishes a bridge between the European Union and the United States and Canada. Political correspondents, David Smith and Eben Black, ask a logical question, "In this context, where does the EU stop?"[77] Bob van den Bos, Dutch member of the European parliament, answered this in part, "The main challenge for an enlarged EU is that it needs to be manageable and governable. In this context, further integration—not looser association—is the only option."[78] He aptly expressed the sentiment of many within the European Union. According to Booker and North, the true goal of the European Union is "to take over the reins of governance for nation states and people who still [think] of themselves as being in the 'democratic' stage of human development..."[79]

Today, the European Union welcomes any nation that seeks the EU's basic aim "of political, economic and monetary union."[80] The potential for growth because of this policy is significant—the EU is currently composed of 450 million citizens from primarily "Christian" nations, but if it were to include the multi-religious nations that adhere to its basic aim, it could easily increase to one billion people.[81]

As more and more nations join the European Union, wealthier nations will be called upon to meet the needs of poorer member nations. This will inevitably force the EU to expand in order to obtain additional needed resources. Canada and the United States may be looked to and eventually included because of their rich natural wealth. Additionally, in the minds of the leadership of the EU, "the extension of the zone [i.e., enlargement] of peace, stability and prosperity in Europe will enhance the security of all its people."[82] Throughout European Union publications, economic stability is portrayed as the driving force behind its support. Following the Monnet method of "gearing up," the EU stresses economic growth as its primary goal because it is already a well-accepted concept. At the same time, the EU conceals its ultimate goal, that of its "role in world affairs—in foreign and security policy, trade policy and the 'other areas of global governance.'"[83] Mark Leonard, British foreign policy thinker, summarizes this ultimate goal:

> Our experience with the European Union has shown that the way to construct a new [world] order will not be to start with a grand constitutional design but to create an interest in working together on the pressing problems. By forming a series of overlapping clubs to deal with trade, nuclear proliferation, economic development, global disease, and propping up failing states, it might one day be possible to bring them together into a single framework.[84]

The European Union's economic policy is the small brick that will establish the major philosophical principle leading to world governance. Under the EU Commission's leadership the EU's powers will be expanded, building upon these small incremental bricks until the global supranational system is in place, being always careful "never to define too clearly what [is] the 'project's' ultimate goal, for fear this would arouse the countervailing forces which might seek to sabotage it before it [is] complete."[85]

Using Monnet's guidelines for "gearing up," the European Union is quickly moving toward a modern-day, worldwide Roman Empire with "the emergence of a world of regions."[86] For the EU, the neighborhood is the world.

In Leonard's definitive work about Europe running the 21ˢᵗ century, he states, "The EU's success has let the genie of regionalism out of the bottle, and it will be impossible to put it back in again."[87] By replacing nations with governed world regions, the globalist's believe that national rivalries and conflicts can be avoided.[88]

Today, the European Union has a committee, The Committee of the Regions, which is designed to work with the many regions encompassing its member nations. The Committee's 317 members seek to be an advisory body representing Europe's regional and local authorities.[89]

The two major problems that the EU must solve if it is to successfully reach its goal of global governance are the following:

- How to unite people of differing backgrounds, languages, and cultures

- How to prevent neighboring nations from threatening the EU's ability to achieve its goal

The official European Union website poses the question, "How are people from so many different backgrounds and cultures to develop the will to live together, so that they will be prepared to pool a part of their sovereignty?"[90]

Regionalism: Divide and Conquer

One solution to this unification problem is to divide nations, weaken them, and then "conquer" them. Noting the historic fact that five hundred years ago, "Europe invented the most effective form of political organization in history: the nation-state," Leonard sees a parallel with today's Europe, as the European Union creates a "new regional world" in the 21ˢᵗ century.[91]

Many attribute the plan to devolve Scotland and Wales from England as a part of this process. Political analyst, Pierre Hillard, believes it is possible to verify through five EU documents plans to "Balkanise Europe into little ethnic parcels."[92] The claim has been made that the German Interior Ministry has given its support to one hundred regionalist organizations in Europe.[93] Employing the Monnet Method, the Committee for Regions has the vision or "sees to strengthen the economic, social and territorial 'cohesion' of the Union."[94] This committee deals with matters relevant to regions within the union. In doing so, the committee can cross national lines and view areas as regions. Today this is a minor committee, but through the effective Monnet Method, it could ostensibly remove national borders within the EU and divide the entire union into regions.

Whether or not the European Union is indeed seeking to redefine borders by creating regions as some have speculated, the underlying issue remains: there is the need for a methodology in uniting the differing peoples of the expanded empire. The EU has offered its Regional Policies as a solution for creating greater cohesion and inclusion with the Union.

One means of achieving these goals is through technological services, specifically, innovative Information and Communications Technologies (ICT). The EU believes ICT could "mean that everyone is far less dependent on their location."[95] Through ICT, the "e-government" can consult with citizens.[96] With time, increased accessibility to information and increased communications between the EU and individuals will reduce dependence and identification with their own national governments. Ultimately, a true European Union citizen will emerge with a newly adopted identity and then national identities and nations will fade away.

The Roman concept of "divide and rule" is one method employed in the past as a means of diminishing national loyalties. This was a process of fragmenting nations into smaller regions governed by civil rulers. Rome could maintain its over-all rule and supremacy since no single region would be strong enough to challenge it.[97] Taking this *divide and rule* concept and applying it to a supranational empire could result in national identities gradually being done away with. Then the empire could be divided into ten regions that are governed by ten rulers. In this way the prophecy of Daniel regarding the ten horns or ten kings could be fulfilled:

> *The fourth beast shall...devour the whole earth, and shall tread it down, and break it in pieces. And the ten horns out of this kingdom are ten kings that shall arise:*
>
> Daniel 7:23b-24a

The words *"tread it down"* seem to imply the subjugation of the nations under its rule. This is followed by the words, *"break it in pieces,"* which suggest a "tearing apart," "shattering"[98] or division of the kingdom. These "pieces" may then be rearranged into new governing zones, thereby eradicating individual nations.

Perhaps the European Dream is not really just a dream but is in fact part of Satan's plan for the age — a world empire under his direction that is in rebellion against God and His people. The seventh resolution of the Congress of Europe in The Hague stated, "The creation of a United Europe must be regarded as an essential step towards the creation of a United World."[99] These words were spoken in the 1950's. More recently, in February 2000, Romano Prodi declared that the Commission will play the "pivotal role" in achieving the EU's following strategic objectives:

> What we are aiming at is a new kind of global governance, Europe's model of integration, working

successfully on the continental scale, is a quarry from which ideas for global governance can and should be drawn.[100]

Certainly, the signs are clear if they are read and heeded. From the table below, countries and relationships are noted with an observable inference—the world is heading in the very direction the prophets foretold.

The Growing Eurosphere as of 2007

Country	EU Member	Euro-Med	Neighbor-hood Policy	Gulf Co-Op Group	Mercosur	SPP	CAFTA
Austria	Yes						
Belgium	Yes						
Cyprus	Yes						
Czech Republic	Yes						
Denmark	Yes						
Estonia	Yes						
Finland	Yes						
France	Yes						
Germany	Yes						
Greece	Yes						
Hungary	Yes						
Ireland	Yes						
Italy	Yes						
Latvia	Yes						
Lithuania	Yes						
Luxembourg	Yes						
Malta	Yes						
Poland	Yes						
Portugal	Yes						
Slovakia	Yes						
Slovenia	Yes						
Spain	Yes						
Sweden	Yes						
The Netherlands	Yes						

Country	EU Member	Euro-Med	Neighbor-hood Policy	Gulf Co-Op Group	Mercosur	SPP	CAFTA
United Kingdom	Yes						
Bulgaria	Yes						
Croatia	Candidate						
Romania	Yes						
Algeria		Yes	Yes				
Egypt		Yes	Yes				
Israel		Yes	Yes				
Jordan		Yes	Yes				
Lebanon		Yes	Yes				
Morocco		Yes	Yes				
Palestinian Authority		Yes	Yes				
Syria		Yes	Yes				
Tunisia		Yes	Yes				
Turkey	Candidate	Yes	Yes				
Armenia			Yes				
Azerbaijan			Yes				
Belarus			Yes				
Georgia			Yes				
Libya			Yes				
Moldova			Yes				
Ukraine			Yes				
Bahrain				Yes			
Kuwait				Yes			
Oman				Yes			
Saudi Arabia				Yes			
United Arab Emirate				Yes			
Argentina					Yes		
Brazil					Yes		
Paraguay					Yes		
Uruguay					Yes		
Venezuela					Yes		
Chile					Associate		
Bolivia					Associate		
USA						Yes	
Canada						Yes	
Mexico						Yes	

Country	EU Member	Euro-Med	Neighbor-hood Policy	Gulf Co-Op Group	Mercosur	SPP	CAFTA
Costa Rica							Yes
El Salvador							Yes
Guatemala							Yes
Honduras							Yes
Dominican Republic							Yes
Nicaragua							Yes

The European Union is on the move in a quest to direct and lead the world's governance. Its "neighborhood" knows no bounds and the methods it employs have been effectively used thus far.

ACT III – SCENE 3
THE SUPRA-NATIONAL GOVERNMENT

—ɷ—

Time: 21ˢᵗ Century
Setting: The Capital of Europe
Enter: Bureaucrats of the European Union

"We are a nation that has a government—not the other way around."[1] These few words from Ronald Reagan's presidential inaugural address proclaimed his view of government and its relationship to its people. For him, government was "to make it work—work with us, not over us; to stand by our side, not ride on our back. Government can and must provide opportunity, not smother it; foster productivity, not stifle it."[2] He also included a warning that remained one of the hallmarks of his presidency, a leadership advisory against the growth of government: "Our Government has no power except that granted it by the people. It is time to check and reverse the growth of government which shows signs of having grown beyond the consent of the governed."[3]

Almost as if the people of the Netherlands had heard this warning by an American president, they rejected the European Union's proposed constitution in June 2005. A leading "No" campaigner in the Netherlands, Geert Wilders, explained the success of the "No" campaign when he said, "If you realise that two-thirds of parliament [Dutch] supported the constitution and two out of three people [Dutch voters] in the land are against, it means a lot is wrong in the country."[4] BBC's Hague reporter, Geraldine Coughlan, commenting on the Dutch voters' perception of EU leadership in Brussels said that they believe it "has too much power and that their national politicians are not protecting them enough."[5]

The fear of "too much power" stems from the fact that the EU's constitution centralizes power to the **existing** government and is an ever-growing compilation of a succession of treaties that establishes its powers and duties.[6] It does not resemble the United States' Constitution, which **created** the government with its three branches (executive, legislative, and judicial) and clearly defined how each is to function while together they form a check and balance upon each other. The overall powers of the central government are also limited, as individual states retain control in many areas of regional concern.

The American process of amending its constitution is the closest approximation to the recently proposed EU constitution. The European Union was already functioning under a series of treaties that it now desires to formally compile, along with additional central powers, under the new title, *the European Union Constitution.* The additional powers caused the objection to its ratification only on the part of the Netherlands where the people feared granting more power to the EU.[7] Because it is already functioning under these treaties, the European Union does not require this new constitution to exist but merely to add the additional central powers. The EU ratification process does not require national referendums in each of its twenty-seven countries for the constitution's approval, as the national parliaments of each country may ratify it without a popular vote or referendum by the people of their respective nations.[8] The EU constitution, in a manner similar to the ratification process of a US constitutional amendment, will take effect only when all member nations ratify it. Prior to that time, the EU government will continue under its current powers granted by its treaties. It is important to understand that the heads of state and governments have already approved it and implemented many of its new provisions prior to ratification. It has been said that "Around 85 per cent of the text can, with some creative interpretation, be implemented" without ratification.[9]

Five of the twenty-seven member EU nations, including France and the Netherlands, did choose to allow their citizens to vote on ratification in a referendum. Four others promised a "consultative referendum," one which merely reflects the peoples' preference and is not binding upon the parliaments. The remaining members will ratify it based upon the decisions of their respective parliaments alone.[10] To date, fifteen members have ratified the constitution and two have rejected it.[11] The method of ratification is not unique, but to a limited degree, does represent the mindset of the European Union's supranational government in which the ruling entity is not obligated to base its decisions on the citizens' consent. Monnet and Salter's (two of the EU's founding fathers) idea of a supranational "United States of Europe" did not include the idea that "the wishes of the people should be consulted."[12] Monnet, believing that national veto powers would always work counter to the supranational goal, would never have favored a ratification process that required unanimous approval.

By its very definition, a supranational government transcends "established boundaries or spheres of influence held by individual nations."[13] Many misunderstand the term "supranational," equating it with the concept of a federation or a co-operative international government of equal sovereign states. However, a **supranational government** is one that is

...beyond the control of national governments, politicians, or electorates. Nation states, governments, and parliaments could be left in place: but only so that they could gradually become subordinated to a new supranational government which was above them all."[14]

The world has witnessed many attempts at government unions prior to the formation of the European Union. Two examples will suffice to illustrate this. In 16th century Europe, city-states merged into nation-states.[15] This traditional type of governmental union requires a uniform population, language, and culture for cohesion.[16] In this example, the unions resulted in a "sovereign territory of a particular nation" with a single system of law and government with "no external authority above the state itself."[17]

Another example is a union of sovereign states. This type of governmental union is formed around a common cause through willing co-operation. The United States of America began in just this way and ultimately emerged as "the first modern democratic federation" in 1787.[18] In this type of governmental union, individual states retain sovereign control within their boundaries but share powers with a central government in matters of mutual concern.

In 1308, the poet and statesman, Dante, first proposed a unique, new form of government, a supranational Holy Roman Empire.[19] Writing of the dream of many Europeans seeking the reunification of Europe in his treatise, *De Monarchia,* he addressed the issue of how Europe might end the wars and conflicts produced by a multitude of nations and city-states.[20] He suggested that one independent governing authority be placed above and independent of national governments, "one 'empire' above them all, with power to control their actions in the common interest."[21] This independent authority was to govern nations and empires in such a way that the governing authority would be free of national loyalties, influences, or spheres of interest. Thus, the governing authority was to base its decisions upon the goals of the union rather than upon the individual member-states' desires or nationalistic interests. Furthermore, this governing authority was to be over the citizens, having few checks and balances on its power. The intention was for the citizens to serve the supranational entity, not for the entity to serve the people. This same goal of supranationalism is what the EU is striving to achieve as Booker and North explain in their book, *The Great Deception*:

> The whole purpose of a supranational body is to stand above the wishes of individual nations and peoples. When Monnet and Salter first conceived their idea of a supranational "United States of Europe", it never entered their minds that the wishes of the people should be consulted. They were technocrats, who thought that the future of Europe would best be served by placing it under the role of a government of technocrats like themselves...unsullied by any need to resort to all the messy, unpredictable business of elections.[22]

Unlike the United States, with clearly defined separation of powers between the executive, legislative, and judicial branches, the European Union is a spider web of inter-related branches and powers. The European Commission, for example, is the single most powerful arm of the European Union's supranational government. Its twenty-seven members are appointed rather than elected, as is the EU Commission president who is appointed by the national government leaders. An EU publication declares, "The Commission is independent of national governments. Its job is to represent and uphold the interests of the EU as a whole."[23] In this independent role, it has three duties: "to propose legislation to Parliament and the Council; to manage and implement EU policies and the budget; and to enforce European law."[24] The European Union Commission represents the modern version of the supra-entity foreseen by Dante.

Dante's 14th century proposal for a supranational system and entity lay dormant until the 20th century. Its success depended upon rapid communication and ease of travel to allow efficient governing of its territories. Throughout history, the extent, size, and control of an empire or nation-state were proportionate to its ruling authority's ability to efficiently execute decrees over vast areas.[25] For this reason, the Roman Empire lacked cohesion despite its Greco-Roman culture.[26] "Difficulties of land transport and communications isolated regions from one another."[27] While the Roman Empire successfully ruled a vast area, it never truly governed it directly; rather, it delegated governance to local ruling bodies. When such bodies went against Rome's goals, the army was able to re-establish Roman control, aided by its Roman road network. As noted earlier, one of the reasons for the decline of the Roman Empire was its loss of control over regions as it delegated away its own power.[28] The essential elements that were needed in the formation of a global government awaited the technological advances that began to appear in the 19th century with the Industrial Revolution. The expansion of the British Empire during this period of history, for example, was largely due to technological advances in communication and transportation.[29] Steam power brought about railroads and improved ocean travel while the telegraph and telephone advanced communication. British culture spread around the globe until it was said, "the sun never set on the British Empire."

Today the British Empire has all but vanished, having become a Commonwealth of independent nations. The technology that encouraged its formation has advanced to such a degree that a new trend has emerged—globalization. The "world community" has now become a reality and appears to be encroaching on the autonomy of individual nations as today's "modern life transcends the nation-state and its government."[30] International commerce has expedited this trend. People now purchase items worldwide via the Internet; international corporations know no borders; worldwide ATM banking, air travel, satellite television, and free trade zones have formed a 20th century "global community." Where generations of families once remained intact within miles of their place of birth, sons and daughters, now separated by multi-time zones from their parents, find their national loyalties out of focus. Thus, "even well-established nation-states can no longer confer an adequate sense of identity upon their peoples."[31]

Spanish Foreign Minister, Miguel Angel Moratinos, recently noted: "The concept of traditional citizenship has been bypassed in the 21st Century....We are witnessing the last remnants of national politics."[32] More in tune with a global point of view, today's citizen is inclined to have a less grounded sense of identity in his or her own nation, which, in turn, gives rise to a less problematic identification with the supra-entity of the supranational system. The ruling entity of the European Union now extends its jurisdiction and its social programs throughout a vast empire of nations in ways that no single national government could do. With time, the EU is becoming legitimized as the government in Europe, in the minds of its multi-cultural and internationally blended citizens, and eventually will replace former nationalistic attachments and loyalties of individuals. This replacement of national identity is furthered by a world of global brands and products of international companies that are no longer recognized as being produced or consumed in a single country.

It is in the area of business and economics that supranationalism finds its principal support from the average citizen. While minority groups and individuals are hurt by EU regulations, the people have been conditioned to accept the concept that everything is done for the over-all good of the majority. They see and experience the universal benefits: the freedom to travel between countries without lengthy delays at border crossings, the convenience of a common currency when exchange is no longer necessary, the ease with which business can be conducted between countries, cross-border services, and the much publicized entitlements (grants). Having been told that the over-all quality of life within the EU is improved by the decision-makers, the people believe and assent to it, not considering and even over-looking the personal and overall economic costs. The EU, by its structure of being above and independent of its subservient national governments,[33] is freer to assist international trade and business.

A prime requirement for members of the EU's ruling authority is impartiality or an independence from personal loyalties to nation or homeland. Ideally, the authority bases its decisions and policies to favor the interests of the overall supranational system without significant consideration for any individual subservient nation or individual's needs. This is a notable difference when compared to the United States' government which was established upon the basic God-given rights of individuals, however flawed as it was at the time concerning slavery and voting qualifications. The constitution of the United States was designed by men who took into consideration the selfish sin nature of humanity and deliberately chose to implement a check and balance system in an attempt to override and thwart its influence. This system will only work if it is adhered to by individuals. Today it is being challenged by those who would destroy democracy by corrupting it from within. As Booker and North observe, those within the EU believe that "Democracy is for nation states, for people who still live under the illusion that human affairs are best decided through rivalry and conflict between competing political parties."[34] The potential for ultimate control of citizens and their commerce is tremendous under a supranational system. Recent acts of EU legislation that have been enforced by the European Union upon its citizens, illustrate this control and its intrusive nature into even the smallest areas of its citizens' lives.

In July of 2003, the EU technocrats declared that the "jugglers, tightrope walkers and acrobats of the Moscow Circus would have to wear protective headgear during their four-month tour of Britain.[35] As Lorne Gunter of the Edmonton Journal sarcastically commented, "There is a tragic report almost daily of some poor unfortunate juggler being bonked to death...."[36] If this were a unique example of the type of legislation coming out of the EU, it would be humorous. Regrettably, it is not unique and this type of legislation often is quite costly to industry.

The EU agriculture department decrees the size of leek, the girth of peaches, and other fruits and vegetables. The Swedish strawberry producers had to change all of their labeling and advertising of strawberries to reflect the EU legislation which declared their strawberries to be "Nordic berries" because they did not meet the EU's 22-millimeter minimum to be called strawberries. The EU bureaucracy also decides the amount of water in a toilet flush and the dimensions of poles in fire departments. This is all done to maintain "level playing fields" in the marketplace.[37] [38]

In Scotland, the EU declared the Scottish fisheries to be depleting its codfish population in Scottish territorial waters. The EU banned Scottish fishermen from fishing in Scottish waters. The EU compensated Spanish fishermen when they enacted a similar ban in Spanish waters, but offered no compensation to the Scots. The only reason for such a disparity appears to be the EU's desire to equalize nations economically. The author's piano tuner is a former Scottish fisherman, forced to find a new occupation to feed his family in order to be "fair" to Spain. This is the story for many former fishermen living in the villages on the east coast of Scotland. The justification for destroying national occupations is, again, that all nations of the EU must be on a "level playing field." These are just a few illustrations of the intrusion of the EU into the life of the average citizen. "The whole purpose of a supranational body is to stand above the wishes of the individual nations and peoples."[39] In doing this, the EU believes that while some national groups may suffer, such as the Scottish fishermen, the EU as a whole, will gain. Another EU publication declares, "the bigger the EU, the greater the benefits."[40] Today's European Union, a **supranational government,** appears to be following the path that President Ronald Reagan warned against, for it is **a government that "has" nations.**

As the European Union continues to append more nations, it will be necessary to govern more and more people. At the same time, the governing body of the European Commission, now composed of twenty-seven members, will grow to an unwieldy size. Anticipating the problems of an increased representation of these peoples and nations, the European Commission has already determined that it must limit the number of commissioners to less than twenty-seven.[41] As a result, a small number of unelected commissioners will govern an increasing number of people. A vast number of technocrats will be needed to implement the decisions of the commissioners. Today, 25,000 technocrats work under the European Commission.[42] In an attempt to reduce its bureaucracy with its cumbersome "red tape," the EU has actually created a "bureaucracy...to fight bureaucracy." The question is whether or not this new agency will actually succeed in down-sizing this colossus of government or simply augment its size.[43] As already noted, this technocratic mentality, combined with the need for ongoing expansion, creates the enormous potential of global control by the first supranational system in the world.

A Key Characteristic—a Diverse Empire

While the expansionist concepts of the European Union potentially fit the *"whole earth"* description of Daniel 7:23, another key characteristic is also required of mankind's final kingdom—that it be *"diverse"* from all kingdoms. Few Bible commentators make note of the significance of the diverse aspect of the kingdom. Yet, this word provides a key to understanding what distinguishes the latter-day phase of the Roman Empire from its previous form or from its current fragmented form. The Aramaic word for *diverse* is repeated several times in Daniel 7 (Dan. 7:3, 7, 19, 23, 24).

Verse 7 states that the fourth kingdom will be diverse from the three previous kingdoms. Verse 23 states that the fourth kingdom will be diverse from *"all kingdoms,"* not just the first three of Daniel. Clearly, understanding the meaning of this word is essential since it is what sets the latter-day kingdom apart from its earlier form and from all of the other kingdoms of history.

The English definition of the word *diverse* is something that is "distinctly dissimilar or unlike"[44] anything else. The ancient Chaldean word means to "be different from"[45] or unique. Summing it up, *diverse* describes something that is unique from everything else. Daniel uses the same word to depict the Antichrist of the Tribulation (Daniel 7:24). Based upon Daniel's use of diverse, it is logical to conclude that the latter day form of the Roman Empire will be unique in history in some distinct aspect. It is imperative to ask, "Is the European Union the diverse kingdom written of by Daniel?" Again, a historical review will help to determine the answer.

Responding to the devastation of World War I, Jean Monnet offered the world a unique, new form of government. He called it a supranational government and defined it as "transcending established national boundaries or spheres of interest."[46] Since this granted power would not belong to a single nation but to a controlling independent entity, it was called supranational. For the first time in history, this unique form of government is possible largely due to technological advances in communication and transportation.

In a supranational system, an independent bureaucracy, composed of civil servants or bureaucrats, determines policies for the member nations, and the member nations must yield to that independent ruling body. Key to this system is the willing subjection of the member nations' individual sovereignties. Unlike a federation, where powers flow voluntarily between the governing authorities, forming an inherent check and balance system while maintaining the sovereignty of individual states, a supra-national governing authority must over-ride state or national sovereignty. The authority is empowered to govern because it is given the final rule of law, the economic control of the single monetary system, and the might of a single army. Furthermore, Monnet himself stated that once a particular power has been yielded to the supranational government, it should never be returned to the individual sovereign nation.[47] Thus, power within a supranational government flows one-way and, logically, can only increase.

The European Union could be considered diverse since it is following the pattern of a supranational government, a form which has existed at no other time in history. Jens-Peter Bonde, co-president of the Independent Democrats, a political power group within the EU parliament, noted that the newly proposed constitution "is a one-way-street with transfer of powers from the voters to mainly civil servants and ministers behind closed doors in Brussels."[48] This means that ultimate control of the EU is in the hands of unelected officials who are not accountable in any way to the people. With no opposition to thwart its progressive absorption of powers, it can only become a more powerful entity. The supplantation of national law by EU legislation created by its bureaucracy well represents this principle. A 1992 study revealed that the European Commission (the main law making body of unelected officials) initiated only 30 of the 535 proposed laws. "The rest came from other sources, ranging from civil servants of member states to an array of anonymous committees."[49] Instead of the power residing in the national lawmaking bodies, it primarily rests with Monnet's technocrats. "The number of EU laws in force in the UK has risen from 1,947 to over 25,000 in just 30 years, and only a handful of these were ever debated at Westminster [the UK parliament]."[50] As a result of actions such as these, the European Union's supranational government can only grow stronger. Britain's Lord Denning stated, "No longer is European law an incoming tide flowing up the estuaries of England. It is now like a tidal wave bringing down our sea walls and flowing inland over our fields and houses, to the dismay of us all."[51] Additionally, with the implementation of the Neighborhood Policy, the EU will continue to absorb neighboring, non-European Union countries in order to prevent conflicts with its member states. In reality, a supranational system requires the ultimate eradication of all national identities outside of itself and precludes the existence of nations and national interests.

As the European Union has noted, it is obligated to be involved in its "neighborhood" in order to assure its own peace and security. It appears inevitable that any government outside of the supranational government is a threat to it. Therefore, a global government is the only plausible outcome of a supranational government. Such a span of control through one entity is reminiscent of the days of Nimrod and the Tower of Babel. Perhaps the design of the Weiss building does indeed proclaim the goal of the European Union—that of uniting all of mankind.

While the idea of a global government is not new, the concept of supranationalism is unique in history. Salter, one of the three founding members of the EU, declared that the proposed form of the European Union's government is "something new in the world's history."[52] A recent Oxford University publication noted, "the EU is neither a conventional international organization nor a (national) state, even though many do not accept that the Union may be considered as a political system or polity in its own right. It is not surprising then that the EU is often defined as a unique or hybrid institution."[53] Others declare that "the EU is indeed unique and distinctive."[54] An EU publication, proudly states, "The European Union's success owes a lot to the unusual way in which it works, unusual because the EU is not a federation like the United States. Nor is it simply an organization for cooperation between governments, like the United Nations. It is, in fact, unique."[55] In the year 2000, after fifty years of existence, the president of the EU vocalized the ultimate outcome of the European Union when he said, "we are aiming at a new kind of global governance, one from which a global government can emerge."[56]

In conclusion, supranationalism is unique in history and, therefore, is a diverse form of government. As has been explained, the European Union with its supranational government must continually expand in order to ensure its ongoing success. Twenty-five hundred years ago, Daniel indicated that the final form of the fourth empire would be diverse or unique and would *"devour the whole earth."* He added that it would *"tread it down"* and *"break it in pieces,"* suggesting governmental control without any consideration for the governed, followed by the restructuring of the entire world into ten regions governed by ten kings.

It is difficult to deny the possibility that the European Union may eventually evolve into the final form of the Fourth Kingdom described by Daniel. On the other hand, it should also be acknowledged that the European Union may not ultimately materialize as the final kingdom of mankind. Nevertheless, it can be concluded that the EU at this point in time has the potential of fulfilling Daniel 7:23. It is certain, however, that God's Word is truthful. The final form of the Fourth Kingdom will manifest itself some day and those who know His Word should be able to recognize it

ACT III – SCENE 4
THE ALLIANCE – GOVERNMENT AND RELIGION

—ɷ—

Time: Shortly after the start of the 7-year Tribulation
Setting: The World
Enter: A Woman Riding a Beast

In 16th century Britain the flame of reformation ignited with great fervor, catching fire throughout the land. Then as the British Empire spread across the globe, Christian beliefs traveled with its expansion. At one time "the sun never set upon the British Empire" and the influence of Christianity was felt around the world. Today, however, no such Christian spiritual fires are burning in the United Kingdom. A recent study found that the current Sunday church attendance will decline to less than two percent by the year 2040.[1] Foreseeing the nationwide closing of 18,000 churches, The *Daily Telegraph* declared the churches to be "on the road to doom."[2] The future of Christianity is uncertain.[3]

Similarly, throughout the twenty-seven nations of the European Union, traditional Christianity seems to be fading away, as evidenced by the latest proposed 250-page European Union constitution.[4] Conspicuously absent from this ponderous document is any reference to God or any recognition of the "Judeo-Christian values ... [which]

shaped European culture."[5] Surprisingly, even Alexander Kwasniewski, the self-described atheist and former president of Roman Catholic Poland, "called the godless tone of the constitution shameful."[6]

Although the European Union gives no official recognition to God and church attendance in Europe has been waning, over 4.5 million people flock to Fatima, Portugal each year to worship at what has become a worldwide ecumenical venue. Once solely a Roman Catholic shrine, Fatima is now "a multi-faith centre where Buddhism, Islam, Christianity, and Pagan religions can rest at ease with each other."[7]

What really lies beneath these spiritual trends and events in Europe? One possible answer is that mankind is nearing the point in history prophesied by John in Revelation 17 and 18 where he describes a latter-day global government and global religion. At the very least, the changes in European governments as well as in Europe's spiritual landscape call for a closer examination.

Throughout history, Christians have set forth possible scenarios depicting the latter day world-uniting government and religion written of by the prophets. Many have speculated that one dominant religion will conquer all of the other religions of the world. Such a scenario foresees the demise of the conquered religions as this dominating religion engulfs the masses. Often personal prejudices and bias against one religion or another is the basis for choosing a candidate for the dominant religion. In some instances, world events involving a specific religion influence the choice. Scenarios based upon prejudices, biases, and world events weaken the cause of Christ and do not motivate people to study the Scriptures. Therefore, an alternative scenario based upon the Word of God and free of prejudices and biases, might counter such distorted concepts. To this end, a possible alternative is explored in this scene. Based upon the European Union's concept of supra-nationalism, a study of Biblical prophecy, and observations of historical religious trends in Europe, a scenario of a latter-day supra-religion that is allied with a supra-national government is offered:

Proposed Scenario of the Supra-Religion

A "supra-religion" is comprised of a ruling body or authority that is over, above, and independent of subservient religions and, therefore, bases its decisions and policies to favor the good of the supra-religion's goals, without consideration for any subservient religion's unique beliefs or distinctives. The ruling-authority is not in and of itself a religion; rather, it is a governing entity that does not favor a single belief system. For example, a supra-religion governing both Muslims and Hindus would not restrict the worship style of either but would merely require loyalty and support to the supra-religion's ruling entity and goals. Key to a supra-religion is the idea that it does not replace or eliminate an existing religion. It merely controls and links the subordinate religions into a united body while allowing them to continue to maintain their own identities and systems of worship as long as in doing this they do not conflict with the supra-religion's purposes. The stated goal of the supra-religion would be identical to that of the supra-government—to prevent conflict and to bring "peace and harmony" to the world through unification.

The description of a supra-religion provides a starting point for establishing an alternative scenario of a latter day world-uniting government and religion. Next, the Scriptures need to be examined. John's prophetic vision in Revelation 17 pictures the future alliance of a global government with a global religion that is designed to unify mankind.

The Alliance—Revelation 17

And there came one of the seven angels which had the seven vials, and talked with me, saying unto me,

Come hither; I will shew unto thee the judgment of the great whore that sitteth upon many waters: With whom the kings of the earth have committed fornication, and the inhabitants of the earth have been made drunk with the wine of her fornication. So he carried me away in the spirit into the wilderness: and I saw a woman sit upon a scarlet coloured beast, full of names of blasphemy, having seven heads and ten horns. And the woman was arrayed in purple and scarlet colour, and decked with gold and precious stones and pearls, having a golden cup in her hand full of abominations and filthiness of her fornication: And upon her forehead was a name written, MYSTERY, BABYLON THE GREAT, THE MOTHER OF HARLOTS AND ABOMINATIONS OF THE EARTH.

Revelation 17:1-5

In the proposed alternative scenario, the *"woman"* is the supra-religion and the *"scarlet coloured beast"* is the supra-government. This alliance of religion and government may well be the latter-day form of the global religion and global government put in place during the first half of the Tribulation and identified by John as *"Babylon the great, the mother of harlots and abominations of the earth."* John Walvoord places the formation of such a global religion before the seven vial judgments, noting that the seven angels still have the seven vials (Rev. 16). Consequently, he places the implementation of this alliance at the beginning of the Tribulation (Daniel's 70th Week) and continuing to the mid-point of the Tribulation.[8] This latter-day supra-religion, described as the *"woman"* (Rev. 17:1), arises as a ruling entity or authority above or "supra" to the existing religions of the world. It is not a new, independent religion but, rather, a ruling authority over all existing religions of the world.

John often uses women as figures to symbolize a religious system in the book of Revelation. For example, in Revelation 2:20 he uses Jezebel to represent "pagan idolatry of the past;" while in Revelation 12:1, a sun-clothed woman represents the nation of Israel. The figurative woman of Revelation 17 is used to represent and describe the union of government and religion during the Tribulation.[9] The imagery relating to this woman discloses three characteristics of the alliance of government with religion:

Three Characteristics of the Alliance — Revelation 17

1) John describes the *"woman"* of Revelation 17 as a *"whore"* or harlot, symbolically indicating that she represents a false religious system.

In the biblical "prophetic language, prostitution, fornication, or adultery is equivalent to idolatry or religious apostasy (Isa. 23:15-17; Jer. 2:20-31; 13:27; Ezek. 16:17-19; Hos. 2:5; Nah. 3:4)."[10] The adjective *"great"* (*megas*) modifies *"whore"* indicating a harlot of great size, age, intensity, and/or rank.[11]

Essentially, the *"woman"* represents "an ecclesiastical or religious facet that is a counterfeit of the real."[12] Therefore, this religious system must have the appearance and attractiveness of a viable religion in order for it to appeal on a worldwide level since a blatant lie deceives only a relatively small number of people. By coupling *"great"* and *"whore,"* it is "beyond dispute that this woman of Rev. 17:1 is the epitome of spiritual fornication or idolatry."[13] Accordingly, it can be expected that the ruling authority of the latter-day supra-religion will be a counterfeit of a genuine ecclesiastical or religious facet of true belief rather than a new religious belief. Such a counterfeit ruling authority will ultimately be triumphed over by Christ and His translated church of Revelation 19:2.[14]

2) Revelation 17:1 depicts the *"woman"* seated *"upon many waters."*

John defines this symbolism later in verse 15 where *"waters"* are *"peoples, and multitudes, and nations, and tongues."* The all inclusiveness of this characteristic shows that this counterfeit religious system will be global in its scope, affecting great multitudes of people of many nationalities and nations.

3) John's inclusion of *"nations"* suggests that this system's influence and power extends beyond people groups and dominates the nations and governments ruling them.

He re-iterates this in verse two, indicating that her fornication extends also to the *"kings of the earth."* Consequently, national governments will ally with this counterfeit religious system.[15] Revelation 18:3 expands this alliance to include the *"merchants of the earth"* meaning that she not only is involved with international governments but also with international commerce as well.

The woman's harlotry and its resultant power over governments and commerce is so overwhelming that the inhabitants of the earth follow her as if they are *"drunk"* and have lost self-control because of her (Rev. 17:2). Clearly, this drunkenness indicates the irrational nature of the drive that compels people and governments to support the religious system she represents.

Revelation 17:3 offers a fuller description of this relationship between the religious system and the government. The woman is seated *"upon a scarlet-coloured beast."* This *"beast"* is the same one of Revelation 13:1 and represents the latter-day worldwide government.[16] In Revelation 13, the "*beast*" symbolizes the Antichrist and his global government, "*his seat, and great authority*," which receives its power from Satan (Rev. 13:1-10). The position of the "*woman*" upon the "*beast*" suggests the power structure of their relationship to be one in which the "*woman*" dominates and controls the "*beast*." Alford comments on this positioning, "…by the woman sitting on the wild-beast, is signified that superintending and guiding power which the rider possesses over his beast."[17]

Interestingly, the European Union frequently uses the image of the mythical goddess Europa, a woman riding a bull, as its universal theme and logo. For example, the EU uses the name "Europa" for its website; and in physical form, a bronze sculpture of Europa stands outside of the European Union's Council of Ministers office building that is directly across from the European Commission building on Schuman Square in Brussels.

EU Artwork - Schuman Square - Brussels Belgium

Europa is historically tied to the continent of Europe since it was named after this mythical goddess. With the exception of English, all European languages, including Greek and Latin, use the word "Europa" when referring to Europe.[18] While the European Union implies that the symbol merely represents a united Europe,[19] the likeness to the woman and beast of Revelation is noteworthy. In Act III, Scene 5, further consideration will be given to this ancient mythology and its probable link with the final global government and global religion.

John's prophetic imagery and the three characteristics evident in Revelation 17 make it possible to better understand the relationship and subsequent alliance of a global, counterfeit religious system with a global government and commerce system. However, it must be noted that before the alliance is formed during the first half of the Tribulation, it is only possible to hypothesize as to the true identity of both *"the beast"* and *"the woman."* Prior to the onset of the Tribulation, identifying plausible embryonic forms can serve to demonstrate the feasibility of this type of an alliance in today's world. The European Union does serve as a powerful example, for it demonstrates just how such an alliance could develop.

The EU and Religion

Today, the European Union has no formal alliances with any supra-religion. Many even object to the idea that there is a link between the European Union and any religious faith whatsoever. Although the European Union's proposed constitution makes no mention of any faith, a close examination of the religious leanings of its founding fathers and some current leaders reveals that there could be an underlying, although informal, religious influence between the European Union and the Roman Catholic Church. While today's unofficial alliance may only be between a supra-government and a single, traditional religion, it may well be the embryo of the final alliance referenced in Revelation 17.

The European Union's Links to Roman Catholicism

On August 26, 2004, Roman Catholic Italian Prime Minister Berlusconi, then the president of the EU, hinted at the European Union's link to the Roman Catholic Church when he stated, "I am profoundly convinced...that the only glue capable of sticking together Europe is Christianity."[20]

Looking to the religious background of the European Union's "official" founding fathers, all were Roman Catholics.[21] Alcide de Gasperi, Robert Shuman, and Konrad Adenauer are being considered for Roman Catholic saint-hood as a "reward for founding the European Community 'on Roman Catholic principles.'"[22] Of Robert Shuman it was said that his "political convictions were informed by his Catholic faith. 'For the father of Europe, Catholicism was not only a faith but a social doctrine.'"[23]

The intention of solidifying faith with the social/political realm of the European Union is supported by the fact that the "Vatican has been given the privilege of being the leader and president of the Diplomatic corps of all the member govern-ments of the European Union. That was the recognition which declared that the EU was reckoned to be an alliance of RC states."[24]

Perhaps the European Union's flag, its prime symbol, reflects these principles. The Council of Europe proclaims it as being "the symbol par excellence of united Europe and European identity."[25] On December 8, 1955, the committee of Ministers of the Council of Europe officially adopted the flag.[26] An unusual coincidence worth noting is that the vote was conducted on the day of the Roman Catholic feast of the Immaculate Conception of Mary.[27]

The flag is described as having a blue background, portraying the sky over the western world, and upon this "sky" is a "circle of gold stars [which] represents solidarity and harmony between the peoples of Europe."[28]

EU and Council of Europe Flag

Since the European Union believes that peace and prosperity can come only through unity, it would seem reasonable that the circle of twelve stars represents this unity and that every star is of equal importance. This leads to the assumption that each star represents a country within the Union, in much the same way that the United States' flag has a star for each state in its union. However, that conjecture would prove to be incorrect since the Council of Europe in 1955 consisted of fifteen members rather than twelve. Furthermore, the EU has stated, "the number of stars has nothing to do with the number of Member States."[29] Rather, the number twelve was chosen to symbolize the number of "perfection, completeness, and unity."[30]

With no relationship between the number of stars and the number of states, interpretation of the meaning of the stars is left to individual imagination. In this way, the twelve stars could represent "the sons of Jacob, the tables of Roman legislator, the labors of Hercules, the hours of the day, the months of the year, or the signs of the Zodiac."[31] Others saw in it the number of the Apostles.[32] In addition to these symbols, a spokesman for the European Union "pointed out that the circle of twelve stars was a Christian symbol representing the Virgin Mary's halo," which they considered to be symbolic of European identity and unification.[33] Here was the first hint of a religious aspect, either direct or implied, to the European Union's flag and therefore, to its purpose and goals. Since its adoption by the European Union in 1986, all EU institutions use the flag to represent Europe.[34] According to the Council of Europe, this flag with its twelve star halo is "the symbol par excellence of united Europe and European unity."[35]

The unveiling of the Council of Europe's stained glass window in the Strasbourg Cathedral in 1955 substantiated this religious aspect to the flag's stars. On this occasion the secretary-general of the Council, Leon Marchal, offered an understanding of the twelve stars when he said that they symbolized the "the woman of the Apocalypse" of Revelation 12.[36] When the flag's designer, Arsene Heitz of Strasbourg, was questioned regarding the interpretation of the flag's design, he indicated that he based his design upon the iconography of the image of the Immaculate Conception of Mary as seen in Paris' Rue du Bac.[37]

At Rue du Bac on November 27, 1830, Catherine Laboure had an apparition of Mary standing on a globe of the world while crushing a snake's head with her feet. Around her head were twelve stars. According to Mary's instructions during the apparition, a medal was to be cast depicting the twelve stars. The interpretation of this apparition was based upon the Roman Catholic exposition of Genesis 3:15 and Revelation 12:1. In 1955, Heitz was inspired to use the stars in his flag's design while reading a description of the apparition. The symbol of twelve stars is linked with the Roman Catholic doctrine of the Immaculate Conception of Mary.[38] This association of the twelve stars with Mary actually originated in 1649 with the Spanish writer and art censor to the

Inquisition, Francesco Pacheco, and has influenced artists ever since.[39]

Mary with Stars — St. Vitus Cathedral, Prague.
Credit: Timothy Heijermans. All rights reserved.

According to several sources,[40] the symbolism of the twelve stars of the European Union reflects the symbolism of Revelation 12:1 and the Roman Catholic interpretation for the *"woman"* as being Mary. While the European Union does not officially declare this verse to be the inspiration for the twelve stars, it does emphasize the symbol as representing "perfection, completeness, and unity."[41] Obviously, it is those within the European Union who establish the meaning for their flag. However, they officially defined all of the symbolism of the flag except that of the twelve stars. Nevertheless, there have been hints to connect the stars with the *"woman"* of Revelation 12.

The Meaning of Revelation 12:1

The Roman Catholic understanding of Revelation 12:1 is that the *"woman"* mentioned is the Virgin Mary.[42] This interpretation for the *"woman"* was not arrived at by following the Bible's own instructions for gaining an understanding of a portion of Scripture—by comparing Scripture with Scripture and by searching the Scriptures (1 Cor. 2:13; Acts 17:11). Thus, the principle of comparing spiritual things with spiritual can be applied to this first verse of chapter 12:

> *And there appeared a great wonder in heaven; a woman clothed with the sun, and the moon under her feet, and upon her head a crown of twelve stars.*

**Artistic Rendition of the
Woman of Revelation 12:1**

The *"woman"* is described as being a *"great wonder."* Literally, the Greek lexicon meaning is a "great or mega symbol."[43] A symbol is never the actual object symbolized, but rather, "something that stands for, represents, or suggests another thing.[44] Since the *"woman"* is a symbol in this situation, it is obvious that she cannot represent an actual woman.

In searching the Scriptures for the interpretation of a symbol, other contexts using the same symbol must be examined.[45] The context may be immediate or remote.[46] A passage containing a similar symbol sheds light upon the context being considered, providing the correlation necessary to explain the use of the symbol. Applying this method discloses a remote context in Genesis that uniquely contains the symbols of the sun, moon, and a specific number of stars, and consequently brings understanding to the symbolic meaning in Revelation 12.

And he [Joseph] *dreamed yet another dream, and told it his brethren* [Jacob had twelve sons, including Joseph], *and said, Behold, I have dreamed a dream more; and, behold, the sun and the moon and the eleven stars made obeisance to me. And he told it to his father* [Jacob], *and to his brethren: and his father rebuked him, and said unto him, What is this dream that thou hast dreamed? Shall I* [Jacob] *and thy mother* [Rachel] *and thy brethren indeed come to bow down ourselves to thee to the earth? And his brethren envied him; but his father observed the saying.*

Genesis 37:9-11

The word *"obeisance"* (bowing) links the symbols of the sun, moon, and stars in the dream to Jacob and his family. Clearly, Jacob understood the symbols. He was the sun, Rachel was the moon, and the eleven stars were Joseph's brothers. It becomes evident later in Genesis that this dream foretold the future experiences of Joseph and his brothers in Egypt.

By combining the understanding that the stars represent Jacob's twelve sons, when Joseph is included, that the sun represents Jacob, or "Israel" as God re-named him, and that the moon is Rachel, it can be concluded that the symbols of Genesis 37:9 represent this historic family, Israel (v. 10). This "search" of the Scriptures has revealed that the stars of the woman's crown in Revelation 12:1 specifically represent the twelve sons or tribes of Israel.[47] It should also be noted that John uses extensive Jewish contextual references in Revelation 7:5-8; 11:19; 14:1ff; and 21:12.[48] In the book of Revelation, John always speaks of the twelve tribes rather than just eleven (Rev. 7:5-8; 21:12).[49] Since the symbols of

Genesis chapter 37 and those of Revelation chapter 12 are identical, there is Scriptural evidence to support the conclusion that the woman symbolizes this historic family and its descendents. Therefore, the *"woman"* is a symbol for the nation of Israel.

Upon further consideration regarding the events described in Revelation 12, it becomes apparent that nothing in this account corresponds with any events in Mary's life. For example, she never *"fled into the wilderness to a place prepared of God"* (Rev. 12:6). Rather, she and Joseph went to Egypt, a very civilized nation. During the future Tribulation, the nation of Israel will flee to a refuge in the wilderness that God has prepared for her.[50]

Satan's evil intentions have been to *"devour her* [Israel's] *child."* Throughout history, Satan has attempted to destroy or corrupt the line of the Messiah. Examples include:

> … his [Satan's] hostility [that] surfaced in Cain's murder of Abel (Gen. 4:8), the corrupting of the line of Seth (Gen. 6:1-12), attempted rapes of Sara (Gen. 12:10-20; 20:1-18) and Rebekah (Gen. 26:1-18), Rebekah's plan to cheat Esau out of his birthright and the consequent enmity of Esau against Jacob (Gen. 27), the murder of the male children in Egypt (Ex. 1:15-22), attempted murders of David (e.g., 1 Sam. 18:1-11), Queen Athaliah's attempt to destroy the royal seed (2 Chron. 22:10), Haman's attempt to slaughter the Jews (Esther 3-9), and consistent attempts of the Israelites to murder their own children for sacrificial purposes (cf. Lev. 18:21; 2 Kings 16:3; 2 Chron. 28:3; Ps. 106:37-38; Ezek. 16:20). The attack of Herod against the children of Bethlehem (Matt. 2:16) and many other incidents during Jesus' earthly life, including His temptation,

typify the ongoing attempt of the dragon to devour the woman's child once he was born.[51]

An examination of the Scriptures discloses many instances in the Old Testament where Israel is depicted as a travailing woman (Isa. 13:8; 21:3; 26:17-18; 61:7-8; 66:7ff.; Jer. 4:31; 13:21; 22:23; Hos. 13:13; Mic. 4:10; 5:2-3).[52] "Though, historically, the nation gave birth to Christ through the Virgin Mary, the implication of verse 2 is that the references are to the sufferings of Israel as a nation rather than to the historic birth of Christ. It may refer to the sufferings of the nation in general over its entire troublesome history."[53] One of Satan's major attacks to stop God's plan, of course, was when he orchestrated Christ's crucifixion. This apparent victory, however, was short-lived when Jesus was raised from the dead and ascended to the right hand of God's throne—Satan was defeated (Rev. 12:5).

Finally, the events described in verses 14 and 15 bear no resemblance to any events Mary ever experienced. Many Bible commentators agree that the "fleeing into the wilderness" refers to a yet future event regarding the nation of Israel during the Tribulation and not to Joseph and Mary's trip to Egypt (Matt. 2:13-15).[543] God will again provide for and protect this nation from her enemies much as he did at her beginning during the Exodus from Egypt.

Replacement Theology, the teaching that God has replaced Israel with the Church, lies behind the displacement of Israel with Mary. Unfortunately, Replacement Theology thwarts an acknowledgement as well as an understanding of God's plan and purpose for the nation of Israel. Despite this, the Roman Church and some within the European Union interpret the *"woman"* as being a symbol for Mary. The European Union makes use of what is perceived as her starry crown on their flag, stamps, euros, buildings, and publications.

The Roman Catholic Links to Europe and the European Union

Throughout history, the Roman Church has expressed a strong interest in Europe and its dream. In 1309, the Vatican consecrated Europe to the Virgin Mary and placed it under her patronage. More recently, on four separate occasions the late Pope John Paul II consecrated "the world to our Lady."[55] In Gibraltar is the shrine of "Our Lady of Europe." The EU recently granted one-half of the total cost of the shrine's restoration.[56] In 1979, Pope Paul II officially approved Mary's title as "Our Lady of Europe" and transferred her feast day to May 5, to coincide with Europe Day.[57][58][59] On this occasion, the Pope expressed the Dream of Europe and how it might be achieved by saying that "...under the patronage of Mary, the human family will be drawn ever more closely into fraternal unity and peaceful coexistence."[60]

From its beginnings until now, the Roman Church has been the primary cord binding the Roman Empire together, albeit, at times a loose and fragmented empire. Even today, many in Europe hope to regain that lost union through the power of the Roman Church. Speaking to the President of the European Commission, the supra-ruling entity of the European Union, John Paul II reminded him that "the Holy See encouraged the formation of the European Union even before it acquired any juridical framework..."[61] Pope John XXIII "insisted that Roman Catholics should be 'in the front ranks' of the unification effort."[62] In 1975 Pope Paul VI declared, "Can it not be said that it is faith, the Christian faith, the Catholic faith that made Europe? ...No other human force in Europe can ...re-awaken Europe's Christian soul, where its unity is rooted."[63] Pope Benedict XVI purposely chose his name to reflect the role of St. Benedict of Norcia because he had spread Roman Christianity throughout Europe. Hence, "he represents a fundamental point of reference for the unity of Europe and a strong reminder of the

unrenounceable Christian roots of its culture and civilization." He also indicated "his reign would be devoted to unity
[among Catholics, Jews, Muslims, Orthodox Christians, and
other branches of Christianity]."[64] On April 27, 2005, Pope
Benedict XVI stated, "St. Benedict...is a fundamental reference point for European Unity and a powerful reminder of
the indispensable Christian roots of its culture."[65]

The Vatican—a world power

As in the past, the Vatican today continues to exercise
both political and religious influence and power in Europe.
It is now the most extensive international organization in
the world outside of the United Nations.[66] It has formal state
relations with 147 countries of the world and represents one
billion people in world matters. If officially united with the
European Union, the Vatican has the potential of becoming
the greatest economic and governmental state in the world.

Its desire for world control might be exemplified by the
late John Paul II's proclamation that Jesus Christ will conquer
through Mary. Expressing his thoughts at the start of the
new millennium, he said, "Here we stand before you [Mary]
to entrust to your maternal care ourselves, the Church, the
entire world....To you, Dawn of Salvation, we commit our
journey through the new millennium."[67]

The implications of this statement imply that Christ
needs His mother to conquer, thus putting her on His level.
Furthermore, John Paul II taught that through her comes
salvation, a doctrine that he referred to and believed when
he called Mary the Co-Redeemer. The Roman Catholic
Catechism states, "The Virgin Mary 'co-operated through
free faith and obedience in human salvation.'"[68] Pictures
taken during Pope John Paul II's funeral reveal his trust in
Mary as Co-Redeemer. He directed the placing of the initial
"M" beside the engraved cross that is on his coffin.

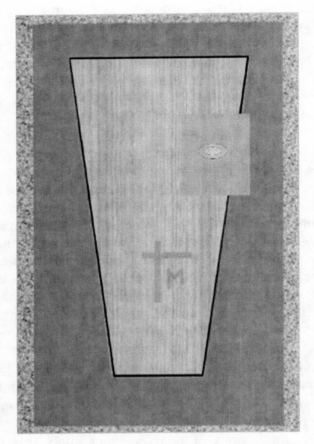

**Artistic representation of Pope John Paul's
Casket Lying in State**

This visual symbol may have been chosen because of its
association with the aforementioned 1830's apparition of
Mary at the Rue du Bac where she communicated that she is
the "advocate, mediatrix, and [is] working with her Divine
Spouse, the Holy Spirit, in preparing for Christ's second
coming, the Co-Redemptrix."[69] The apparition indicated
that in addition to the previously mentioned twelve stars that

were to be cast on the commemorative medal, the design was to incorporate images signifying Mary's role as Co-Redemptrix. The commissioned medal was designed and cast with a cross surrounded by the twelve stars, representing the twelve apostles, and with the initial "M" below to represent "Mary's part [Co-Redeemer] in our salvation and her role as mother of the Church."[70]

This brief review has sought to demonstrate the informal linkage between the supra-national government of the European Union and the Roman Catholic Church. Throughout history, certain common denominators are detected. These include the Roman Church's ongoing interest in the unity of Europe, its persistent desire to ally with state governments of Europe, its desire to dominate the policies of those governments, and its insistence on placing Mary and her Immaculate Conception at the forefront. Today's informal relationship between the European Union and the Roman Catholic Church continues that pattern of history and appears to be bringing about the form foretold by both Daniel and John.

Conversely, just as the Roman Empire did not control the entire world, neither does the Roman Catholic Church; it is just one independent religion among many in the world. While many Bible scholars have speculated that the Roman Church will become the final dominating religion of the world, this may not be the case. Such a view ignores the power of other world religions, religions such as Islam, Hinduism, Buddhism, etc. Certainly, world history is fraught with many religious conflicts which demonstrate the difficulty of uniting the world's religions into one cohesive organization. For this reason, the concept of a "supra religious" controlling entity seems to provide the solution for establishing a one world religious system.

ACT III – SCENE 5
UNITING THE WORLD'S RELIGIONS

—⧟—

Time: Today
Setting: The World
Enter: Dan Brown with his best Seller Book

A work of fiction, but much more than that, *The DaVinci Code* has prompted outrage throughout Christendom. Forty million have purchased copies, and the movie based upon it has gained worldwide attention. While many debate the historical correctness and the factual nature of the book, its subtle underlying theme is overlooked. Within the first twenty pages, Dan Brown introduces his readers to the "sacred feminine," the ancient goddess of Babel in another guise. The book records the quest of its two prime characters to find the Holy Grail, the actual bones of Mary Magdalene whom Brown indicates is the sacred feminine of history. For most people of the 21st century this is something they have never heard of. Some simply view it as a form or modern feminism, but when considered from a Biblical perspective the concept suggests the re-emergence of the feminine goddess, Semiramis, first introduced by Satan in ancient Babylon. Within the concept of the sacred feminine, also known as the Magna Mater, lie the roots of the final global religion described in the book of Revelation by John.

And upon her forehead was a name written,
MYSTERY BABYLON THE GREAT, THE MOTHER
OF HARLOTS AND ABOMINATIONS OF THE
EARTH.

Rev. 17:5

In the previous scene it was noted that the most likely scenario for this final false global religion is not a new belief system but an alliance of the world's religions. This scene will demonstrate that the "sacred feminine" of Babylon may very possibly facilitate this union by providing the focus or means for opposing religions of the world to come together.

In today's world, such an alliance must include Islam and Roman Catholicism, which represent over one-third of the world's population. It must also embrace ecumenical Protestantism as well as a host of other faiths. History, however, argues against such an alliance, for in the past, adherents to one religion often resorted to military or political power to overcome those of another faith. Memories of past conflicts are very long term as the author has discovered while living in the United Kingdom, a "Christian" nation. For example: At local Scottish football games, fans base their loyalty not on the towns represented by the teams, but on the religious history of the towns. Sports events often reflect the conflict between Roman Catholics and Protestants, all rooted in the Reformation of the 16th Century. In September of 2006, Pope Benedict spoke in Germany about the history of Islam and religious aggression. His speech inflamed Muslims and sparked religious fervor in the Muslim community. There are other "hotspots" around the world where tensions exist between various religious groups. Even within religious faiths, there is conflict. In Iraq, three branches of Islam are at odds, and there is disunity between "Christian" groups as well. Many perceive religion as being divisive. The feasibility of the emergence of a single global religion would seem to be impossible unless either one religion conquers all others or a single unifying factor draws them into unity.

History is full of examples of one religion trying to conquer another through political or military strength. Today many believe that the resolution of religious conflict requires political enforcement. They are looking for a strong governing authority to quell religious violence and bring peace to the world. The European Union may provide the governance necessary to attain this. The Council of Europe has already passed a law, the Genocide Treaty, regarding the crime of intolerance.[1] This law states that it is illegal for any individual to declare that his or her religion is the only true faith. While this law may have been intended to disarm Islamic extremists, it is also a potential weapon against true Christians who proclaim Jesus Christ as the only way of salvation. Although many nations have signed this law, it has not been enforced as yet; but the close ties of the Council of Europe to the EU make its potential enforcement quite possible. As the EU expands to 109 nations and develops its global army, it would appear that it could impose a superficial religious peace upon people groups. While this could bring peace on a global scale, it would not preclude religious terrorist attacks within the EU. The European Union could not assure peace throughout every area within its control. It is apparent that a unifying agent is needed, one that could unite all religions rather than divide, subjugate, conquer, or destroy them. This agent, however, would have to use a new method of control, for history shows the futility of political or military force.

The following scenario proposes the means of uniting all religions without the need for a new or dominant religion. Admittedly, it is a proposal or educated guess but it is based upon observations as well as Scripture. It avoids the power struggles of the past and is supported by descriptions of humanity's final false religious system described in

Revelation 17. This scenario brings "peace" to the religious world through a new, unique form of religious "control," one that is over all, above all, and supreme to all—a supra-religion. Thus, just as a new form of governing authority is needed to bring "peace" to Europe, (one above all, independent to all, and supreme to all) so too, the world may seek a religious controlling entity that is above all others while allowing subordinate religions to continue their distinctive practices, thereby creating peace through a unique unity.

A satisfactory scenario would require the supra-religion to offer:

- a system that tolerates religious differences, but negates any differences which could undermine the "peace" of the global community

- an alliance with a supra-government to enforce the necessary religious toleration in order to assure political and religious peace in the world

- a unifying factor or controlling entity having a form of godliness but without genuine power—a counterfeit of true Christianity

The "New Toleration"

This scenario begins by redefining the world's concept of toleration regarding religious differences. Even today, the Monnet Method, which uses a seemingly insignificant step to establish a principle that can be "geared up" to a larger scale, is subtly introducing the "new toleration." This newly defined toleration is in the interest of unity and peace. Without such tolerance, conflicts inevitably develop as history has shown. In the past, toleration meant that individuals of different faiths could express their differences to one another and even attempt to "convert" each other by expressing the belief that their faith was the true faith. Neighbors on one street may hold many different religious beliefs, talk about them with one another, and yet live peacefully side by side. Toleration meant being able to disagree and still live peacefully with each other. Although it seems to be changing, the United States of America has long held this definition of toleration. The new toleration promotes the concept that all faiths are equally valid and lead to God. This definition has largely been promoted in an attempt to disarm radical Islam, which believes in conversion by force rather than heart-changing faith. While it is true that other religions have attempted to use force in the past, this is the first time in history that adherents to a religion have employed massive terror and force on a global scale. As a result, it is considered the height of intolerance to claim one's religious beliefs as the only true faith. This concept is being promoted throughout Europe and is even beginning to surface in the United States. In a spirit of "fairness" it is being applied to all religions. The following examples of the "new toleration" in the United Kingdom and the United States will suffice to demonstrate this method:

Example 1: Churches Together and the Emergent Church

Through Churches Together, hundreds of churches in the United Kingdom are uniting by setting aside their doctrinal differences. The driving force behind this movement is the drastic decline of Sunday church attendance and with it, the fear of extinction. With this fear comes the concept that since "we are so few in number" we cannot allow "minor" doctrines to divide us. Thus, individual church members who persist in defending what are considered to be divergent "minor" doctrines are pressured to keep silent. One such divisive "minor" doctrine is the premillennial view of Christ's Second Coming.[2] Believing such divisiveness "hurts the cause of Christ," church leaders and members seek to eliminate its cause. As a result, the premillennial view is rapidly disappearing in the United Kingdom with the intent of promoting "unity" among Christians. With this "small step", people are being "geared up" to a larger aspect of doctrinal compromise through ecumenicalism. Churches Together states:

> Being ecumenical means looking up to see the big picture: what God is doing through the whole Church in the whole world. It means engaging with others in ways that bring in the Kingdom of God[3], where God's will is done on earth as it is in heaven. It means holding our remaining differences in conversation rather than conflict, engaging in dialogue rather than denouncing each other.
>
> Unity is not singing in unison and losing our distinctiveness: Unity is singing in harmony, each person and tradition enriching the others.
>
> Churches Together respects the distinctiveness of the "Churches", but looks to a time when they will be "Together".[4]

Membership in Churches Together includes the Church of England, the Church of Scotland, Methodist, Presbyterian, Roman Catholic, Greek Orthodox, Quaker, and many independent groups.

The Emerging Church Movement that has begun to develop in the United States is following the same pattern. Just as the hippie movement of the 70's sought to break the moral "bands" of society, the emerging church seeks to break the doctrinal bands between religions, thereby reflecting the protest and rebellion of the 70's only in a refined version. Emergent means something "coming into view, arising from or occurring unexpectedly, requiring immediate action... characterized by evolutionary emergence, or crossing a boundary..."[5] Its prime spokesperson, Brian McClaren, believes that "Jesus' secret message in word and deed makes clear that the kingdom of God will be radically, scandalously inclusive."[6] He adds, "...the kingdom of God seeks to include all who want to participate in and contribute to its purpose, but it cannot include those who oppose its purpose."[7]

Their organization, Emergent Village, proclaims that this movement and its people are committed "to lives of reconciliation and friendship, no matter our theological or historical differences."[8] McClaren summarizes it by saying:

> Wouldn't it be fascinating if thousands of Muslims, alienated with where fundamentalist and extremists have taken their religion, began to "take their places at the feast," discovering the secret message of Jesus in ways that many Christians have not? ...Or if Buddhists, Hindus, and even former atheists and agnostics came from "east and west and north and south" and began to enjoy the feast of the kingdom in ways that those bearing the name *Christian* have not?[9]

Example 2: Reunification

Beginning in the 1940's, amillennialism (the teaching that Christ's kingdom is present today as an invisible, spiritual kingdom rather than a literal future kingdom) has displaced premillennialism (the teaching that Christ literally will rule and reign on earth for one thousand years) in most churches throughout England and Scotland. With the establishment of the principle that Christian groups should not allow such "divisive minor" doctrines to hinder unity, UK church leaders are gearing up for the next major move toward union, the formal reunification of the Roman Catholic Church with the Church of England. When complete, England will have peacefully reversed the events of the English Reformation. This unification will benefit both the European Union and the Roman Church. Today the individual nations and the leaders that make up the European Union are predominantly Roman Catholic. Thus, unification of the Protestant UK churches and Roman Catholicism strengthens the unity of the European Union alliance.

The Anglican-Roman Catholic International Commission (ARCIC) is following a three-step process that is the mechanism for resolving the historic division between Rome and the Church of England. **Step one** was accomplished with their first resolution in May of 1999, when it was agreed that the Pope will have primacy over the Anglican Archbishop of Canterbury if a "new united church" were established.[10]

Step two was reached in 2005 with the agreement on the doctrines of the Immaculate Conception of Mary and her assumption of "body and soul into heaven at the end of her earthly life." The Church of England participants proclaimed these doctrines to be "consonant" with Anglican readings of the Bible.[11]

Step three will undoubtedly advance the doctrine of Mary as co-redeemer, a doctrine that the late Pope John Paul II believed and promoted. Through this three-step process, the Church of England will unite with the Roman Catholic Church by removing "divisive" doctrines and establishing peace within the "Christian" sects.[12] However, the reality will be the elimination of the properly divisive doctrine of the exclusivity of Jesus Christ and salvation through Him alone, a doctrine held today by only a minority within the Anglican Church. In April of 2007 the Church of England's Archbishop of Canterbury, Rowan Williams, suggested that the conservative Christian understanding of texts, such as John 14:6, may be a "partial or even distorting use" of texts.

He notes that this text does not declare the exclusively of Jesus Christ, rather it answers the question posed by chapter 14 of John and "is about the move from desolation in the face of the cross...to the confidence that the process is the work of love coming from and leading to the Father"[13] (a seemingly profound but inexplicable statement).

An Alliance with a Supra-Government

Outside of the church community, the typical Brit today has been conditioned through the educational system and the media to reject the proclamation that Jesus Christ is the only way to heaven and to regard it as being intolerant, divisive, and hateful toward other beliefs (John 14:6, Acts 4:12). Under the guise of protecting its states from incitement to terrorism, the European Union is promoting laws prohibiting exclusivity of any one religious belief. The previously mentioned Genocide Treaty is a step in that direction. In order to eliminate "intolerant" people who are perceived as a threat to both peace and the supra-religion, a supranational government must not allow anyone to express his or her contrary beliefs publicly. Thus, the new toleration will bring religious peace to Europe while the European Union will bring governmental peace. The re-unification of the Roman Church with the Anglican Church will eliminate the last significant Protestant influence in Europe.

The EU's Neighborhood Policy could well be the instrument that enables those who are promoting the European Dream to unite the countries of the ancient Roman Empire, which included countries of the Muslim Middle East and even Israel. Furthermore, longer-range plans are to add all of the Mediterranean countries, including those practicing African religions. After these goals are completed, it is possible that the EU will expand the "Union" to include the entire western hemisphere. Thus, Canada and the United States would be brought into this alliance of global government and the Roman Catholic Church. South America is already predominantly Roman Catholic and working with the European Union through Mercosur. This final expansion may explain, in part, the expanding French Roman Catholic influence in Canada and the massive Hispanic movement into the United States. If the supra-national government of the European Union were to fully ally itself with the Roman Church in these countries, it would become a very powerful governmental/spiritual alliance indeed.

However, this expansion does not solve the problem of how to integrate the Muslim, Hindu, Jewish, and African Pagan religions into this alliance. Certainly none of these religions would accept Roman Catholicism or its dominance. History demonstrates that force will not work.

The Unifying Factor

The solution to the unification of the world's religions into a single global "religion" lies in finding a "unifying agent or factor," one having the ruling authority of a supra-religion. Such a factor must:

- be accepted by all the religions of the world and the supra-government

- reflect a common denominator that is acceptable to all

- be a counterfeit of genuine Christianity

Governmental Acceptance

Following a worldwide congress on religion, the French Interior Minister spoke of the need for a "'one world religion' where individual faiths can live side-by-side under one umbrella...to establish peace and prosperity in the European Union."[14] As noted previously, the European

Union frequently uses the image of the mythical goddess, Europa, as a unifying theme. The mythical story of Europa tells of how the god, Zeus, disguised as a bull, carried her off resulting in a child who later was miraculously resurrected. This story is often seen as a parallel to the story of Mary, as the virgin mother of Jesus. The European Union's national anthem, designed to unify the people of the many member-states, continues this mother-goddess theme.

Owing to the need for a universal anthem that transcends the nationalities of its member states and which eliminates translation problems, the European Union did not assign lyrics to their anthem. The anthem they chose was Ludwig van Beethoven's *Ode to Joy*. While they disavow any lyrics, it is hard to disassociate the original German lyrics of *Ode to Joy* from the European Union's anthem. A translation of these lyrics suggests a possible unifying factor within the anthem. The lyrics are as follows:

Ode to Joy[15]
Joy, Oh! Divine scintillation
Sparkling from Elysium[16],
With a cheerful animation
Goddess, to thy shrine we come

These our nations once divided
Now your magic spells unite,
Where your wind does beat around them
Brotherhood and love delight.

With a kiss bestowed on millions
Embraced in fraternity,
Let us build a world of union
And peace for all humanity

Clearly, these lyrics express a connection to the mythical Europa and her ability to unite the world. The EU's desire to work with the Roman Church and the Roman Church's equally significant desire to lead in the European Union, assure the willingness of the European Union to accept any female "goddess" who could unify the world's religions.

Even the New Age movement speaks of a unifying "goddess." New Age adherent, Beatrice Bruteau, triumphantly says: "the presence of the Goddess herself has never departed from her holy place in our consciousness, and now, as we enter what may fall to be a 'new age,' we sense that the Goddess is somehow making her way back to us. But in just what guise is so far unclear."[17] Apparently, some New Age followers are ready to accept the "goddess" in whatever form she appears.

Surprisingly, even some humanists with a global view recognize the usefulness of religion in bringing about worldwide social stability and are calling for world unification through a supra-national government and a world church. The American Humanist Association stated, "We deplore the division of humankind on nationalistic grounds. We have reached a turning point in history where the best option is to transcend the limits of national sovereignty and to move toward the building of a world community in which all sectors of the human family can participate."[18] They [the humanists] continue to support a "movement toward one-world government and a single church or religion."[19]

Rome not Ready for a Unifying Factor?

However, considering the power of the Roman Church it is difficult to understand how it could accept a unifying factor coming from outside of it. Speaking of a recent ecumenical gathering suggesting such a unifying factor outside of the Roman Church, Peter Scott of the Ignatian Society of Saint Pius X stated:

Such a humanitarian dream [the union proposed at the Congress] to bring about a one-world super religion, more universal than the Catholic Church, uniting all men of all religions, without in any way diminishing their personal religious convictions, is not something new in the history of the Church.[20]

He went on to call such a move of unification a "religious indifferentism." He cited the example of the Roman Church's reaction to a similar movement called *Sillon* at the turn of the last century in France, which Pope Pius X had denounced, pointing out how such a movement would lead to a one-world religion and apostasy of the Roman Catholic faith.[21] Pope John Paul II then offered a counter- proposal.

A Roman Solution for a Unifying Factor
The late Pope John Paul II offered the Roman Catholic Virgin Mary[22] as the unifying factor when he said, "...under the patronage of Mary, the human family will be drawn ever more closely into fraternal unity and peaceful coexistence."[23] When this is properly studied, it will become evident that not only would the various Christian groups acknowledge her, but so, too, would the Muslims, Hindus, African Pagans, and other religious groups. The Roman Catholic Mary is a distortion of the Mary of the Bible as many traditions have been added to the Biblical account of her. This counterfeit aspect grows greater when one considers Mary as immaculately conceived, bodily assumed into heaven, interceding in heaven, and co-redeemer, aspects never attributed to her in the Scriptures.

A universalistic "Global Mary"[24] of the supra-religion who is based upon the Roman Catholic Mary would also be a distortion or counterfeit of the Biblical Mary. Pope John Paul II believed that the Roman Mary would bring about the ultimate victory of the Universal Church. In his book,

217

Crossing the Threshold of Hope, he said, "On this universal level, if victory comes it will be brought by Mary. Christ will conquer through her, because he wants the Church's victories now and in the future to be linked to her."[25] In the largest gathering of the Roman Church since Vatican II, Pope John Paul II entrusted humanity and the third millennium to Our Lady of Fatima. In his lengthy prayer he began by saying "Everything in you is fiat: you are the Immaculate One, through you there shines the fullness of grace."[26] He then committed the future to her and expressed his entrusting of the world to her; "Here we stand before you to entrust to your maternal care ourselves, the Church, the entire world."[27] Concluding he said, "To you, Dawn of Salvation, we commit our journey through the new millennium..."[28]

Throughout the world Marian followers are found, but a particular group called the Blue Army has over 20 million members.[29] A second group, the Marian Movement of Priests, has a membership of 100,000 priests, twenty-five percent of the Roman Church's 400,000 priests.[30] In a Marian apparition to Fr. Gobbi, Mary supposedly said:

> But in the furious struggle of these last times, this struggle between heaven and earth, between the heavenly spirits and the demons, between the Woman and the Dragon, I appear as a great sign of my greatest victory . . . for this great victory, I have formed for myself the cohort of all my little children who, from every part of the world, have responded to me with a yes....I have formed for myself my victorious army.[31]

In another message to Gobbi, Mary reportedly said, "With extraordinary signs which I am giving in every part of the world...I am pointing out to everyone the approaching of the great day of the Lord."[32] With her warnings concerning the times, she emphasized that she has come as the "Blessed

Mother" for all people of the world, regardless of their religion.[33] In the same message, she urged all to pray, "...for all religions, because we know that we have divided ourselves by religion."

In a message given to Ida Peerdeman of Alkmaar, Holland, on May 31, 1954, Mary supposedly indicated that when the dogma, the last Marian dogma of history,[34] has been proclaimed she will give peace, true peace to the world. She stipulated that the nations must say "My prayer in union with the Church" and proclaim her co-redemptrix, mediatrix, and advocate.[35]

De Montfort, a past devotee of Our Lady, predicted, "The power of Mary over all devils will be particularly outstanding in the last period of time. She will extend the Kingdom of Christ over the idolaters and Moslems, and there will come a glorious era in which Mary will be ruler and queen of human hearts."[36]

Perhaps Muslims will allow this "extension of the kingdom" over them in part because some of Mary's most famous apparitions have occurred at Fatima. The village of Fatima was named after the daughter of Mohammed, founder of Islam. Her Arabic name means, "shining one." She was born (c. 605) in Mecca of Saudi Arabia and died in Medina in 633.

Since Mary's appearances at Fatima and Lourdes, France, additional appearances have been recorded around the world. Many eyewitness accounts describe the apparition as being brilliant to behold and arrayed with every splendor. Fifteen to twenty million followers visit the Marian shrine in Guadalupe, Mexico every year.[37] Here the Roman Mary first appeared on December 12, 1531 to Juan Diego. In 1999, over five million people came to honor "Our Lady" on the anniversary of this apparition.[38] This was the first time in church history that all bishops and priests of the Western Hemisphere honored her feast. She also has appeared in

Bosnia, the state of Georgia, Poland, Venezuela, Egypt, Israel, Rwanda, Japan, Australia, Chile, Canada and many other places.[39]

On 31 May 1954, at her appearance to Ida Peerdeman, she proclaimed herself the "Lady of All Nations" and expressed the desire that the Roman church proclaim her the co-redemptrix.[40]

Newsweek stated: "In many ways, the 20th century has belonged to Mary. From almost every continent, visionaries have reported more than 400 'apparitions' of the Virgin — more than in the previous three centuries combined. Taken together, these visions point to what the Marian Movement believes is a millennial 'Age of Mary.'"[41]

Mary's message at Medjugorje, Bosnia—Herzegovina sums up the messages of her many appearances:

> Dear children, today I invite you to peace. I have come here as the Queen of Peace and I desire to enrich you with my Motherly Peace. I invite you to become carriers and witnesses of my peace to this unpeaceful world. Let peace rule in the whole world which is without peace and longs for peace.[42]

With the exception that she once referred to Him as "the little Jesus," there has been no mention of the Lord Jesus Christ or the need of redemption through Him.[43] In another quote, she declared that Muslims and the Orthodox, for the same reason as Catholics, are equal before "my Son and I. You are all my children."[44]

Through these appearances, the Roman Mary of the 21st century appeals to people of all nations, all beliefs, and all cultures. Her message of peace is what many want to hear. The Los Angeles Times noted that unprecedented numbers outside of Roman Catholicism have received comfort from Mary.[45]

In 1983 hundreds of Palestinian Arabs "saw the Virgin Mary" near Bethlehem. She has appeared also in Rwanda, Japan, Australia, Chile, Poland, Canada, Cairo, Amsterdam, and in many other locations.[46]

Muslims Might Accept Her

While Roman Catholicism could certainly accept Mary as the unifying factor, could Islam also accept her? Muslims do show considerable interest in Mary. In the Koran, Mohammed spoke of Mary, either directly or indirectly, over thirty-four times in Suras (chapters) 3, 4, 33, 43, 57 and 66.

For example, the Koran says Mary was a virgin (Sura 19:20) and her Son will be "a sign for the people" (Sura 19 v.21).[47] Mary is "chosen over all women in the world (Sura 3 v.42).[48] Mary is highly honored in Islam and has an entire chapter (Sura 19) of the Koran named after her. "From the Hadith and from verses 35-37 of Sura III, Moslem commentators have deduced and affirmed the principle of Mary's original purity."[49] Therefore, it supports the same concept of Immaculate Conception that is also a key common denominator for reunification between the Church of England and the Roman Church. Interestingly, all references to Jesus Christ are "Jesus son of Mary" rather than "Son of God." While denying Christ's deity, Islam does hold Jesus and Mary in high esteem.[50]

Hindus ready?

Other religious leaders have also made the pilgrimage to Fatima. In May 2004, the Dali Lama visited and prayed at the Fatima shrine. After a Hindu priest, Sha Tri, prayed at the altar, the Rector of the shrine said such meetings gave them the opportunity to "remind ourselves that we live in community."[51] The Hindu priest placed a Hindu priestly shawl, engraved with inscriptions from the Begavad Gita, "on the shoulders of the highest representative of the Church in Fatima...”[52] Following these events there were rumors of the removal of the Rector of the shrine by the Bishop of Lisbon, but by October of 2004, the Bishop related the Vatican's support of him and the “personal instructions” from the Pope regarding inter-religious dialogue.[53]

The movement in Fatima reveals that some foresee a pan-representative religious system emerging that is centered on a common denominator. A congress was sanctioned by leaders within the Roman Church with a purpose that suggests that they are supra-religionists and prime for a supra-religion.

Transforming the Roman Mary to the Global Mary

The Vatican, uniting with the United Nations, sponsored an inter-faith congress at Fatima's shrine on October 10-12, 2003, entitled “The Present of Man—The Future of God.”[54] The Bishop of Leiria—Fatima instigated the congress and the Cardinal Patriarch of Lisbon and the Prefect of the Vatican's Pontifical Council for Inter-religious Dialogue presided over it.[55] [56] The choice of Fatima reflected the fact that the Fatima shrine is rapidly becoming the center of worship for many of the world's religions. Over 4.5 million people visit Fatima each year. This latest congress included Hindu, Muslim, Jewish, Eastern Orthodox, Buddhist, and African Pagan representatives.

At the congress, the shrine's rector said, “The future of Fatima, or the adoration of God and His mother at this holy Shrine, must pass through the creation of a shrine where different religions can mingle....the Shrine of Fatima is not indifferent to this fact and is already open to being a univer-salistic place of vocation.”[57]

This outreach to the Roman Mary far exceeded what most people anticipated. Speaking to the congress in Fatima, the Hindu representative, Ansshok Ansraj, pointed out that “in the Far East millions of Hindus are getting ‘positive vibrations' from visiting Marian shrines without endangering their faith."[58]

Anticipating the fear of proselytizing, the congress released a statement that prohibited this act by all religions. "No one religion can eradicate another or strengthen itself by downplaying others and an open dialogue is the way to building bridges and tearing down walls of centuries of hate. What is needed is that each religion be true to its faith integrally and treat each religion on the same footing of equality with no inferior or superiority complexes."[59]

The Coming of the Anti-Mary before the Antichrist

Clearly, the intent of these groups is to allow existing religious actions and beliefs to continue while united by a common entity and purpose. Father Jacques Dupuis, one of the principle speakers of the Fatima congress called for just such a union. "The religion of the future will be a general converging of religions in a universal Christ that will satisfy all."[60]

The ultimate "universal Christ" will be the Antichrist, brought to power by Satan (Revelation 13:2). It seems most probable that the Anti-Mary will proclaim and present him. In her role as a counterfeit of the true Biblical Mary, she will most likely promote the idea of a universal Christ in a mode similar to the Biblical Mary's proclamation concerning God and her Savior in the Magnificat of Luke 1:47-55. This counterfeit role expands as we delve further into the actual history of mother/child goddesses. Thus, it seems probable that this global, Anti-Mary is the woman seated upon the scarlet colored beast of Revelation 17:3; the one who will serve as co-redeemer and intercessor between man the "universal Christ" (the Antichrist) prior to his assumption of all worship in the second half of the Tribulation (Revelation 13:7, 8). In this role, **the global Mary would serve as a unifying factor**, drawing the world's religions together in preparation for the acceptance of the Antichrist and his worship system.

The ongoing growth in the ecumenical movement as exemplified at Fatima lends credibility to the speculation that Roman Catholicism may play a major part in bringing about the whole system that places Mary with her declarations in the role of supra-ruling entity of the supra-religion. With a following consisting of both Muslims and Roman Catholics, over two billion people potentially could be directed by Mary. If we add the Protestant groups and others who would likely subscribe to the pan-religious perspective, half of the world's population could be under the supra-religion centered upon the "sacred feminine" or Magna Mater (as she is often called) of Fatima.

In addition to the world's desire for unity and religious peace, the desire for power, influence, and prosperity are also contributing factors bringing these religious groups together. Fatima, one of the most lucrative religious venues in the world, netted a profit in excess of 8.4 million euros in 2003.[61]

A Credible Scenario—The Supra-Religion

Having laid out the essential background information, it is now possible to present a credible scenario for the future supra-religion and to explain why events leading to this one world religion may proceed along a different path than many Bible scholars have previously supposed, for many theologians have concluded that Roman Catholicism will ultimately prevail on the world stage. This alternative scenario is a viable possibility for it satisfies the descriptions found in Revelation 17 and 18. In so doing, it sets the stage for God's ultimate triumph, glorification, and the establishment of Jesus Christ's earthly millennial kingdom and the restoration of the earth as God promised.

Encouraged by the rising power of the European Union as it seeks global governance, it is quite possible that the Global Mary will arise out of the spirit of "new toleration." The people of the world, desiring not only political peace but religious peace as well, would willingly turn to her. Perhaps through a grand apparition, she will offer a lie or great deception to explain the disappearance of the true believers, at the Rapture of the true Church and offer the comfort sought by those left behind (2 Thessalonians 2:11). They would see in her all the graces, gifts, beauty, comfort, and love of a mother for mankind. The world's religions, already positive to the Roman Mary, would acknowledge her countless apparitions and accept her as the Global Mary, uniting under her direction, authority, and rule. She will be the supra-religion's governing authority, issuing decrees through various apparitions. As the supra-entity, she will be independent of all religions while favoring none. She will leave their various worship rites and lesser doctrines intact, requiring only the acceptance of her immaculate conception and her intercessory and co-redemptive powers. Allied with the supra-government, she will then direct the people of the world toward unity and the acceptance of her son, the Antichrist, who promises to solve all remaining problems (Revelation 17:2, 5, 18). He will then assume all supra-governmental authority and all supra-religious authority, eventually replacing the Global Mary as he takes on the role of global political leader and god of this world. He will, in fact, be empowered by Satan himself as he seeks to fulfill his desire of being *"like the Most High* (Isaiah 14:14)." This is the goal that began in Heaven with the angelic rebellion and was first manifested in the kingdom of ancient Babylon where he led humanity in uniting government and religion. One might ask how this connection back to Babel or Babylon can be made.

Where it All Began

In Revelation 17:5, John wrote of a harlot whose forehead bears the name, *"Mystery, Babylon the Great, the mother of harlots and abominations of the earth."* Thus, John linked the harlot (the proposed Global Mary) with the land of Babylon.

In the Bible, a name is applied to an individual with the intention of describing qualities about the person bearing the label. In Revelation 19 Christ is described as having *"a name written, that no man knew, but he himself"* (Rev. 19:12). He returns as the *"Word of God"* (Rev. 19:13) to the earth to conquer and reclaim the earthly kingdom. At that time He receives the name *"King of kings and Lord of lords"* (Rev. 19:16). True believers also will have God's name written on their foreheads as an indication that they belong to Him (Rev. 14:1, 22:4).

In ancient Roman times, harlots were identified by names written on their foreheads,[62] a practice that provided the obvious function of distinguishing one harlot from another. Just such a label declares the name of the harlot of Revelation 17 to be a *"mystery."* Her name *"Babylon"* is a mystery, a hidden thing, a secret thing.[63] Thus, at the appropriate time "...the true character and identity of the woman, previously kept concealed, are now objects of clear revelation."[64] Additionally, the syntactical grammar of this verse suggests that the woman's complete name is *"Babylon the Great."*[65] Consequently, we would expect that during the time from Babel to the Tribulation, the identity of the harlot will be hidden until fully revealed as the mother of religious harlots who does not have a legal or rightful relationship to the God of the Bible.

While many would attach mystical or allegorical references to the name, *"Babylon the Great,"* the obvious, literal meaning seems more likely, especially as Iraq takes the forefront on the world stage. By this term, God's intention is to draw the reader's attention back to ancient Babel upon the plain of Shinar. As many have rightly concluded, the satanic governmental and religious unity begun with Nimrod will end in a final attempt to reach its pinnacle in the latter days.[66] This seems a very appropriate conclusion, for Babylon is where the first organized false religion began and, as such, is the "mother" of counterfeit religions. Babylon has been a source of problems, which have troubled Israel, the church, and the world right up to the present day.[67]

Therefore, allied with a supra-religion, Babylon will once again become the center for the world's idolatrous worship system; one that will epitomize satanic worship and opposition to God.[68] Just as Nimrod in ancient days attempted to provide mankind with a central location for Satan worship and rule, so too, in the latter days, mankind again will return to this locality in an attempt to regain the unity lost at Babel. Theologian, John Walvoord, concluded that the term "Babylon" is "the name for a great system of religious error."[69] It may be that Walvoord's "great system" is the same system that began at Babel, deceptively "morphing" or changing its outward guise through the centuries of world history while maintaining its essential elements of harlotry or rebellion against God and supporting Satan's goals of being a counterfeit of God.

Ancient Babel's Harlotry

The "system" is the abominable religion of ancient Babel. In his rebellion, Satan has always sought to mimic God's worship with a counterfeit religion, a counterfeit woman, and a counterfeit Christ or Antichrist. He has also attempted to limit mankind's expansion throughout the world in opposition to God's commandment to *"fill the earth."* He seeks to limit mankind's reproductive efforts through abortion and homo-sexuality, countering God's command to *"be fruitful and multiply."* Therefore, we would expect a form of worship that is a counterfeit of the worship of God in humanity's final religious system.

Any religious system that deprives God of His rightful glory and worship is guilty of spiritual harlotry and is an abomination to Him. This is seen throughout the Old Testament where God many times equated Israel's religious unfaithfulness to harlotry. This final system rightly would be called the *"mother of harlots"* for having spawned other systems of "spiritual harlotry" throughout history. Therefore, it is essential to discover the true nature of the original Babylonian harlotry and then to determine if it has continued on to the present day in various guises. If this is the likely case, then the final harlot of Revelation may manifest herself as the Global Mary/Magna Mater.

In Revelation 17:3, the Spirit took John into the wilderness, a solitary or desolate place.[70] Apparently this location gave John a better perspective from which to study this "woman."[71] It was from here also, that John viewed *"the beast"* as he stood upon the *"sand of the s*ea (Rev. 13:1)." Combining the picture of the *"sand of the sea"* with the *"wilderness,"* along with John's discussion of Babylon in Revelation 17 and 18, we are led back to Isaiah 21 where Isaiah also sees a fallen Babylon by the desert or wilderness of the sea.[72]

> *The Burden of the desert of the sea. As whirlwinds in the south pass through; so it cometh from the desert, from a terrible land.*
>
> Isaiah 21:1

In this chapter God speaks through Isaiah to encourage Israel during the Babylonian Captivity, by promising to judge Babylon and her false gods.

> *...Babylon is fallen, is fallen; and all the graven images of her gods he hath broken unto the ground.*
>
> Isaiah 21:9

This promised judgment is quite similar to the judgment of Babylon in Revelation 18:10, *"Alas, alas, that great city Babylon, that mighty city! For in one hour is thy judgment come."* Isaiah had spoken previously of this judgment in Isaiah 14:4, *"That thou shalt take up this proverb against the king of Babylon, and say, How hath the oppressor ceased! The golden city ceased!"*

Bible scholars propose that while Isaiah begins with the king of Babylon he moves from the lesser to the greater and in reality is describing the fall of Satan, the power behind Babylon, in the same chapter (Isa. 14:4, 15). Therefore, in verses 13 and 14, Satan declares his goal of being *"upon the mount of the congregation in the sides of the north: I will ascend above the heights of the clouds; I will be like the Most High."* In verse 15, God proclaimed Satan's ultimate defeat by declaring *"Yet thou shalt be brought down to hell, to the sides of the pit."* Therefore, the Biblical evidence appears to link Babylon, with its false religion and idols, to Satan's desire for world conquest and worship.[73]

Since ancient Babel began by seeking to unite governmental and religious elements, logic would suggest that humanity's final governmental and religious system will seek to re-establish the unity lost at Babel. Therefore, the beast "controls the system politically, but the woman represents the false religion that gives spiritual cohesion to the system."[74] Ancient Babylon was known for its abundance of clay, which explains the use of fire-dried clay bricks instead of stone as the prime building material at Babel (Gen. 11:3).[75] Recalling Nebuchadnezzar's image with its feet and toes of iron and clay, which Daniel interpreted as representing the final form of the Roman Empire, it is reasonable to conclude that the clay symbolically pictures the final supra-religion that binds the diverse peoples (the *"many waters"* of Revelation 17:1) together in the supra-national governmental world.

Ancient Babel's Influence throughout History

Based upon this background, it is now necessary to examine Babel's ancient abominable belief that is centered in the land of Shinar, for Biblical references to this location suggest a rather "sinister" tone. It was in Shinar that Nimrod attempted to unite the world's people by building the Tower of Babel (Gen. 10:10). Interestingly, it was to this same land that King Nebuchadnezzar removed the vessels of God from the temple. We are told that Shinar is one of the lands from which re-gathered Israel will return when the Millennial age is established (Dan. 1:2; Isa. 11:11). The prophet Zechariah wrote of the woman in the ephah who epitomized evil and of her removal to Shinar where a temple was built for her (Zech. 5).[75] Theologians have long regarded Shinar as "the major center for the development of a culture and civilization built on counterfeit religion."[76]

Tradition relates how Nimrod's wife, Semiramis, initiated Babel's counterfeit religion. There are many views regarding this false religion, but one aspect is very consistent—a worship cult developed around Semiramis that transcends time and cultures. She appears throughout the ancient world under various names and descriptions, thereby hiding her true identity. In her role as mother-child goddess she appears as Nina (Assyria), Ishtar (Samaria), Isis (Egypt), Aphrodite/Astarte (Greece, Phoenicia, and Syria), Cybele (Phrygia), and Venus (Rome). Legends always involve her son, Tammuz, also known as Adonis (Greek)[77] and Osiris (Egyptian).[78] Sometimes his birth is described as miraculous, as is his death and resurrection.[79] Ezekiel 8:14 records the circumstances of Israel's "abominable" commemoration of this death and resurrection.[80] Often Tammuz worship included prostitution or harlotry.[81] The common theme of these ancient records appears to be a "satanic anticipation of the resurrection of Christ."[82]

In Akkadia, this false goddess is part of an astral triad consisting as Venus, along with Shamash, the sun god, and Sin, the moon god. In this triad, a circle of six, eight, or sixteen star rays symbolize her.[83] This imagery bears a remarkable likeness to the false interpretation given to the "*woman*" of Revelation 12:1. Even a cursory study of these ancient forms of worship of the mother goddess shows certain common elements passing down from culture to culture throughout history. These elements include: a mother giving birth to a miraculous child, a close relationship between mother and child, the resurrection of the child, some aspect of a bull, the sprinkling of holy water, virgins for prostitution, and other abominable practices.[84]

The Counterfeit

This false religion originated in Babel as Satan's counterfeit of God's plan. Semiramis' son, Tammuz was presented to the people as "the Anointed"[85] or savior, a counterfeit fulfillment of God's promise to Eve and her seed (Gen. 3:15).[86] Semiramis was the satanic version of the "woman" who's "seed" brings salvation. Once again, Satan offered his substitute for that which God would accomplish. Instead of the Biblical Mary giving birth to Jesus of Nazareth, Semiramis was the anti-Mary giving birth to the anti-Jesus, Tammuz. In the ancient world, the emphasis shifted from the "*seed*" to the great mother, Semiramis. Since we believe the true "Seed" is Jesus Christ, God Himself, then any diversion to another savior is an abomination and those who follow the woman instead of Christ have gone after a "*harlot*," worshipping incorrectly.

From this, we see a principle: By offering a false savior, Satan creates a counterfeit religion that diverts people to him

instead of God. The actions of the false mimic the characteristics of God's true Savior, Jesus Christ. God destroyed the
false unity of Babel by forcing the people to spread out upon
the earth, but sadly, they took with them the false religion of
Semiramis, sometimes called the "Queen of heaven."[87] Even
Israel was subject to her infection, for they prepared cakes
for the "queen of heaven" and burned incense to her (Jer.
44:17-19, 25). Even today, Roman Catholics often refer to
Mary as the "Queen of Heaven."

Queen of Heaven Mausoleum, Hillside, IL

In her "motherly goddess role" Semiramis became the
"model and original of every goddess and female cult figure
in the ancient and modern worlds (either directly or by deri-
vation)...."[88] The spread of this evil cult and the commonality
of its concepts, found in most ancient societies, evidences
the worship of Semiramis as the "great mother (Magna

232

Mater)" and the deified "queen of heaven." Ultimately the church at Pergamos evidenced its evil and was warned by God (Rev. 2:13-14). The Bible records that from Babel to AD 90, the influence of Semiramis' religion was evident and will continue on into the Tribulation.

Considering these ancient records of cults and the evidence seen in the Bible, one concludes that the original form of pagan Babel's harlotry was a religion centered upon a mother goddess whose son was resurrected. While the son was worshipped, the emphasis always moved to his mother. Today the Roman Mary fulfills a similar role. With the start of the Tribulation, or shortly before, it is quite possible that she will "morph" into the Global Mary or the Magna Mater whom John calls the *"mother of harlots."*

There are two reasons that would explain why humanity succumbs to and accepts this counterfeit form of religion. **First**, mankind is nearly always sympathetic to motherhood and the high place given to mothers. The **second** is that the sensual nature of man finds any evil worship that involves virgins and prostitution appealing. In the religion of the Magna Mater, these two incongruous concepts blended to create spiritual harlotry, the exact opposite of the true Bible teaching regarding womanhood and the virgin birth.

The following is a summary of our conclusion concerning the counterfeit Magna Mater of history:

- Semiramis of Babel is the original harlot, the Magna Mater of Satan's counterfeit religions.

- All forms of the Magna Mater are perverted attempts by Satan to distract from the true teaching of Genesis 3:15, which gives Jesus Christ His rightful position as Savior and bestows on the Biblical Mary the correct position as His earthly mother, a sinner who found redemption through her Savior (Luke 1: 46-47), not an immaculately conceived co-redeemer.

- The Magna Mater is the counterfeit anti-Mary, a substitute for God's Biblical Mary.

- The Magna Mater detracts from true godly worship by centering attention on herself as the mother goddess.

- Those who worship the Magna Mater are partaking of a spiritual harlot and diverting worship away from the true God.

- By incorrectly interpreting Revelation 12:1, the Magna Mater falsely replaces Israel.

- The son of the Magna Mater is a false savior offering a false gospel.

By the fourth century, Christianity had become the preferred religion of the Roman Empire and with "acceptance," the Greek-Roman pagans began to infect the church with the counterfeit, resulting in:

Thousands of the people who entered the church brought with them the superstitions and devotions which they had long given to Isis, Ishtar, Diana, Athena, Artemis, Aphrodite, and other goddesses, which were then conveniently transferred to Mary. Statues were dedicated to her, as there had been statues dedicated to Isis, Diana, and others, and before them the people kneeled and prayed as they had been accustomed to do before the statue of the heathen goddesses.[89]

234

By the fifth century, the Romans renamed "Isis" and "Horus," calling them "Mary" and "Jesus."[90]

Ongoing Harlotry

Going by various names and configurations from Babel to the Roman Empire, the Magna Mater's counterfeit religion has been the invisible entity holding people in spiritual bondage. These counterfeit religions have all been propagated by Satan and designed to bring him to the position of being, *"like the Most High."* The mother-child goddess image spanned ancient history.

That image continues on into the 21st century and can be seen in the European Union's symbols: symbols such as the metal sculpture of Europa outside the European Council of Ministers' office building in Brussels (cf. Act III, Scene 4), the colossal painting of a woman riding a beast on the dome of the new £8 million Parliament Building in Strasbourg, or the hugh painting of a nearly naked woman upon a beast in the Parliament's office building.[91] The Euro currency shows a similar figure. Using such imagery, the European Union revives and strengthens the ancient Greek myth, Europa.

Another Form of the Magna Mater?

In Greek mythology Europa, the daughter of a Phoenician king of Tyre was out gathering flowers by the seashore. The god Zeus spied her and fell in love with her. Desiring her, he took the form of a beautiful chestnut colored bull and enticed her onto his back. Before she could jump off, he took her across the sea to the island of Crete where she bore him a son. Artists have painted the image of the woman on the beast throughout history. Archaeology attests to the antiquity of the image.[92] Europa is merely the Greek version of Semiramis, the Magna Mater.

It is very difficult to find any definitive basis for the naming of Europe after Europa. One can only note that her many legendary travels in the land now called Europe gave the continent its name. Many stories seem to indicate that her travels reflect her journey from maidenhood to full maturity, from life to death to rebirth.[93] Perhaps this is why the European Union chose this symbol, for in the supra-national European Union is seen the rebirth of Europe and the Roman Empire. If the European Union is the embryonic form of Daniel's latter day, fourth global empire, then perhaps the supra-religion of the Magna Mater is also near. While this may sound incredible, the author's visit to the EU's Louise Weis parliament building in Strasbourg confirmed just such a connection.

The approach to this Tower of Babel-like structure is impressive. The EU flag and the flags of every EU member nation greet each visitor. Nestled beneath them is a unique sculpture of a Madonna and child.

Europe A Coeur Sculpture by Ludmila Tcherina, Strasbourg

This modernistic representation of the mother and her infant seem to spring from a human heart and is entitled "Europe in Heart."[94] It is the creation of the late French ballerina and sculptress, Ludmila Tcherina, a devout Catholic. Symbolically, the sculpture is said to represent the European Union warmheartedly and tenderly encircling the people of its Union with love. Perhaps more than Peace and security are depicted by this image for it may be intended to portray the message that is at the heart of the EU's entire system of government: that the "salvation" of this present age can only be obtained by the union of global government with the global supra-religion of the Magna Mater.

However, Paul informs us that Jesus Christ *"gave himself for our sins, that He might deliver us from this present evil world* [age], *according to the will of God and our Father"* (Galatians 1:4). Just four verses later, he warns that *"though we, or an angel from heaven, preach any other gospel unto you than that which we have preached unto you, let him be accursed"* (v. 8). Certainly, any angel from heaven preaching another, i.e., a counterfeit gospel, would have to be a fallen angel. Thus, through true faith in the Lord Jesus Christ, we are delivered from this evil age, a term referring to the age before the Messianic Kingdom. However, for those without such a trust in Christ, they are in danger of believing a counterfeit gospel as Paul warned.

In his letter to the Thessalonians, Paul indicated that in this present age, the *"mystery of iniquity doth already work"* (2 Thess. 2:7). This *"mystery"* is none other than the counterfeit religious system that will reach its height when the Antichrist is revealed and Satan's power behind him is made known. It will also become apparent to all that the Antichrist's as well as the Magna Mater's power is *"after the working of Satan with all power and signs and lying wonders"* (2 Thess. 2:9). Those individuals who rejected the truth will be the victims of a *"strong delusion, that they should believe a lie"*

(2 Thess. 2:11). The Bible does not reveal what this lie is, but perhaps the Magna Mater will offer a comforting answer to those who wonder what has happened to Christians who have disappeared in the Rapture and offer her son, the Antichrist, as the solution to world problems. In the end, the Lord Jesus Christ will *"consume"* all this wickedness *"with the spirit of His mouth, and shall destroy with the brightness of His coming"* (2 Thess. 2:8).

The supra-religion and Magna Mater may or may not be the religious system represented by *"mystery Babylon"* of Revelation, but it can be said that world events surrounding us strongly suggest that God's true Son, Jesus Christ, may soon come for His Bride *"that where I am, there ye may be also"* (John 14:3).

ACT III – SCENE 6
CONNECTING THE DOTS OF GOD'S HISTORY

—ᗕᗕ—

Time: 21ˢᵗ Century
Setting: The Real World
Enter: Students of the Bible

M ost people share a common experience of childhood:
The teacher hands each student a sheet of paper with
numbered dots spread throughout the page. Using an over-
sized pencil for little hands, the child begins to connect Dot
1 to Dot 2 to Dot 3 and so on. At first the meandering lines
puzzle the child until suddenly they almost magically begin to
reveal a picture. Some children recognize the picture sooner
than others, but with the last dot connected, every child
understands what the picture is. This book has attempted to
clarify Biblical truths that serve as dots; dots that can help us
to picture and understand the unseen spiritual battle that lies
behind world events and how these events may be leading to
the final act of earth's history.

Connecting the Dots

Dot 1 explained God's plan for history as declared in the
Bible—His plan to reveal Himself and His glory by establishing an earthly kingdom for God the Son Who is the ultimate revelation of God Himself. For this reason God created
the earth with Adam as His authorized ruler. Together with

his wife Eve, Adam was to populate the entire earth with righteous citizens. With this preparatory work completed, it was God's intention that God the Son rule earth's kingdom. When Adam sinned and the earthly kingdom with its citizens was placed under Satan's authority, God promised to provide redemption through the *"seed"* of the woman. It is that seed, Jesus Christ, Who will ultimately defeat Satan. This is why Satan views Him as his enemy.

Dot 2 revealed Satan's counter plan—to glorify himself by being *"like the Most High"* and usurping the rule of the earth from God the Son. Ever since Satan's rebellion and fall from his position as archangel, every effort of his has been to imitate the Most High God by governing the earthly kingdom and receiving worship from its citizens. The fulfillment of this plan requires a satanically authorized ruler and an earthly realm with citizens that are loyal to Satan. When Satan was successful in tempting Adam to sin, he usurped ownership of the earthly kingdom and its citizens. This usurped kingdom represents Satan's ultimate rebellion in his opposition to God. His continued success depends upon his ability to counter God's plan of redemption and to ultimately receive worship from humanity; worship that belongs to God the Son alone. Thus, instead of Jesus Christ becoming the ultimate ruler of the earthly kingdom, Satan desires to substitute his own Antichrist. Throughout history he has persisted in his attempt to do this through a counterfeit woman and her *"seed."* When viewed in light of this conflict, all of history becomes clearer.

Dot 3 was ancient Babel, the scene of Satan's prototypical worldwide government and system of worship. Having failed to stop the seed of the woman through the death of Abel and the corruption of humanity prior to the Flood, Satan renewed his attempt through Nimrod at Babel. This *"mighty hunter"* gathered the earth's population with the intent of forming a manmade kingdom and government. Semiramis, his wife, developed the first worldwide religion with herself as the feminine mother-goddess and her son, Tammuz, the child. Beginning at the first high place of Babel, Satan continues to direct worship away from the true God to himself through a counterfeit woman and her "seed." Blinded by the "*god of this world*," humanity appears to be ready and willing to accept Satan's plan in its quest for peace and prosperity.

When God thwarted his efforts at Babel, Satan was forced to seek alternative ways of uniting the world under his single government and religion. Each of his attempts has followed the prototype of Babel. Satan has employed different religious forms, customized to specific types of people. Many false religions share the common ancestry of Babel and the sacred mother-goddess, Semiramis. Satan continues his attempt to unite false religions with a worldwide government and to establish the rule of his Antichrist. Achieving this goal would signal success and victory for Satan in his quest to be like the Most High.

Dot 4 is the nation of Israel, God's prototype for nations and governments. Through the laws He gave them, this tiny nation revealed God's standards for holy living to the world. He also demonstrated His love, compassion, mercy, and grace as He dealt with their sins and failings. The times of His chastening showed humanity that God takes sin seriously. It was through Israel that the promised "*seed*" came and although Israel was willfully blinded to His identity at His First Advent, the gentile world has benefited as the Church of true believers has grown. Israel's blindness was largely due to a lack of prophetic teaching and understanding. This, coupled with unholy living left most Jewish people unprepared and unwilling to recognize Him. Israel will have the "scales" removed from her eyes at His Second Advent and serve God mightily in the Millennium. The Bible tells us that her "*blindness in part is happened to Israel until the fullness of the Gentiles be come in*" (Rom. 11:25). The Church would do well to learn from Israel's error by teaching prophecy and giving heed to holy living. The Bible refers to the Church as the Bride of Christ and God often called Israel His wife. Is it any wonder that Satan hates both Israel and the true Church for this very reason? He will use all of his *"wiles"* in an attempt to destroy Israel and true Christians in order to prevent Christ's return.

It is reasonable to conclude that Satan's persistent attempts to annihilate Israel and the Jewish people will be intensified as the time of Christ's second appearing approaches because he knows that they play a prominent roll in God's plan. Satan desires to replace Israel and true Christians with his own citizens and fallen angels. This certainly explains why both Jews and Christians are increasingly persecuted and vilified today. His plan is an imitation of God's plan. He will have a counterfeit Elijah, or false prophet, prepare the way for the Antichrist (Rev. 13:11-12).The Bible indicates that in the latter days Satan's ultimate Antichrist will even mimic Christ's resurrection (Rev. 13:3). Instead of peace on earth through Christ's millennial kingdom, Satan will offer false peace and prosperity through worldwide government and religion (Rev. 13:4). Instead of Christ ruling the kingdom from Jerusalem, Satan's Antichrist presumably will rule from Babylon (Rev. 17). Instead of Christ's earthly throne being on the highest mountain of the earth, Satan desires to be on the highest place, *"on the sides of the north."* In all ways, Satan's plan is in opposition to God's plan.

	GOD's PLAN	SATAN's IMITATION
Being Worshipped	The Most High God Dan. 7:27	Satan Isa. 14:13,14
Ultimate Ruler of Earthly Kingdom	Jesus Christ Rev. 20:6	Antichrist Rev. 13:4
Mother of Ruler	Biblical Mary Luke 1:30	Magna Mater Rev. 17:5
Prophet	Elijah Mal. 4:5	The Second Beast Rev. 13:11-12
First Kingdom location	Eden Gen. 2:8	Babel Gen. 10:10
First ruler of kingdom	Adam Gen. 2:28	Nimrod Gen. 10:9-10
Last Kingdom Capital	Jerusalem Zech. 14:16,17	Babylon Rev. 17:18
Location of King's Throne	Jerusalem, David's Throne Isa. 9:7	The Sides of the North Isa. 14:13
Redeemer	Jesus Christ Matt. 1:21	Antichrist Rev. 13:8
Redeemer's Resurrection	Jesus Christ, Matt. 28:6	Antichrist Rev. 13:12-14
Citizens of the Earthly Kingdom	Righteous Jewish and Gentile People of every nation	Unrighteous People and fallen angels
Source of peace for the earth	Jesus Christ's Worldwide Millennial Government Rev. 20:4	Satan's Worldwide Government and Religion Rev. 13:4

These four dots yield a pattern by which history and world events can be perceived and understood. When the conflict between God's and Satan's plans is clarified and the methods Satan employs are recognized, one inevitably comes to the conclusion that our world may well be catapulting toward the final act of earth's history. It becomes possible to recognize the potential direction of a particular world system of government and to knowledgably speculate as to whether or not it may be heading in Satan's direction. The probability that the EU is indeed spearheading Satan's final attempt is quite valid in light of this pattern. Only time will reveal if it is growing into Satan's final worldwide government united with a world religious system.

The Final Act?

Today, at the beginning of the 21st century, it appears that Satan is gaining in momentum as he maneuvers humanity toward the achievement of his plan. It seems that he is using the European Union as his instrument in uniting many people groups and nations. Peace and prosperity are the "carrots" used to entice the world's population that is motivated by fear of terrorism, violence, economic collapse, and ecological disaster into believing that a single worldwide government is the only solution. Knowingly or unknowingly, those who are promoting the EU may be setting the stage for the final act described by the book of Daniel. The EU's ever-increasing expansion to other areas of the world lead to the plausible conjecture that the European Union could eventually become a world-wide government, possibly called the "Union of Unions."[1] However, as the European Union steadily progresses toward its goal of uniting more than 100 world nations, it must remove the barriers created by the many religions of the world. Books such as Brown's *DaVinci Code*, New Age music and writings, ecumenical movements such as the emerging church, and the many apparitions of the

Virgin Mary throughout the world appear to be promoting a world religion. If this is true, the stage is nearing readiness for the last act and its primary player, the Antichrist. With the growing economic and political strength of the European Union, the time may soon be ripe for the EU to peacefully unite with a world religion. How is this feasible since there are so many conflicting religions within the EU?

In Europe today the trend toward religious toleration is strong, as long as one religion does not declare that it offers the only way to God. Because of this, true Christianity is viewed as exclusive, divisive, and dangerous. At the same time, Islam's exclusive claims are causing much fear and upheaval and there is a growing demand for a peaceful solution. In light of the fact that Marian apparitions are on the increase it is conceivable that the Roman Catholic Mary could appear and offer herself as the Magna Mater, the universal mother of all religions of the world. She could represent herself to all religions as the mother-goddess of all humanity, causing the people of the world to respond to her motherly love and care by accepting her spiritual guidance. As previously mentioned, even Islam acknowledges her greatness. Were she to declare all religions of the world acceptable and allow them to continue their distinctive traditions with her as head, resistance could be eliminated. Recognizing her historical ties to the Roman Church, she could conceivably distance herself from it by moving her center of authority to a newly rebuilt Babylon, re-establishing herself as the original mother-goddess that the Bible calls *"Mystery Babylon the Great, the Mother of Harlots"* (Rev. 17:5).

Even today, the Vatican is laying the foundation for unity among three of the major religious groups of the world. In November of 2006, Pope Benedict XVI visited the ancient city of Ephesus in Turkey where "the Virgin Mary lived during the last days of her life. Here the holy site is visited by tens of thousands of Christians and Muslims every year."[2]

He then went to Istanbul, formerly known as Constantinople, capital of the Eastern Roman Empire. During this visit he not only sought dialogue with Muslim leaders, but he celebrated Mass with his peer, Orthodox Christianity's Patriarch (Pope) Bartholomew in an attempt to "patch an age-old rift" between the two major segments of Christendom.[3] That division occurred during the time of the ancient Roman Empire when the Roman Church split into the Eastern Orthodox and Roman Catholic churches.[4] Reunification of these two sects would re-establish the religion of the ancient Roman Empire. During the same visit, the Pope announced his strong support of the European Union and the need to include the Muslim nation of Turkey in the Union.[5] In his statements, he noted that modern Turkey's relationship with Europe may be "realized in a new way in a different historic and religious context."[6]

Another prime purpose of his trip, however, was to appease the Islamic world for remarks he had made concerning Islam's history regarding violence. In his attempt to pacify the offended Muslim world, he actually prayed in a mosque while facing in the direction of Mecca.[7] This event received little attention by the American media.

It is feasible that other world leaders may advance this type of appeasement by offering to rebuild Iraq with Babylon as its capital; for the Bible indicates that it will exist in the latter days (Rev. 18:2-3). This could happen quite rapidly for in the United Arab Emirates, Dubai City has amazingly and rapidly become a focal point for the world-famous to live and vacation in.[8] Babylon may quickly be rebuilt and regain its former greatness in the eyes of the entire world (Isa. 14:4). Certainly, Islam would welcome this offer to make Babylon a burgeoning commercial center that is the centerpiece of the Middle East. The Bible indicates that this will be accomplished. Under the power of the Union's ten-region supranational rule that is encouraged and supported by the Magna Mater, much of the world would enjoy a *Pax Romana* for the first time since the Roman Empire. Terrorism would appear to be outdated as the Magna Mater resolves religious conflicts, for allied with the Union; she would become ruler of the earth during the first half of the Tribulation (Rev. 17:1-3).

It is also possible that the Magna Mater could humbly announce that her role has been only to prepare people for her son, the Christ (Antichrist). He then would move to center stage as leader of the Union. Despite world catastrophes and wars, the Union will grow ever more powerful under his leadership. Following his apparent death and resurrection, he would supersede and displace the Magna Mater as he steps forward as god (Rev. 13). Loyalty to and worship of him would then become mandatory, demonstrated by the taking of his mark and worshipping the image he has set up (Rev. 13:14-17). This act is Satan's proclamation of victory over the Most High God. However, there remains one significant barrier to Satan's desire of being like God, the nation of Israel and the Jewish people.

Through the prophets, God has declared that He will turn again to Israel when that nation repents of her national sin and cries out to the Messiah for deliverance.

And it shall come to pass in that day, that I will seek to destroy all the nations that come against Jerusalem. And I will pour upon the house of David, and upon the inhabitants of Jerusalem, the spirit of grace and of supplications: and they shall look upon me whom they have pierced, and they shall mourn for him, as one mourneth for his only son, and shall be in bitterness for him, as one that is in bitterness for his firstborn. In that day shall there be a great mourning in Jerusalem, as the mourning of Hadadrimmon in the valley of Megiddon.

Zech. 12:9-11

> *In that day there shall be a fountain opened to the*
> *house of David and to the inhabitants of Jerusalem*
> *for sin and for uncleanness.*
>
> Zech. 13:1

Satan knows this and, therefore, strives to destroy every Jewish person on earth before repentance can take place. At this time the Antichrist will unleash the greatest holocaust known to man in his last attempt to annihilate Israel.

The final event in this final act is Jesus Christ's second coming to the earth. When He appears in answer to the nation's cries His word alone will deliver her, for it is quick and powerful and sharper than any two-edged sword (Rev. 19:15). It is the same powerful word that created the heavens and the earth (Col. 1:16). He will cleanse the earth of all unrighteousness, restoring it to its original Eden-like conditions.

> *Thus saith the Lord GOD; In the day that I shall*
> *have cleansed you from all your iniquities I will also*
> *cause you to dwell in the cities, and the wastes shall*
> *be builded. And the desolate land shall be tilled,*
> *whereas it lay desolate in the sight of all that passed*
> *by And they shall say, <u>This land that was desolate is</u>*
> *<u>become like the garden of Eden</u>; and the waste and*
> *desolate and ruined cities are become fenced, and*
> *are inhabited.*
>
> Ezekiel 36:33-35

Then Jesus Christ will gloriously rule and reign from David's Throne in Jerusalem (2 Sam. 7:12; Acts 2:29, 30). Church-Age believers will co-reign with Him for a thousand years (Rev. 20:4). The restored nation of Israel will regain its place of prominence in God's plan by leading the nations of the world in worship (Zech. 8:23). Through the fulfillment of

prophecy as God has ordained it, He will display His attribute of truthfulness to all beings.

Contrary to Satan's plan, he will be cast into the bottomless pit for one thousand years (Rev. 20:1-3). Recalling his
boast of ruling from the highest place on earth; "*I will exalt
my throne above the stars of God: I will sit also upon the
mount of the congregation in the sides of the north*" (Isa.
14:13), God will place him in the lowest place in the earth.

Many wonder why Satan is released for a short time
at the conclusion of the Millennium (Rev. 20:3). God will
use him at this time to demonstrate the true condition of the
human heart or will. Although the Millennium begins with
the redeemed individuals of the earth who have survived the
Great Tribulation, children will be born to them who need
to turn to the Lord Jesus Christ for salvation just as those
born before the Millennium did. Families raised during the
Millennium will experience Eden-like conditions and the
earth will once again be filled with people. Many will accept
and trust King Jesus Christ as Savior and Lord but some
will secretly reject Him, worshipping Him only outwardly.
This time will serve as a demonstration: With Satan bound
and with the Lord Jesus Christ visibly reigning justly and
righteously from His throne there are still those who will
inwardly and secretly reject Him. This will reveal the truth
that the real problem with humanity is within the heart just
as God said: "*the heart is deceitful above all things, and
desperately wicked: who can know it?*" (Jer. 17:9). Human
sin cannot be blamed on Satan, the environment, or the
inability to see, and therefore believe, that God exists. With
the release of Satan, the facade will drop and the true heart
condition revealed as some individuals unite with Satan for
a final rebellion. At this point, Christ will cast Satan into the
Lake of Fire (Rev. 20:10) and judge the unredeemed of all
ages at the Great White Throne. These individuals, too, will
be cast into the Lake of Fire for eternity (Rev. 20:11-15). The

Millennium serves a very important and essential purpose in the plan of God. To ignore its significance leads to a misunderstanding of God's full plan.

The prophet Isaiah re-iterates the significance of God's prophecies:

> *Remember the former things of old: for I am God, and there is none else; I am God, and there is none like me, Declaring the end from the beginning, and from ancient times the things that are not yet done, saying, My counsel [purpose]*[8] *shall stand, and I will do all my pleasure: Calling a ravenous bird from the east, the man that executeth my counsel [purpose] from a far country: yea, I have spoken it, I will also bring it to pass; I have purposed it, I will also do it.*
> Isaiah 46:9-11

As the final curtain closes upon the old heavens and earth at the end of the Millennium, God will have demonstrated His truthfulness, trustworthiness, and uniqueness. Those who trusted Him for salvation will enter the new heavens and earth where righteousness dwells. Those who do not believe His declarations of coming wrath will experience the Lake of Fire for eternity (John 3:36).

> *Hearken unto me, ye stouthearted, that are far from righteousness: I bring near my righteousness; it shall not be far off, and my salvation shall not tarry: and I will place salvation in Zion...*
> Isaiah 46:12, 13

God's word will not fail. Just as Adam and Eve had to make a choice, to trust either God's or Satan's word, so too, human individuals throughout history have had to make the same decision. That choice establishes each person's eternal destiny. Every individual must decide now, for the Bible says, *"now is the accepted time, now is the day of salvation"* (2 Corinthians 6:2).

Clearly history presents more than just a play in which the audience goes home and soon forgets about it. Each individual in the audience is also a player who must decide whom he or she will follow, the one who wants to be like the Most High God or the Most High God Himself. It is the hope of this author that each reader will choose the Most High before the final act. To God be the glory!

EPILOGUE

—⟋⟋⟍—

It seems that the curtain is about to rise on human history's final act. The set may soon be in place as the European Union expands its empire that increasingly appears to be the resurgence of ancient Rome. Many prominent world players are proclaiming that the only answer to peace is a united world government. The world's religions are seeking peace through ecumenical union as well and it appears that this may be enhanced by a feminine goddess or Magna Mater. Governmental and religious barriers are being set aside, just as God foretold in the Bible. The climax of Satan's rebellion is about to commence. The Bible indicates that true believers of the Church Age will be removed prior to the curtain's rise on this final act (1 Thess. 5:9). Therefore, one must decide how he or she will live in these last days.

To sit idly by, ignoring the urgency of the hour and the spiritual significance it holds in individual lives would be folly indeed. This urgency demands that earnest believers understand the Biblical foundation of God's plan for the ages. Church and Bible study leaders throughout the world must teach this foundational material along with current events. No subject is more relevant or important in the lives of people; for it offers purpose, meaning, direction, and hope to a lost and perishing world. Proclaiming the coming kingdom of God the Son glorifies and blesses God (Psalm 145:11, 12).

For the Christian, the sense of urgency should result in action; action that motivates evangelization of the lost, for the days are coming when modern "toleration" will not allow the free declaration of the Gospel of salvation through Jesus Christ alone. The author has spoken to American missionaries in Europe who have informed him that should the EU begin issuing visas, which would replace individual national visas, they may be denied the new EU visa and forced to leave the field. The denial would be based on the new toleration and anti-hatred climate that views the spreading of the gospel as proselytizing and possibly inciting unrest. Although such views may have originated because of fears regarding Islam, the spirit of "fair play" would certainly apply it to Christianity. The missionaries referred to have earnestly begun to train up nationals to replace them should this transpire. The future of missions within the EU is uncertain and bears watching, for the opportunities to share the gospel may be shorter than many could have imagined. To delay could tragically affect the eternal destinies of many individuals for "...*faith cometh by hearing, and hearing by the Word of God*" (Romans 10:17).

Christians must also realize the significance of Israel and the Jewish people in God's plan and stand with them when Satan and the world seek their extermination. As Christians read and view the news relating to Israel, a Biblical perspective gives a truer understanding of what is happening behind the scenes on a spiritual level, "*for we wrestle not against flesh and blood, but against principalities, against powers against the rulers of the darkness of this world, against spiritual wickedness in high places*" (Ephesians 6:12). Such an understanding gives Christians a worldview and prevents an insular Christianity. The coming of Christ opens the eyes of Christians as nothing else can do.

Sadly, when a Christian loses sight of Christ's return, he or she loses spiritual direction and purpose in life, conforming more and more to the world with its desires and goals that are contrary to God's will. A mindset that is worldly rather that godly stunts Christian growth and spiritual atrophy sets in: *"be not conformed to this world: but be transformed by the renewing of your mind, that ye may prove what is that good, and acceptable, and* perfect, *will of God"* (Romans 12:2). The purpose of this book is to counter this atrophy by impressing individual Christians and churches leaders with the fact that this age is drawing to a close with all of its transitory things. The recognition that Jesus Christ could come at any moment for all true believers should transform an empty, self-centered, and materialistic Christianity into a vibrant solid Christianity that proclaims purposeful, holy living (1 John 3:1-3). Instead of encountering a country club atmosphere, searching individuals would find churches offering answers to life's important questions. Instead of living to please self, Christians would live to please God only to discover that this is where true happiness and joy is found. Instead of wasted time and useless activity, Christians would evaluate daily pursuits from an eternal perspective, never losing sight of the fact that they are to rule and reign with Christ in the millennium as well as in eternity (Rev. 1:5; 20:4; 22:5). Rather than an aimless existence, the goal of all who understand God's plan and purpose of history should be to find the unique role that God has for each believer.

God recognizes that not all Christians will understand the impact of the doctrine of Christ's return to His earthly kingdom. Just as only a few were looking for His first advent, so too, only a relatively small minority will be looking for His second. For that small number, God promises a crown: *"Henceforth there is laid up for me a crown of righteousness, which the Lord, the righteous judge, shall give me at that day: and not to me only, but unto all them also that love his appearing"* (2 Timothy 4:8). The Bible indicates that crowns are awarded in recognition of proper attitudes and actions. The Crown of Righteousness is for those eagerly looking for Christ's appearing, in contrast to those who would turn away from the truth of this important teaching (2 Timothy 4: 1-4, 8).

Each individual must make a choice as to the role he or she will play in human history, to carry out either God's plan or Satan's plan. God plan will prevail over Satan; ultimately every knee shall bow, giving glory to His Son. Some will do it willingly while others will do it unwillingly, but all will be to the glory of God the Father:

> *That at the name of Jesus every knee should bow, of things in heaven, an things in earth, and things under the earth; And that every tongue should confess that Jesus Christ is Lord, to the glory of God the Father.*
> Philippians 2:10-11.

It is my prayer that every reader will choose God and will be looking up for His return, living moment by moment with that expectation.

A companion study guide is available for adult Sunday School classes, home and church Bible studies, and Bible Institutes.

For more information on this subject, this ministry, our free email newsletter, or to contact us, write or email:

Congdon Ministries International
PO Box 1362
Oak Park, IL 60304

email: **rcongdon@InternetBibleInstitute.com**

website: **www.Congdon-Ministries.com**

END NOTES

—∿∿—

Prologue

[1] William Shakespeare. *As You Like It*. Act 2 Scene 7.

[2] Christopher Booker and Richard North. *The Great Deception: a Secret History of the European Union*. (London: Continuum, 2003), p. 1.

Act I - Scene 1: God's Plan and Purpose for Humanity

[1] "Genesis 1:1." *Jamieson, Fausset, Brown Commentary* (JFB). CD-ROM. Online Bible Edition version 2.00, 19 Jan. 2005. Winterbourne, ON. Canada: Online Bible, 1992-2005.

[2] Charles H. Spurgeon. "Psalm 19:1" *Treasury of David—Vol.1.* (Nashville, TN: Thomas Nelson Publishers, n.d.), p. 269.

[3] Merrill Unger. "Glory" *Unger's Bible Dictionary—3rd ed.* (Chicago: Moody Bible Institute, 1960), p. 409.

[4] Lewis Sperry Chafer. *Systematic Theology—Vol. 1* abridged ed. John F. Walvoord, ed. (Wheaton, Il.: Victory Books, 1988), p. 141.

[5] David K. Huttar. "Glory" *Evangelical Dictionary of Biblical Theology, ed. Walter A. Elwell*. (Grand Rapids: Baker Books, 1996), p. 288.

[6] Chafer. *Systematic Theology*. p. 140.

[7] Arthur W. Pink. *Gleanings in the Godhead* (Chicago: Moody Press, 1975), p. 11.

[8] Alva J. McClain. *The Greatness of the Kingdom—an Inductive Study of the Kingdom of God.* (Winona Lake, IN: BMH Books, 1974), p. 17.

Act I - Scene 2: Satan's Counter-Plan and Purpose for Humanity

[1] Romano Prodi. "Shaping the New Europe—Strategic Objectives 2000-2005 COM(2000) 154 Final. 9 Sep. 2000. *Europa* website. (Brussels:

Commission of the European Communities, 2000), p. 4. http://europa.
eu.int/comm/off/work/2000-2005/com154_en.pdf (9 February 2000).

[2] Booker, p. 368, quoting "Today Europe, Tomorrow the World."

[3] Chafer, p. 170.

[4] Ibid.

[5] Ibid., p. 140.

[6] A. W. Tozer. *The Knowledge of the Holy*. (New York: Harper and Row
Publishers, 1961), p. 40.

[7] Based upon Nehemiah 9:6, angels were created on the first day of
Creation.

[8] Renald E. Showers. *Those Invisible Spirits Called Angels*. (Bellmawr,
NJ: Friends of Israel Gospel Ministry, 1997), p. 79.

[9] Henry C. Thiessen. *Lectures in Systematic Theology*. (Grand Rapids:
William B. Eerdmans Publishing Co., 1979), p. 25.

[10] Chafer, p. 140.

[11] "Daniel 8:10" *JFB*.

[12] "Ephesians 6:11" *JFB*.

[13] TWOT, 1865, p. 750 and Showers, *Invisible Spirits*, p. 43.

[14] Showers, *Invisible Spirits*, p. 37.

[15] Ibid., p. 87.

[16] Joseph A. Alexander. *Commentary on Isaiah. 2 Volumes in 1*. (Grand
Rapids, MI: Kregel Publications, 1992), p. 297.

[17] "Isaiah 14:14" *JFB*.

[18] F. Delitzsch, F. *Commentary on the Old Testament Vol. 7, Isaiah*.
(Peabody, Massachusetts: Hendrickson Publishers, 2001), p. 202.

[19] Alexander, p. 298.

[20] The term, Shekinah Glory, is not found in the Scriptures, but it is used
by later Jews and Christians to designate the divine presence of God. In
the Aramaic and late Hebrew, it means residence or dwelling of God.
Unger. "Shechinah," pp. 1008-1009.

[21] Alexander, p. 298.

[22] Arnold G. Fruchtenbaum. *Israelology: The Missing Link in Systematic
Theology*. (Tustin, CA: Ariel Ministries Press, 1992). pp. 781-785.

Act I - Scene 3: God's First Earthly Kingdom

[1] James Strong, "Strong's # 07287." *Strong's Extensive Concordance of
the Bible*. CD-ROM. Online Bible Edition version 2.00, 19 Jan. 2005.
Winterbourne, ON. Canada: Online Bible, 1992-2005.

[2] "Genesis 1:26" *JFB*.

[3] Note: in the English Bible the Hebrew word is translated "fill or full"
155x and replenish only 7x. "Genesis 1:22." Strong's #04390.

Act I - Scene 4: Satan's First Earthly Kingdom

[1] Renald E. Showers, *There Really is a Difference—a Comparison of Covenant and Dispensational Theology*. (Bellmawr, NJ: The Friends of Israel Gospel Ministry, Inc., 1990), p. 37.

[2] C. F. Keil. *Keil & Delitzsch—Commentary on the Old Testament, Vol. 1—The Pentateuch*. (K&D) (Peabody, MA: Hendrickson Publishers, 2001), p. 79.

[3] Showers, *Difference*, p. 36.

[4] K&D, *Pentateuch*, p. 86.

[5] Ibid., p. 79.

[6] Ibid.

[7] John Whitcomb, *The Genesis Flood—the Biblical Record and Its Scientific Implications*. (n.l.: The Presbyterian and Reformed Publishing Co., 1961), p. 26.

[8] Showers, *What on Earth is God Doing?—Satan's Conflict with God*. Updated and Revised. (Bellmawr, NJ: The Friends of Israel Gospel Ministry, Inc., 2003), p. 23.

[9] Ibid.

[10] Ibid.

[11] McClain, *Greatness*, p. 46.

[12] K&D, *Pentateuch*, p. 97.

[13] Ibid.

[14] McClain, *Greatness*, p. 47.

[15] McClain, *Greatness*, pp. 46-7.

[16] Showers, *Invisible Spirits*, pp. 92-105.

[17] McClain, *Greatness*, p. 44.

[18] Henry Alford, *The Greet New Testament Revised by Everett F. Harrison, Vol. 1*. (Chicago: Moody Press, 1958), p. 797.

[19] K&D, *Pentateuch*. p.71.

[20] John Gill. "Genesis 10:8" *John Gill's Expositor*. CD-ROM. Online Bible Edition version 2.00, 19 Jan. 2005. Winterbourne, ON. Canada: Online Bible, 1992-2005.

[21] Henry H. Halley. *Halley's Bible Handbook*. (Grand Rapids: Zondervan Publishing House, 1962), p. 69. Also "Eden" *Wycliffe Bible Encyclopedia Vol. 1*, Charles F. Pfeiffer, Howard F. Vos, and John Rhea ed. (Chicago: Moody Press, 1975), p. 489.

[22] William Whiston. *The Works of Josephus*. (Peabody, MA: Hendrickson Publishers, 1987), p. 35.

[23] TWOT, 2097, p. 826.

[24] Alfred Edersheim. *Bible History—Old Testament*. (Peabody, MA: Hendrickson Publishers, 1995), p. 42.

[25] K & D, *Pentateuch*, p. 105.
[26] Edersheim, p. 42.
[27] Ibid., p. 43.
[28] Ibid.
[29] McClain, *Greatness*, p. 47.
[30] John F. Walvoord. *The Revelation of Jesus Christ.* (Chicago: Moody Press, 1966), p, 246.
[31] "Marduk." *Wikipedia—The Free Encyclopedia.* 17 Jan. 2006. Wikimedia Foundation, Inc. http://en.wikipedia.org/wiki/Marduk (24 Jan. 2006).
[32] J. D. Douglas. "Babel" *New Bible Dictionary—*2nd ed. (Wheaton, IL: Tyndale House Publ., 1982), p. 111.
[33] "Marduk." *Wikipedia.*
[34] Douglas, "Babel," p. 111.
[35] Bryce Self. "Semiramis, Queen of Babylon." *Lambert Dolphin's Library* website. 28 Apr. 1984. http://www.ldolphin.org/semir.html (27 Feb. 2006).
[36] Walvoord. *Revelation*, p. 247.
[37] Ibid.
[38] Ibid.
[39] Ibid.
[40] Robert deLeon. "Soul-Surfing—June 1, 2003." *Holy Cross Family Ministries* website. http://www.familyrosary.org/main/prayer-soul-archieves.php?iContentID=1760 (4 Jan. 2006).
[41] Strong's # 2161 and TWOT 556, p. 244.

Act II - Scene 1: The Kingdom of Israel

[1] Charles F. Pfeiffer, ed. *Baker's Bible Atlas.* (Grand Rapids: Baker Book House, 1979), p. 47.
[2] Ibid.
[3] Note: The land of Babylon, approximately 350 miles long, is named for its capital city, Babylon, located in the center of the land.
[4] "Ur" *University of Pennsylvania Museum of Archaeology and Anthropology* website. http://www.mnsu.edu/emuseum/archaeology/sites/middle_east/ur.html (13 Apr. 2006).
[5] Ibid.
[6] H. W. F. Saggs. *The Greatness that was Babylon.* (NY: Mentor Books, The New American Library, Inc., 1962), p. 72.
[7] Saggs, p. 500.
[8] "Ur" *University of Pennsylvania.*
[9] Saggs, pp. 76-78.

[10] Ibid. p. 317.

[11] Ibid. p. 79.

[12] Ibid. p. 72.

[13] Ibid. pp. 46, 529.

[14] "Abraham." *Easton's Bible Dictionary*. CD-ROM. Online Bible Edition version 2.00, 19 Jan. 2005. Winterbourne, ON. Canada: Online Bible, 1992-2005. Also, Strong's #87.

[15] C. Donald Cole. *Abraham: God's Man of Faith*. (Chicago: Moody Press, 1977), p. 9.

[16] "Abraham." *Easton's Bible Dictionary*.

[17] Saggs, p. 76.

[18] Cole, p. 47.

[19] Ibid.

[20] Douglas. "Edom," *New Bible Dictionary*, p. 299.

[21] John J. Davis. *Moses and the Gods of Egypt—Studies in Exodus—2nd ed*. (Winona Lake, IN: BMH Books, 1986), p. 293.

[22] John F. Walvoord. *Major Bible Prophecies—37 Crucial Prophecies That Affect You Today*. (Grand Rapids: Zondervan Publ. House, 1991), p. 55.

[23] Ibid., p. 85.

[24] John F. Walvoord. *The Millennial Kingdom*. (Grand Rapids: Zondervan Publ. House, 1959), p. 195.

[25] Ibid., p. 196.

[26] Ibid.

[27] Ibid.

[28] "Assyria." Charles F. Pfeiffer, Howard F. Vos, and John Rhea ed. *Wycliffe Bible Encyclopedia— vol. 1*. (Chicago: Moody Press, 1975), p. 166.

[29] Ibid, p. 868.

[30] Ibid.

[31] Pfeiffer, *Wycliffe*, p. 169.

[32] John J. Davis and John C. Whitcomb. *Israel—From Conquest to Exile*. (Winona Lake, IN: BMH Books, 1971), p. 481.

[33] Ibid. p. 487.

Act II - Scene 2: God Reveals Future Kingdoms

[1] Whitcomb. *Daniel*. (Chicago: Moody Press, 1985), pp. 92-93.

[2] Renald Showers, *The Most High God—A Commentary on Daniel*. [Bellmawr, NJ: The Friends of Israel Gospel Ministry, Inc., 1982], p. 17.

[3] Showers, *Most High*, p. 18

[4] Ibid., pp. 75-76.
[5] Walvoord, *Daniel*, p. 156.
[6] C. F. Keil. K&D, vol. 9, p. 685.
[7] Walvoord, *Daniel*, p. 184.
[8] Walvoord, *Daniel*, pp. 68-69, quoting Leuopold, *Daniel*, p. 119.
[9] Ibid., p. 68.
[10] Ibid., p. 69.
[11] Ibid.
[12] Showers, *Most High*, pp. 84-85.
[13] Ibid.
[14] Walvoord, *Daniel*, p. 72.
[15] Ibid.
[16] Whitcomb, *Daniel*, p. 98.
[16] J. Dwight Pentecost, "Daniel," *The Bible Knowledge Commentary: Old Testament* (Wheaton, IL: Victor, 1985), p. 1351.
[17] Whitcomb, *Daniel*, p.47, quoting Edward N. Luttwak, *The Grand Strategy of the Roman Empire from the First Century A.D. to the Third* [Baltimore: Johns Hopkins U., 1976].
[18] Ibid., p. 98.

Act III - Scene 1: The Grand Dream of Humanity's Last Kingdom
[1] "The Grand Design" 17 May 1948 *TIME Magazine Archieve* website. Time Inc, 2006. http://www.time.com/time/achive/0,23657,798604,00.html (24 Jun. 2006).
[2] Ibid.
[3] Ibid.
[4] Ibid.
[5] "Christian" referring more to political powers than religious faith.
[6] "The Grand Design."
[7] Pascal Fontaine. *Europe in 12 Lessons.* (Brussels: European Commission, 2004), p. 57.
[8] Booker, p. 43, quoting Lord Boothby. *Boothby—Recollections of a Rebel.* (London: Hutchinson, n.d.), p. 264.
[9] The European Union has two buildings for its parliament, in two separate cities; Brussels and Strasbourg. Parliament sessions are divided between both each month.
[10] "Travel-Strasbourg/EU" *Ordo Praeicatorium-The Order of Preachers-the Domician Family Website. The Domican Order of the Roman Catholic Church.* http://www.op.org/steinkerchner/travels/strasbourg/eu.htm (2 Jun. 2004).
[11] Booker, p. 4.

[12] "Message to Europeans." 22 Sep. 2004. *The European Movement International* website. http://www.europeanmovement.org/history.cfm (22 Jun. 2006).
[13] Adrian Hilton. *The Principality and Power of Europe: Britain and the Emerging Holy European Empire*. (Rickmansworth, UK: Dorchester House Publications, 2000), p. 32.
[14] Booker, p. 12.
[15] Avro Manhattan. "The Vatican in World Politics." 1949. *Gaer Associations, Inc*, Chapter 9. http://www.ephas-library.com/catholic/catholic_vatican_in_world_politics_chpt_9.html (15 Mar. 2006). p. 1.
[16] Ibid., p, 4.
[17] Ibid., p. 5.
[18] Ibid., p. 6.
[19] Hilton, pp. 31, 33.
[20] Ibid.
[21] Francois Duchene. *The First Statesman of Interdependence*. (London: W. W. Norton & Co., 1994), p. 30.
[22] Ibid., p. 31.
[23] Ibid., p. 29.
[24] Frederic Fransen. *The Supranational Politics of Jean Monnet: Ideas and Origins of the European Community*. (Connecticut: Greenwood Press, 2001), p. 1.
[25] Ibid, p. 15.
[26] Ibid.
[27] Booker, p. 15.
[28] Duchene, p. 41.
[29] Ibid., p. 40.
[30] Booker, p. 15.
[31] Ibid., p. 16, quoting Bromberger, Merry and Serge (1969), Jean Monnet and the United States of Europe (New York, Coward-McCann), p. 19.
[32] Ibid., p. 17.
[33] Ibid.
[34] Hilton, p. 34.
[35] United Nations" CD-ROM *Encarta Encyclopedia Standard 2001*. Redmond, WA: Microsoft Corp. 1993-2000.
[36] Booker, p. 33.
[37] Kenneth Frampton. *Le Corbusier*. (London: Thames & Hudson, 2001), p. 161.
[38] Booker, p. 453.
[39] Ibid.

[40] "Thousand Delegates at The Hague" *Council of Europe* website. http://www.coealb.org/o2.htm (22 Jun 2006).

[41] "Greater and Smaller Europe." *Council of Europe* website. http://www.coealb.org/04.htm (22 Jun. 2006).

[42] Jean-Claude Juncker. *Council of Europe-European Union: A Sole ambition for the European Continent* (Brussels: Council of Europe, 2006), p. 18.

[43] Ibid., p. 29.

[44] Booker, p. 48.

[45] Ibid.

[46] Ibid., p. 51.

[47] Ibid.

[48] Ibid., pp. 51, 52.

[49] Mark Leonard. *Why Europe Will Run the 21ˢᵗ Century.* (London: Fourth Estate, 2005), p. 10.

[50] Booker, p. 428.

[51] Ibid.

[52] Ibid.

[53] Leonard, *Why Europe,* p. 10. Monnet was referring to American politics and applied it to his plan for success.

[54] Honor Mahony. "EU Nervous and Introspective at Fifty Years of Age." 21 Mar. 2007 *Euobserver.com* website. http://euobserer.com/9/23536 (4 Apr. 2007).

[55] Leonard, *Why Europe,* p. 10.

Act III - Scene 2: The European Union's Neighborhood

[1] Benita Ferrero-Waldner. "Europe's Neighbours-Toward Closer Integration." *Europa* website. http://europa.eu.int/comm/external_relations/news/ferrero/2005/sp05_253.htm (30 Sep. 2005)

[2] Ibid.

[3] Benita Ferrero-Waldner. "The European Neighborhood Policy-Welcome." 21 Dec. 2004. *Haaretz-Israel News.* http://www.haaretz.com/hasen/spages/517071.html (8 Jan. 2005).

[4] "F.A.Q." Europa website. http://europa.eu.int/comm/world/enp/components_en.htm (9 Sep. 2005).

[5] Herb Keinon. "Israel Okays wider Europe action plan." *Jerusalem Post,* 9 Dec. 2004. http://www.jpost.com/servlet/Satelite?pagename=JPost/JPArticle/Printe&cid=110260 (16 Feb. 2005).

[6] Waldner, "Neighborhood Policy."

[7] CIA-World Factbook-Israel. http://www.cia.gov/cia/pulbications/fact-book/geos/is.html (29 Jun. 2006).

[8] Sergio della Pergola. "World Jewish Population 2002," *American Jewish Year Book*. http://www.jafi.org.il/education/100/concepts/demography/demjpop.html (1 Jul. 2006).

[9] Waldner, "Neighborhood Policy."

[10] Ibid.

[11] Ibid.

[12] Ibid.

[13] Martin Walker. "Analysis: Israel Weighing EU Membership." *United Press International*, 2 May 2003. http://www.upi.com/viwe.cfm?StoryID=20030521-112245-2333r (24 Sep. 2005).

[14] Ibid.

[15] Robert Anderson. *The Coming Prince*. (Grand Rapids: Kregel, 1957), p. 67.

[16] Ibid., p. 127.

[17] Showers, *Most High*, p. 128.

[18] Anderson, p. 198.

[19] Showers, *Most High*, p. 131.

[20] Ibid. p. 132.

[21] Showers, *Most High*, p. 132.

[22] J. Dwight Pentecost. *Things to Come: A Study in Biblical Eschatology*. (Grand Rapids, MI: Zondervan Publ., 1958), p. 328.

[23] Ibid., pp. 328-330.

[24] Ibid., p. 351.

[25] "Meeting of the First Zionist Congress-August 29, 1897" *Hagshama Dept.-World Zionist Organization* website. http://www.wzo.org.il/en/resources/view.asp?id=1057 (29 Jun. 2006).

[26] Ibid.

[27] Elwood McQuaid. *It is No Dream-Biblical Prophecy: Fact or Fanaticism?* (Bellmawr, NJ: The Friends of Israel Gospel Ministry, Inc., 1978), pp. 90-91.

[28] Ibid., p. 92.

[29] Ibid., p. 91, quoting *Facts About Israel 1973* (Jerusalem: Division of Information, Ministry of Foreign Affairs, 1973), p. 34.

[30] "Jordan, Hasemite Kingdom of" CD-ROM *Encarta Encyclopedia Standard 2001*. Redmond, WA: Microsoft Corp. 1993-2000.

[31] McQuaid, p. 97.

[32] Strong's # 398.

[33] TWOT, p. 85.

[34] Literally "to eat up" (Strong's #0399). The concept is that it will absorb the conquered countries rather than destroy them. To "devour the earth" describes Ancient Rome's method that "added government to conquest, and instead of treading down and breaking in pieces the nations it subdued, sought rather to mould them to its own civilization and polity." Sir Robert Anderson. p. 276.

[35] Walvoord, "*Daniel*," p. 175.

[36] Pentecost. *Things to Come*. p. 326 Quoting F. C. Jennings, "The Boundaries of the Revived Roman Empire," *Our Hope*, xlvii: 387-389, December, 1940.

[37] Kevin Byrne. "Euromed, an Economic Failure?" 28 Nov. 2005. *CaféBabel.com—The European Magazine*. Babel International, 2006. http://www.cafebabel.com/en/dossierprintversion.asp?ID-234 (27 Jan. 2006).

[38] "Euro-Mediterranean Partnership/Barcelona Process." *Europa* website. http://www.europa.eu.int/comm/external_relations/euromed/ (27 Jan. 2005).

[39] "Is Africa Next Target for EU Expansion?" *Midnight Call Magazine, December 2003* (Midnight Call Ministries, Inc.)

[40] Gamal Nkrumah. "Mare Nostrum." *Al-Ahram Weekly Online 16-22 October 2003, Issue No. 660*. http://weekly.ahram.org.eg/w003/660/eg4.htm (27 Jan. 2006).

[41] Ibid.

[42] "EU Opens Door to Turkey." *BBC News UK edition 17 December 2004*. http://news.bbc.co.uk/1/hi/world/europe//4103397 (17 Apr. 2006).

[43] "EU-Turkey Relations." Europa website. http://europa.eu.int/comm/enlargement/turkey/eu_relations.htm (27 Jan. 2006).

[44] "Making the EU a Factor in the Middle East." *Europa* website. http://europa.eu.int/comm/external_relations/gr/index.htm (27 Jan. 2006).

[45] Walker. "Analysis."

[46] "EU a Factor."

[47] "Euro-Mediterranean Partnership."

[48] Herb Keinon. "Israel Okays Wider Europe Action Plan." Jerusalem Post website. 9 Dec. 2004. http://www.jpost.com/servlet/Satellite?pagename=JPost/JPArticle?printer& cid=110260 (16 Feb. 2005).

[49] "Commissioner Ferrer-Waldner Announces €250 million Support to the Palestinians in 2005." IP/05/157 *Europa* website, 9 Feb 2005. http://europa.eu.int/comm/external_relations/gaza/intro/index.htm (9 Feb. 2005).

[50] CIA-World Factbook.

[51] Jeremy Rifkin. *The European Dream.* (Cambridge: Polity Press, 2004), p. 61.

[52] Ibid., p. 298.

[53] Ibid., p. 299. Quoting Romano Prodi, Speech at the Institu d'Etudes Politiques in Paris, May 29, 2001.

[54] Mark Leonard. "Europe's Transformative Power" CER Bulletin. http://markleonard.net/journalism/eurotranform/ (26 Jan. 2006).

[55] Leonard. *Why Europe*, p. 55.

[56] Ibid.

[57] Hilton, p. 120 quoting *English Churchman*, no. 7452, 11th April 1997, p. 1 and *Protestant Truth*, Jan-Feb 1998, p. 7.

[58] Ibid., quoting *Evangelicals Now*, May 1997, p. 1.

[59] Steven Mather. "MERCOSUR: Does it Have a Role in Fulfillment of Simon Bolivar's Dream?" Venezuelanalysis.com 22 Jun. 2006. http://www.venezuelanalysis.com/articles.php?artno-1756 (30 Jun. 2006).

[60] Ibid.

[61] Leonard, *Why Europe*, p. 137.

[62] "EU and Mercosur meet at ministerial level, Brussels 2 September 2005" IP/05/1081 *Europa* website. http://europe.eu.int/comm/external_relations/mercosur/intro/ip05_1081.htm (16 Sep. 2005).

[63] "The EU's Relations with Mercosur." *Europa* website. http://www.europa.eu.int/comm./external_relations/Mercosur/intro/index.htm (9 Feb. 2005).

[64] Ibid.

[65] Ibid.

[66] "Senate Votes in Favor of CAFTA" *Fox News Channel*, 30 Jun. 2005. http://www.foxnews.com/printer_friendly_story/0,3566,161192,00.html (1 Jul. 2005).

[67] "House Approves CAFTA in 217-215 Vote" *Fox News Channel*, 28 Jul. 2005. http://www.foxnews.com/printer_friendly_story/0,3566,163891,00.html (28 Jul. 2005).

[68] "Bush 'Super-state' Documents Sought." *WorldnetDaily*.com. 20 Jun. 2006 http://www.worldnetdaily.com/news/printer-friendly.asp?ARTICLE_ID=50719 (23 Jun. 2006).

[69] Ibid.

[70] Ibid.

[71] "Creating a North American Community – Chairmen's Statement." *Council on Foreign Relations*, March 2005. http://www.cfr.org/publication/7912/creating_a_north_american_community_chairmen (30 Jun. 2006).

[72] "Bush 'Super-state' Documents."

[73] "Bush Sneaking North American Super-State Without Oversight?" *Worldnetdaily.com.* http://www.worldnetdaily.com/news/printer-friendly.asp?ARTICLE_ID=50618 (23 Jun. 2006).

[74] "The EU's relations with the United States of America." *Europa* website. http://www.europa.eu.int/cgi-bin/etal.pl (9 Feb. 2005).

[75] Ibid.

[76] Ibid.

[77] David Smith and Eben Black. "How Big Can it Get?" *The Sunday Times* 15 Dec. 2002. Focus Section, p. 23.

[78] "Viewpoints: Where is the EU heading?" *BBC News UK edition, 4 May 2004.* http://news.bbc.co.uk/1/hi/world/europe/3659659.stm (22 Mar. 2006).

[79] Booker, p. 444.

[80] Smith and Black, "How Big Can it Get?".

[81] Ibid.

[82] "Enlargement—Basic Arguments." *Europa* website. http://europa.eu.int/comm/enlargement/arguments/index.htm (18 Mar. 2003).

[83] Ibid.

[84] Leonard, *Why Europe*, citing Ann-Marie Slaughter, *A New World Order* (New Jersey: Princeton University Press, 2004), p. 143.

[85] Booker, p. 428.

[86] Leonard, *Why Europe*, p. 135.

[87] Ibid., p. 139.

[88] Ibid., p. 138.

[89] *How the European Union Works.* (Luxembourg: Office for Official Publications of the European Communities, 2005), p. 32.

[90] "Europe in the 21st Century: the Shape of things to come." *Europa* website. http://europa.eu.int/comm/publications/booklets/eu_glance/12/txt_en.htm (22 Mar. 2006).

[91] Ibid., pp. 140, 145.

[92] Pierre Hillard. "minorities et regionalismes, Enquete sur le plan allemande qui va bouleverser l'Europe." Editions Francois-Xavier de Guibert, 3rd edition augmentee, 2002 quoted by the *Campaign for an Independent Britain*: London. 23 January 2006. http://www.bullen.demon.co.uk/frenchcn.htm (1/27/2006).

[93] Ibid.

[94] *Working for the Regions.* (Luxembourg: Office for Official Publications of the European Communities, 2004), p. 3.

[95] "Europe's Regions and the Information Society." *Europa* website. http://europa.eu.int/information_society/regwor/reg/index_en.htm (26 Mar. 2006).

[96] Ibid.

[97] Hilton, p. 64.

[98] Strong's # 1855, corresponding to 1854

[99] Hilton, p. 79. Dennis Behreandt. "Abolishing Our Nation – Step by Step." Stop the FTAA, *John Birch Society* website. http://www.stop-theftaa.org/artman/publish_142.shtml (30 Jun. 2006).

[100] Booker, p. 374.

Act III - Scene 3: The Supra-National World of the EU

[1] Ronald Reagan. "President Reagan's First Inaugural Address" January 20, 1981. *The Reagan Information Page. August 1993-present.* http://www.presidentreagan.info/speeches/in1.cfm (25 Jan. 2006).

[2] Ibid.

[3] Ibid.

[4] "Dutch say 'No' to EU Constitution." *BBC News Online*, (2 Jun. 2005). http://news.bbc.co.uk/2/hi/worlod/europe/4601439.stm. (26 Jan. 2006).

[5] Ibid.

[6] *A Constitution for Europe – Presentation to Citizens.* (Luxembourg: EU Commission – European Communities Publication, 2004), p. 7.

[7] The basis of the French rejection was more a consequence of France's internal politics rather than a rejection of the proposed constitution.

[8] *A Constitution for Europe – Presentation to Citizens.* p. 6.

[9] Daniel Hannan. "So, You Thought the European Constitution was Dead, Did You?" *Opinion.Telegraph – Daily Telegraph Online*, (20 March 2006). http://www.telegraph.co.uk/opinion/main.jhtml?xml=/opinion/2006/03/20/do2001.xml (26 Mar. 2006).

[10] "The Ratification of the Constitution – the Status Across Europe. *ALD – Alliance of Liberals and Democrats for Europe.* http://alde.europarl.eu.int/content/default.asp?pageID=607# (3/26/2006).

[11] Ibid.

[12] Booker, p. 443.

[13] "Supranational." *The American Heritage® Dictionary of the English Language, Fourth Edition* Copyright © 2004, 2000 by Houghton Mifflin Company. Answers Corporation, 2006. http://www.answers.com/supranational&r=67 (26 Jan. 2006).

[14] Booker, p. 1.

[15] Leonard. *Why Europe*, p. 140.

[16] "Nation-State." *Wikipedia, the Free Encyclopedia, 23 January 2006.* (Wikimedia Foundation, Inc.). http://en.wikipedia.org/wiki/Nation-state (26 Jan. 2006).

[17] "Nation-State."

[18] "World Government." *Wikipedia, the Free Encyclopedia, 19 March 2006.* (Wikimedia Foundation, Inc.). http://en.wikipedia.org/wiki/World_Government (22 Mar. 2006).

[19] Dante Alighieri" *CD-ROM. Microsoft Encarta Encyclopedia 2001.* (Microsoft Corporation, 1993-2001), 1.

[20] Booker, p. 12.

[21] Ibid, p. 12.

[22] Ibid., p. 443.

[23] *How the European Union Works – Your Guide to the EU Institutions.* (Luxembourg: Office for Official Publications of the European Communities, 2005), 20.

[24] Ibid., p. 21.

[25] William Anthony Hay. *Challenges of Empire, Vol. 3 No. 5, May 2002.* Foreign Policy Research Institute, 2001-2005. http://www.fpri.org/ww/0305.200205.hay.chalendgesofempire.html (3/22/2006).

[26] Mary T. Boatwright. *Hadrian and the Cities of the Roman Empire – Book Description.* (New York: Princeton University Press, 2000), 4. http://www.pupress.princeton.edu/chapters/s6878.html (22 Mar. 2006).

[27] Chester G. Starr. *The Roman Empire* (New York, 1982), 3-4. Quoted by Mary T. Boatwright. *Hadrian and the Cities of the Roman Empire – Book Description*

[28] Brayn Ward-Perkins. *The Fall of Rome and the End of Civilization.* (Oxford: Oxford University Press, 2005), p. 9.

[29] "United Kingdom." CD-ROM. *Microsoft Encarta Encyclopedia 2001.* (Microsoft Corporation, 1993-2001), p. 1.

[30] Nico Colchester. "The Nation-State." *FT.com Financial Times Special Report.* First published in *The New York Times,* July 12, 1994. http://specials.ft.com/nicocolchester/FT3EZT7SEIC.html (26 Mar. 2006).

[31] Colchester.

[32] Fernando Navarro. "We Are Witnessing the Last Remnants of National Politics" *CaféBabel.com – The European Magazine, 28 February 2005.* Babel International, 2006. http://www.cafebabel.com/en/printversion.asp?T=T&Id=3285 (27 Jan. 2006).

[33] Michelle Cini, *European Union Politics.* (Oxford: Oxford University Press, 2003), 1.

[34] Booker, pp. 443-4.

[35] Lorne Gunter. "Eurocrats are a Bunch of Clowns." *The Edmonton Journal/National Post July 28, 2003* (CanWest Interactive, a div. of CanWest Global Communications Corp, 2003). http://www.national-post.com (31 Jul. 2003).

[36] Ibid.

[37] Ibid.

[38] Ibid.

[39] Booker, p. 443.

[40] *Going for Growth – The Economy of the EU.* (Luxembourg: Office for Official Publications of the European Communities, 2003), p. 6.

[41] *How the European Union Works*, p. 24.

[42] Ibid., p. 21.

[43] "More Bureaucracy to Reduce Bureaucracy" The European Foundation Intelligence Digest- March/April 2006. (London: The European Foundation), p. 4,

[44] "Diverse." *WordNet Dictionary*, (Hyperdictionary.com, 2000-2005), http:hyperdictionary.com/dictionary/diverse (25 Mar. 2006).

[45] BDB, p. 1116. TWOT 2419, p. 941, vol. II.

[46] "Supranational" *WordNet Dictionary*, (Hyperdictionary.com, 2000-2005), http:hyperdictinary.com/dictionary/supranational (25 Mar. 2006).

[47] Booker, p. 103.

[48] Jens-Peter Bonde. "Why Shouldn't Spain Re-run its Referendum?" *EU Observer* http://euobserver.com/?aid=19174&sid=7. (26 May 2005).

[49] Booker, p. 294.

[50] Hilton, p. 81.

[51] Ibid.

[52] Booker, p. 17 quoting Slater, Arthur, *The United States of Europe* (London, Allen & Unwin), p. 92.

[53] Cini, p. 1.

[54] Cini, p. 3.

[55] *How the European Union Works*, p. 3.

[56] Booker, p. 374.

Act III - Scene 4: The Alliance—Government and Religion

[1] Jonathan Petre. "Churches on Road to Doom if Trends Continue." *The Daily Telegraph*, Saturday Sept 3, 2005. No. 46,729, page 1- Scottish Section. (1 Mar 2005).

[2] Ibid.

[3] Louise Gray. "In the Land of Knox, Religion Isn't What It Was" *The Scotsman.com*, http://news.scotsman.com/scotland.cfm?id=225032005 (1 Mar. 2005).

[4] Note: the constitution is merely the latest treaty amending the operation of the European Union by incorporating the previous treaties and adding additional roles for the EU. The rejection by two members does not signify the complete rejection of the constitution nor the end of the

European Union. Great efforts are underway to approve the constitution by circumventing the referendum of France and the Netherlands.

[5] Governments of Portugal, Spain, Ireland, Poland, the Czech Republic, Lithuania, Slovakia, Italy, and Malta – "EU Constitution Omits Reference to Christianity," *The New American*, July 26, 2004, (Appleton, WI: American Opinion Publishing Inc., 2004), p. 7. Also, Thomas Dixon. "Ignoring God in the Constitution" *Christianity Today*. 25 Jun 2003. http://www.christianity today.com/ct/2003/007/18.26.html (3 Mar 2005).

[6] Dixon.

[7] "The Portugal News Reports the Facts on Fatima Congress" *The News, Portugal's English Language Online Newspaper*. 15 Nov 2003. www.the-news.net (3 Mar 2005).

[8] John Walvoord. *Revelation*, 243. See also, David Levy, *Revelation, Hearing the Last Word*. (Bellmawr, NJ: The Friends of Israel Gospel Ministry, Inc., 1999), p. 189.

[9] Herman A. Hoyt. *Studies in Revelation*. (Winona Lake, IN: BMH Books, 1977), p. 111 and Walvoord, p. 188.

[10] Robert L. Thomas. *Revelation 8-22, An Exegetical Commentary*. (Chicago: Moody Press, 1995), p. 282, quoting Ford, *Revelation*, p. 277; Wall, *Revelation*, p. 205.

[11] Strong's # 3173.

[12] Thomas, p. 282.

[13] Thomas, p. 282; Johnson, "Revelation," 12:555; Hailey, Revelation, p. 343; Philip Edgcumbe Hughes, T*he Book of Revelation* (Grand Rapids: Eerdmans, 1990), p. 182.

[14] Herman Hoyt. *Studies in Revelation*. (Winona Lake, IN: BMH Books, 1977), p. 111 and Thomas, p. 282.

[15] Walvoord, *Revelation*, p. 243.

[16] Walvoord, *Revelation*, p. 244.

[17] Henry Alford. *The Greek Testament - Vol. 4*. (Chicago: Moody Press, 1958), p. 706.

[18] "Europa" Wikipedia—*The Free Encyclopedia 23 Mar 2006* (Wikimedia Foundation, Inc.) http://en.wikipedia.org/wiki/Europa_(mythology) 3/28/2006.

[19] Ibid.

[20] "Yes to Reference to Christianity, Berlusconi Said." *Italy On Line—Agenzia Giornalistica Italia—News in English*. 25 Aug 2003. http://www.agi.it/english/news.pl?doc=200308252011-   0146-RT1-POL-0-NF82&page=0. (26 Aug 2003).

[21] Jean Monnet and Arthur Salter are the true founding fathers of the EU, but much of their work was "behind the scenes," hence they are not the recognized founders.

[22] Hilton, p. 39, quoting *Church of England Newspaper, 10 December 1999* and *The Tablet, 30 October 1999* issue.

[23] Jacques Paragan quoted by Luke Coppen, *Catholic Herald Newspaper* 23 May 2003 and reported by Ian Paisely "Architect of European Union Advancing to RC Sainthood." *European Institute of Protestant Studies* 23 Jun 2003 http://www.ianpaisley.org. (13 Nov 2005).

[24] Paisley.

[25] "Council of Europe's Emblems" *The Council of Europe.* http://www.coe.int/T/e/Com/About_coe/flag.asp. (25 Sep 2004).

[26] "Council of Europe's Emblems".

[27] "Coincidences" of European Flag" *Zenit News Agency 7* Dec 1999, ZE00120707. http://www.zenit.org/english/archive/9912/ZE991207.html , (14 Nov 2005).

[28] "The EU at a glance—The symbols of the European Union" *Europa – EU website.* http://europa.eu.int/abc/symbols/emblem/index_en.htm, (26 May 2004).

[29] Ibid.

[30] Ibid.

[31] Booker, p. 218 fn., also, *Europa - EU website.*

[32] Ibid., also Hermann Schafer: Sterne und Staaten, in : Koch, Thilo (Ed.), Euopre und ich. Personliche Eindrucke und Eriebnisse, Boon, 1993. Quoted in HDG.

[33] Booker, p. 218 fn.

[34] "European Symbols" *Wikipedia – the Free Encyclopedia* 27 Oct. 2005. http://en.wikipedia.org/wiki/Europe_Day 11/14/2005.

[35] Council of Europe's Emblems"

[36] Dr. David R Reagan, "Europe in Bible Prophecy", *Lamb and Lion Ministries,* http://www.lamblion.com/New10.php. His footnote: Remarks of Leon Marchal were reported by Dr. William Crampton, executive director of The Flag Institute in York, England. The remarks were made in 1973.

[37] "Coincidences" of European Flag" Zenit.

[38] "Unity of Hearts" *Daily Catholic October 2001.* http://www.dailycath-olic.org/issue/2001Oct/redebac.htm (14 Nov 2005).

[39] Joseph Phelan. "The Immaculate Conception" *ArtCyclopedia.* http://www.artcyclopedia.com/advent/feature-2002-12-day9.html. (14 Nov 2005).

[40] Booker, Regan, and Zenit.

[41] "The EU at a glance – The symbols of the European Union".

[42] John Paul II, Evangelium vitae, 3/25/1995. The Vatican See. http://www.vatican.va/edocs/ENG0141/_P13.htm . (13 Nov 2005).

[43] Strong's # 3173 and 4592.

[44] Victoria Neufeldt, ed. "Symbol." *Webster's New World Dictionary of American English, 3rd ed.* (NY: Prentice Hall, 1994).

[45] Bernard Ramm. *Protestant Biblical Interpretation 3rd ed.* (Grand Rapids: Baker Book House, 1970), 234.

[46] Paul Lee Tan. *The Interpretation of Prophecy* (Winona Lake, IN: BMH Books, Inc., 1974),

[47] Thomas, p. 121.

[48] Ibid., pp. 120, 121.

[49] Ibid.

[50] Ibid., p. 127

[51] Ibid,, p. 125; quoting Robertson, *Word Pictures*, 6:389; Chilton, *Days of Vengeance*, pp. 307-8.

[52] Ibid., p. 121.

[53] Walvoord, *Revelation*, p. 188.

[54] Walvoord, *Revelation*, p. 191.

[55] Dave Hunt. *A Woman Rides the Beast.* (Eugene, OR: Harvest House, 1994), p. 459.

[56] "The Shrine of Our Lady of Europe." 4 Aug 2003. www.gibraltar.gov.gi/tourism/lady_of_Europe.htm (24 Jun 2004).

[57] Ibid.

[58] "The European Emblem".

[59] On May 9, 1950, Robert Schuman presented his proposal calling for the European Union. In 1985, the EU adopted the 9 May as Europe Day to honor Schuman. However, many still observe the earlier designated Europe Day of 5 May. "European Symbols" *Wikipedia, the Free Encyclopedia.* http://en.wikipedia.org/wiki/Europe_Day. (14 Nov 2005).

[60] "The Shrine of Our Lady of Europe."

[61] John Paul II. "Address to Hon. Mr. Romano Prodi, President of the European Commission." 28 Oct 2004. *The Vatican See.* http://www.vatican.va/holy_father/joh_paul_ii/speeches/2004/October/documents/hf_jp_ii_spe _20041028_romano-prodi_en.htm (13 Nov 2005).

[62] Hilton, p. 35.

[63] Ibid., pp. 35-36.

[64] Ian Fisher. "Pope Explains Christian Roots in Choice of Name" *International Herald Tribune*, 29 Apr 2005. http://www.iht.com/aritcles/2005/04/28/news/vatican.php, (14 Nov 2005).

[65] Clive Gillis. "Rome's Secret Weapon for Recatholicising the EU" *The European Institute for Protestant Studies* 30 June 2005. http://www.ianpaisley.org/article.asp?printerFriendly=true&ArtKey=secret_weapon (14 Nov 2005).

[66] Hunt, p. 469

[67] John Paul II. "Act of Entrustment to Mary, Jubilee of Bishops, 8 October 2000" *The Vatican See*. 2000. http://www.vaticanva/holy_father/john_paul_ii/speeches/documents/hf_jp-   ii_spe_20001008_act-entrustment-mary_en.html (14 Nov 2005).

[68] "Paragraph 2. 'Conceived by the Power of the Holy Spirit and Born of the Virgin Mary'" *the Vatican See*. http://www.vatican.va/archive/ENG0015/_P1K.HTM. (15 Nov 2005).

[69] "The Message and Meaning of Rue de Bac." *Daily Catholic October*. 2001. http://www.dailycatholic.org/issue/2001/Oct/ruedebac.htm. (14 Nov 2005).

[70] "The Miraculous Medal and Its Meaning." *The Association of the Miraculous Medal*. http://www.amm.org/medal.htm (14 Nov 2005).

Act III - Scene 5: Uniting the World's Religions

"European Convention on the Non-Applicability of Statutory Limitations to Crimes Against Humanity and War Crimes, ETS 82, 13 I.L.M. 540, Jan. 25, 1974." *University of Minnesota Human Rights Library*. http://www1.umn.edu/humanrts/instree/1974a.htm (18 Apr. 2007).

[2] Militant amillennialism in the UK plays down the significance of eschatology by calling it a minor area of doctrine.

[3] Note the use of "bringing in the kingdom" reflects the doctrinal position of both post- millennialists and militant amillennialists (Replacement Theology groups in the United Kingdom). Thus, the "minor" doctrine concept concerning the Millennium removes a barrier in their ecumenical alliances.

[4] "Why Unity Matters." *Churches Together Association*. http://www.churches-together.org.uk/whoweare_why_unity_matters.htm. (12 Nov. 2005).

[5]. "Emergent." Emergent Village website. http://www.emergentvillage.com/about/1 (17 Apr. 2007).

[6] Brian D. McLaren. The Secret Message of Jesus - Uncovering the Truth that could Change Everything. (Nashville, TN: W Publishing Group, 2006), p. 94.

[7] Ibid., p. 167.

[8] "Emergent."

[9] McLaren, pp. 216-217.

[10] Oliver Poole. "Churches Agree Pope Has Overall Authority." *Electronic Telegraph Issue 1448*. 13 May 1999. http://www.telegraph. co.uk. (14 Nov. 2005).

[11]"Churches Close Rift." *Sky News*. (May 19, 2005). http://www.sky. com/skynews/article/0,,30200-1182464,00.html. (14 Nov. 2005).

[12]Both historically hold to the same amillennial view of the kingdom.

13 Rowan Williams. "The Bible Today: Reading & Hearing." Archbishop William's Sermons and Speeches, 16 Apr. 2007. http://www.archbish-opof Canterbury.org/sermons-speeches/070416.htm (28 Apr. 2007).

[14]"The Portugal News reports the facts on Fatima Congress." *The Portugal National Weekend Newspaper in English*. 15 Nov 2003. http:// the-news.net.

[15] Hannah Salter. "Ludwig van Beethoven's Ode to Joy." *Ludwig van Beethoven – Dominique Prevot*. http//www.lvbeethoven.com/Oeuvres/ Music_Odetojoy.html. (4 Dec. 2003). Note, latest page http://www. lvbeethoven.com/Oeuvres/Music-EuropeanAnthem-OdeToJoy.html (18 Apr. 2007) revises the translation to be politically correct—many other translations to confirm their first version.

[16] Elysium — "plain of the departed, dwelling place of virtuous people after death." *Webster's New World Dictionary of American English – 3rd College Ed.* (New York: Prentice Hall, 1994).

[17] Samuel Bacchiocchi. "The Co-Redemptive Role of Mary in *The Passion*." *Endtimes Newsletter No. 118*. http://www.biblicalperspectives. com/endtimeissue/et_118.htm (16 Nov. 2005) quoting Beatrice Bruteau, "The Unknown Goddess," *The Goddess Re-Awakening*, compiled by Shirley Nicholson, (Wheaton, IL: the Theosophical Publishing House, 1992), p. 68.

[18] *Humanist Manifest II, American Humanist Association*, www.ameri-canhumanist.org/about/manifesto2.html1. (17 Apr. 2007).

[19] Showers, *What on Earth*, p. 100, quoting John Dillenberger and Claude Welch, *Protestant Christianity*, pp. 290.

[20] Peter R. Scott. "Fatima Inter-Religious Congress" *Holy Cross Seminary Newsletter. December 1, 2002* (Bathurst, N.S.W.Australia: Holy Cross Seminary), http://www.holycrossseminary.com/2003_December.htm. (3 Mar 2005).

[21] Ibid.

[22] Note the term Roman Virgin Mary, Virgin Mary, Roman Mary, Mary refers to the Mary of the Roman Catholic doctrinal view. The term, Biblical Mary, refers to the Mary of the Scriptures.

[23] "The Shrine of Our Lady of Europe." *Gibraltar Government Tourism.* 22 Apr 2003. http://www.gibraltar.gov.gi/tourism/lady_of_europe.htm. (4 Aug 2003).

[24] Global Mary will be the term to indicate the supra-religion's unifying factor or controlling entity.

[25] Adela Galindo. "At the End My Immaculate Heart Will Triumph." http://www.piercedhearts.org/mother-adela/immaculate_heart_triumph. htm (18 Apr. 2007), quoting Pope John Paul II, Vittorio Messori, editor, *Crossing the Threshold of Hope.* (New York: Alfred A. Knopf, Borzoi Book, 1994), p. 215.

[26] John Paul II, "Entrustment."

[27] Ibid.

[28] Ibid.

[29] Jim Tetlow, Roger Oakland, and Brad Myers. Queen *of Rome, Queen of Islam, Queen of All.* (Fairport, NY: Eternal Productions, 2006), p. 22 quoting Thomas W. Petrisko. *The Last Crusade* (McKees Rock, PA: St. Andrews Productions, 1996), p. 70.

[30] Ibid.

[31] Ibid., p. 20 quoting Fr. Don Stefano Gobbi, *To the Priest, Our Lady's Beloved Sons* (St. Francis, ME: The National Headquarters of the Marian Movement of Priests in the United States of America, 1998), pp 923, 924. Message given to Father Gobbi, Oct 13, 1996, Tokyo Japan.

[32] Ibid., p. 24 quoting Gobbi, p. 419. Message given in Como, Italy, Dec. 31, 1984.

[33] Wayne Weible. *Medjugorje the Message.* (Brewster, MA: Paraclette Press, 1989), p. 344.

[34] Believed by many Marian theologians.

[35] Jim Tetlow. "Will Mary Unite All Religions?" *Endtime Issues Newsletter No. 116* p. 19. http://www.biblicalperspectives.com/endti-meissues/et_116.htm. (17 Nov 2005). Section "Dogma, then Peace." Quoting Kunzli, editor, *The Messages of the Lord of All Nations*, p. 85.

[36] Tetlow, *Newsletter*, section "Queen over All," quoting Petrisko, *Call of the Ages*, p. 449.

[37] Tetlow, *Newsletter*, section "The Numbers are Staggering.

[38] Ibid. Quoting "5 Million Pilgrims Visit Virgin's Shrine," *Orange County Register*, Dec. 13, 1999, p. 20.

[39] Hunt, p. 453.

[40] Tetlow, *Newsletter*, section "Marian Apparitions Everywhere," quoting Josef Kunzli, editor, *The Messages of the Lady of All Nations*, (Santa Barbara, CA, Queenship Publishing, 1996), p. 85.

[41] Tetlow, *Newsletter*, section "Growing Worldwide Popularity," quoting Kenneth L. Woodward, "Hail Mary," *Newsweek*, August 25, 1997, p. 50.

[42] "Our Lady of Medjugorje - Message given July 25, 1990." http://www. medjugorje.org/msg90.htm. (3 Mar 2005).

[43] Ibid.

[44] Tetlow, *Newsletter*, section "Our Lady's Ecumenical Peach Plan," quoting Richard J. Beyer, "April 6, 1993 Meditation" *Medjugorje Day By Day*, (Notre Dame, IN: Ave Maria Press, 1993).

[45] Tetlow. *Queenl*, p. 12. Quoting Elaine Gale, "Mary's Rising Popularity Goes Beyond Faith," *Los Angeles Times*, Dec. 25, 1998, p. A41.

[46] Hunt, p. 453.

[47] "Sura - 19 Mary." *Submission.org* website. http://www.submission. org/suras/sura19.html1 (17 Apr. 2007).

[48] "Sura - 3 The Amramites." *Submission.org website.* http://www. submission.org/suras/sura19.html1 (17 Apr. 2007).

[49] Giancarlo Finazzo. "The Virgin Mary in the Koran." *Catholic Culture* website. Trinity Communications 2007. http://www.catholicculture.org/ docs/doc_view.cfm?recnum=412 (17 Apr. 2007).

[50] Ibid., Surah 3:40-3:46.

[51] "Hindus Worship at Fatima Altar" *Portugal's National Weekend Newspaper in English*. 22 May 2004. http://the-news.net/cgi-local/story. pl?title=Hindus worship at Fatima altar&edition=all. 3 Jan 2005.

[52] Ibid.

[53] "Bishop – Fatima open to all" *Portugal's National Weekend Newspaper in English*. 16 Oct 2004. http://the-news/cgi-local/story.pl?title=Bishop-Fatima open to all&edition=all. (3 Jan 2005).

[54] "Fatima to Become Interfaith Shrine" *Portugal's National Weekend Newspaper in English*. 1 Nov 2003. http://the-news.net/cgi-local/sotry. pl?title=Fatima to become interfaith shrine&edition=all. (3 Jan 2005).

[55] John Vennari. "Fatima to Become Interfaith Shrine? An Account From One Who Was There." http://www.fatima.org/news/newsview/ sprep111303 (3 Jan 2005).

[56] "Fatima Inter-Religious Congress" *Holy Cross Seminary Newsletter*.

[57] "Fatima to Become Interfaith Shrine."

[58] Ibid.

[59] Ibid.

[60] Ibid.

[61] "Rome to Control Fatima?" *Portugal's National Weekend Newspaper in English*. 2 Oct 2004. http://the-news.net/cgi-local/sotry.pl?title=rome to control Fatima?&edition=all. (3 Jan 2005).

[62] A. T. Robertson, "Revelation 17:5" *Robertson's Word Pictures*.(Online Bible Edition — Version 2.0, 19 Jan 2005).

[63] Ibid.

[64] Thomas quoting Hailey, p. 289.

[65] Ibid.

[66] Lenski, Bullinger, Seiss – Thomas, p. 289.

[67] Thomas, quoting Walvoord, p. 290.

[68] Thomas, p. 290.

[69] Walvoord, *Revelation*, p. 246.

[70] Strong's #2048.

[71] Walvoord, *Revelation*, p. 244.

[72] Thomas, p. 285.

[73] Alford, p. 707.

[74] Thomas, p. 286.

[75] "Babel." Pfeiffer, Wycliffe, p. 187.

[76] TWOT, 2424, p. 943 vol. II.

[77] Will Durant. *The Story of Civilization: Part 1 - Our Oriental Heritage.* (New York: Simon and Schuster, 1954), p. 120.

[78] Ibid.

[79] "Ezekiel 8:14,"*Matthew Henry Commentary*,

[80] "Ezekiel 8:14,"*JFB*. Also, Levy, p. 193.

[81] Ibid.

[82] Durant, p. 239.

[83] Walvoord, *Revelation*, p. 247.

[84] Durant, 239.

[85] Walvoord, *Revelation*, p. 247.

[86] Durant, fn. p. 241.

[87] David Levy. Revelation: Hearing the Last Word. (Bellmawr, NJ: The Friends of Israel Gospel Ministry, Inc., 1999). p. 193. Also, Hoyt, p. 110.

[88] Loraine Boettner. *Roman Catholicism*. (New Jersey: The Presbyterian and Reformed Publishing Co., 1962), p. 142.

[89] Bryce Self. "Semiramis, Queen of Babylon" Page 1. http://Idolphin. org/semir.html. (2 Mar 2005).

[90] Boettner, 136.

[91] Hunt, p. 419.

[92] Alan Franklin. EU: The Final World Empire. (Hampshire, UK: Banner Publishing Ltd., 2004). p. 49.

[93] Judith M. Barringer. "Abstract: Europa and the Nereids: Wedding or Funeral." *American Journal of Archaeology*. http://www.ajaonline.org/ archive/95.4/barringer_judith_m.html. (26 Feb 2005).

[94] Ibid.

[95] "Ludmila Tcherina" Telegraph Media Group Ltd. 7/4/2004. http://www.telegraph.co.uk/news/main.jhtml?xml=/news/2004/04/07/db0703.xml&sSheet=/opinion/2004/04/07/ixopright.html 12/2/2006.

Act III – Scene 6: Connecting the Dots of God's History

[1] Leonard, *Why Europe*, p. 142.

[2] "Pope Holds First Mass in Turkey." *EuroNews* website. 29 November 2006. http://www.euronews.net/crate_html.php?page=detail_info&article=393299&lng=1&option=1 (29 Nov. 2006).

[3] "Pope Celebrates Mass With Patriarch." *EuroNews* website. 30 Nov. 2006. http://www.euronews.net/create_html.php?page=detail_info&article=393490&lng=1 (30 Nov. 2006).

[4] "Orthodox Church." CD-ROM *Encarta Encyclopedia Standard 2001*. Redmond, WA: Microsoft Corp. 1993-2000.

[5] Lucia Kubosova. "Turkey Claims Pope Supports its EU Membership Bid." 29 Nov.2006 Euobserver.com. http://cuobserver.com/9/22974/?print=1 (29 Nov. 2006)

[6] Ibid.

[7] "The Pope in Turkey: 'Istanbul Peace.'" *Evening Echo: News* website. 1 Dec. 2006. http://www.eveningecho.ie/news/bstory.asp?j=13225874&p=y3zz59zx&n=13225962 (2 Dec. 2006)

[8] "Dubai Internet City – A Real Broadband Oasis." Cisco Systems. 1999-2005. http://www.cisco.com/en/US/netso/ns341/ns396/ns223/ns227/networking_solutions. (17 Nov. 2005).

[9] Strong's #6098.

BIBLIOGRAPHY & REFERENCES

—〜〜—

Alexander, Joseph A. *Commentary on Isaiah. 2 Volumes in 1*. Grand Rapids, MI: Kregel Publications, 1992.

Alford, Henry, *The Greet New Testament Revised by Everett F. Harrison, Vol. 1*. Chicago: Moody Press, 1958.

Anderson, Robert A. The Coming Prince. Grand Rapids, MI: Kregel Publ., 1957.

Boettner, Loraine. Roman Catholicism. Philipsburg, NJ: Presbyterian and Reformed Publ. Co., 1962.

Booker, Christopher and Richard North. *The Great Deception: a Secret History of the European Union*. London: Continuum, 2003.

Brown, Francis, S. R. Driver, and Charles A. Briggs. *Hebrew and English Lexicon of the Old Testament*. Oxford: Clarendon Press, 1978.

Chafer, Lewis Sperry. *Systematic Theology—Vol. 1 abridged ed. John F. Walvoord, ed.* Wheaton, Il.: Victory Books, 1988.

Cini, Michelle ed. *European Union Politics*. Oxford: Oxford Press, 2003.

Cole, C. Donald. *Abraham: God's Man of Faith*. Chicago: Moody Press, 1977.

Constitution for Europe. Luxembourg: European Communities, 2004.

Davis, John J. and John C. Whitcomb. *Israel—From Conquest to Exile*. Winona Lake, IN: BMH Books, 1971.

Davis, John J. *Moses and the Gods of Egypt—Studies in Exodus—2ⁿᵈ* ed. Winona Lake, IN: BMH Books, 1986.

Durant, Will. *The Story of Civilization: Part 1—Our Oriental Heritage.* NY: Simon and Schuster, 1954.

Douglas, J. D. ed. *New Bible Dictionary, 2ⁿᵈ ed.* Wheaton, IL: Tyndale House Publishers, Inc., 1982.

Duchene, Francois. *Jean Monnet—the First Statesman of Interdependence.* NY: W. W. Norton & Co., 1994.

Edersheim, Alfred. *Bible History—Old Testament.* Peabody, MA: Hendrickson Publishers, 1995.

Fonatine, Pascal. *Europe in 12 Lessons.* Luxembourg: European Communities, 2004.

Franklin, Alan. *EU: The Final World Empire.* Hampshire, UK: Banner Publ. Ltd., 2004.

Frampton, Kenneth. *Le Corbusier.* London: Thames & Hudson, 2001.

Fransen, Frederic. *The Supranational Politics of Jean Monnet: Ideas and Origins of the European Community.* Connecticut: Greenwood Press, 2001.

Fruchtenbaum, Arnold G. Fruchtenbaum. *Israelology: The Missing Link in Systematic Theology.* Tustin, CA: Ariel Ministries Press, 1992.

Going for Growth: The Economy of the EU. Luxembourg: European Communities, 2003.

Halley, Henry H. *Halley's Bible Handbook.* Grand Rapids: Zondervan Publishing House, 1962.

Hilton, Adrian. *The Principality and Power of Europe.* Norfolk, UK: 2000.

How the European Union Works. Luxembourg: European Communities, 2005.

Hoyt, Herman A. *Studies in Revelation.* Winona Lake, IN: BMH Books, 1977.

Hunt, Dave. *A Woman Rides the Beast*. Eugene, OR: Harvest House Publ., 1994.

Huttar, David K. *Evangelical Dictionary of Biblical Theology, ed. Walter A. Elwell*. Grand Rapids: Baker Books, 1996.

Kiel, C. F. and F. Delitzsch. *Keil & Delitzsch—Commentary on the Old Testament 10 vol*. Peabody, Massachusetts: Hendrickson Publishers, 2001.

Leonard, Mark. *Why Europe Will Run the 21st Century*. London: Fourth Estate, 2005.

Levy, David M. *Revelation: Hearing the Last Word*. Bellmawr, NJ: The Friends of Israel Gospel Ministry, Inc., 1999.

McClain, Alva J. *The Greatness of the Kingdom—an Inductive Study of the Kingdom of God*. Winona Lake, IN: BMH Books, 1974.

McLaren, Brian D. The Secret Message of Jesus. Nashville, TN: W Publ. Group, 2006.

McQuaid, Elwood. *It is No Dream: Bible Prophecy: Fact or Fanaticism?* Bellmawr, NJ: The Friends of Israel Gospel Ministry, Inc., 2000.

Neufeldt, Victoria, ed. *Webster's New World Dictionary of American English, 3rd ed*. NY: Prentice Hall, 1994.

Pentecost, J. Dwight. *Things to Come: A Study in Biblical Eschatology*. Grand Rapids, MI: Zondervan Publ. House, 1958

_____ *The Bible Knowledge Commentary: Old Testament* Wheaton, IL: Victor, 1985.

Pfeiffer, Charles F. ed. *Baker's Bible Atlas*. Grand Rapids: Baker Book House, 1979.

Pfeiffer; Charles F, Howard F. Vos and John Rhea, ed. *Wycliffe Bible Encyclopedia 2 vol*. Chicago: Moody Press, 1975.

Pink, Arthur W. *Gleanings in the Godhead*. Chicago: Moody Press, 1975.

Ramm, *Bernard. Protestant Biblical Interpretation 3rd ed.* Grand Rapids, MI: Baker Book House, 1970.

Rifkin, Jeremy. *The European Dream: How Europe's Vision of the Future is Quietly Eclipsing the American Dream.* Cambridge: Polity Press, 2004.

Saggs, H. W. F. *The Greatness that was Babylon.* NY: Mentor Books, The New American Library, Inc., 1962.

Showers, Renald. *The Most High God—A Commentary on Daniel.* Bellmawr, NJ: The Friends of Israel Gospel Ministry, Inc., 1982.

_____. *There Really is a Difference!* Bellmawr, NJ: The Friends of Israel Gospel Ministry, Inc., 1990.

_____.*Those Invisible Spirits Called Angels.* (Bellmawr, NJ: Friends of Israel Gospel Ministries, Inc., 1997).

_____.*What on Earth is God Doing? Satan's Conflict with God.* Bellmawr, NJ: The Friends of Israel Gospel Ministry, Inc., 2005.

Spurgeon, Charles H. *Treasury of David.* Nashville, TN: Thomas Nelson Publishers, n.d.

Tan, Paul Lee. *The Interpretation of Prophecy.* Winona Lake, IN: BMH Books, 1974.

Tetlow, Jim, Roger Oakland, and Brad Myers. *Queen of Rome: Queen of Islam: Queen of All.* Fairport, NY: Eternal Productions, 2006.

Thiessen, Henry C. *Lectures in Systematic Theology.* Grand Rapids: William B. Eerdmans Publishing Co., 1979.

Thomas, Robert L. *Revelation: An Exegetical Commentary— 2 vols.* Chicago: Moody Press, 1992.

Tozer, A. W. *The Knowledge of the Holy.* New York: Harper and Row Publishers, 1961.

Laird, Harris, R., ed., Gleason L. Archer, Jr. and Bruce K. Waltke, assoc. ed. *Theological Wordbook of the Old Testament, 2 vol.* Chicago: Moody Press, 1980.

Unger, Merrill. *Unger's Bible Dictionary—3rd ed.* Chicago: Moody Bible Institute, 1960.

Walvoord, John F. *Daniel*. Chicago: Moody Press, 1985.

_____. *Major Bible Prophecies—37 Crucial Prophecies That Affect You Today*. Grand Rapids: Zondervan Publ. House, 1991.

_____. *The Millennial Kingdom*. Grand Rapids: Zondervan Publ. House, 1959.

_____. *The Revelation of Jesus Christ*. Chicago: Moody Press, 1966.

Ward-Perkins, Bryan. *The Fall of Rome and the End of Civilization*. Oxford: Oxford Press, 2005.

Whiston, William. *The Works of Josephus*. Peabody, MA: Hendrickson Publishers, 1987.

Whitcomb, John C. *Daniel: Everyman's Bible Commentary*. Chicago: Moody Press, 1985.

_____. *The Genesis Flood—the Biblical Record and Its Scientific Implications*. n.l.: The Presbyterian and Reformed Publishing Co., 1961.

Wiseman, D. J. *New Bible Dictionary—2nd* ed. J. D. Douglas ed. (Wheaton, IL: Tyndale House Publ., 1982).

Working for the Regions. Luxembourg: European Communities, 2004.

INDEX

289

Printed in the United States
115233LV00004BA/112-144/A